D0063965

To Sue —

Enjoy the trip
down Memory Lane!

Jay Strouse
3/23

Beyond the Broken Window

JOY STROUSE

Ordering information: For details contact Joy Strouse at joyfulimagesllc@ gmail.com or follow us on Facebook: @joystrouseauthor

Print ISBN: 978-1-66781-771-2
eBook ISBN: 978-1-66781-772-9

Printed in the USA
First Edition

Dedicated to those who lived it

Beyond the Broken Window

Chapter 1

JUNE 1987

Julie had some thinking to do and had come back to her roots. Just yesterday, she had discovered a terrible truth that struck her with such force it splintered her reality. It turned over and over in her thoughts with no clear path of resolution, so here she was, parked in front of the house where she grew up.

The house was a typical suburban split-level. Beneath the bay window, shrubbery grew, dark and dense. New growth sprouted here and there, so it looked as if the needles were spattered with bright chartreuse paint. There were her mother's morning glories, faces open to the sun, still climbing up the lamppost at the start of the walk. Below them, marigolds gave the air a pungent smell that blended with the nose-tickling scent of a newly trimmed lawn.

Looking at this house brought back memories of a happy childhood surrounded by a loving family. She hadn't been here for years, since her parents moved to a condo, but this was the place she always felt safe.

She released the seat belt from beneath her prodigious pregnant belly, hauled herself out of the car, and wandered up the drive. Julie wanted to see the backyard where she and her friends ran through sprinklers, chased fireflies, and dreamed of their future. The nostalgia made her smile, and she longed for that carefree innocence again.

As she moved toward the yard, a murder of crows lifted from the woods and flew across the sun, dappling the lawn with light and shade. How appropriate, she thought.

At the top of the driveway, she stopped short; her heart leapt in her chest.

There it was, its spikey branches reaching out and up 20 feet tall, piercing the sky, its dark shadow spreading toward her, its knotty roots twisting beneath her feet. To think just ten years ago, this piney beast was a humble sapling rooted in burlap.

How did I forget it was here? It was the Christmas tree from the year she was first married.

They put off getting a tree, so by the time they journeyed out, there were none left on the lots. She remembered Rick fuming about how the stupid Boy Scouts should stock enough trees. She also remembered him turning that anger on her when she said they shouldn't have waited until Christmas Eve. How naïve she'd been!

They ended up at the local garden center, just as the worker was locking the door. There was the saddest little fir sitting by the entrance, its dozen skinny branches reaching out to her.

"A Charlie Brown tree!" she said. "Please let us in. We need to rescue that tree!"

The weary salesman saw Rick pull a ten from his pocket. He grabbed the money and pushed the tree into Julie's arms. "Sold," he said, "Merry Christmas!" and pulled the door closed with a bang.

The scraggly tree looked festive once they wrapped the burlap in gift paper, hung a few balls on its fragile arms, and crowned it with a paper star.

By the end of January, little "Charlie Brown" was relegated to the porch of their first-floor apartment, to be planted once the ground thawed. There, he patiently sat through the bitter winter and into March.

One evening, just as spring was peeking around the corner, they came home to find the tree planted in the ground next to the parking lot. Rick went ballistic. His face turned red, his fists clenched as he stomped around to the super's apartment and banged on the door. With a string of expletives, he demanded the tree be dug up and put back where it was.

She remembered the shell-shocked super stumbling through an apology. "The poor thing didn't look so good. Thought I was doing a favor, you dealing with the trial and all." He shrugged his shoulders, grabbed a shovel and dug up the tree.

Then Rick and Julie took Charlie Brown to her parents' home, and there it still grew, a remnant of nightmares Julie would prefer to keep buried.

But the excavator in her brain would not let that happen. Memories uprooted and tumbled over one another as they clamored toward the light of consciousness.

So much had transpired since the planting of this tree—between that life and the one she lived now, and this was the place it all began. Three fat crows returned and perched on the telephone wire to provide a soundtrack with their raucous confabulation . . . *Caw caw! Caw, caw!*

Julie shook her head to release her sadness to the crows and rubbed her belly where a little foot was tap dancing within. She looked out on the lush lawn behind the tree and could almost see two unsuspecting girls lounging in the June heat . . .

There are days, she thought, that you look back on and know . . .

That's the day my life changed.

One small decision lays the path for what's to come. If she could go back to that one moment of that one day and tell herself, "Don't go."

If she could lay back down on the warm grass and daydream instead of plowing forward into her future as it now is, would she?

JUNE 1977

It was the first day of summer, a sweltering afternoon. The air rippled with humidity. It felt thick and alive, making movement arduous. It clung to the skin, leaving one sticky with sweat and craving cool drinks.

Colleen and Julie lay on beach towels spread on the grass in Julie's backyard. They were wearing short shorts and bikini tops on their slender eighteen-year-old bodies. High school graduation was behind them, and they were enjoying a few empty days. They planned to do nothing: no work, no school, no college preparations.

Julie lay on her stomach with her chin propped on folded arms. Perspiration beaded on her forehead and trickled into her eye. She slid her sunglasses down and wiped at it with a ring-clad hand.

"It's hot," she murmured, too lazy to speak with much effort.

"Supposed to be hot, it's summer vacay!" Colleen replied. She propped herself up on her elbows and glanced at her friend. "I wish I tanned like you do."

"You have Irish skin, Lassie, what can you do?" Julie poked Colleen in the ribs as she flipped herself over to her back and stared up at a wisp of cloud.

"Guess I could catch a leprechaun and wish for golden skin," Colleen said and sighed.

"You'd look like that Oscar statue," Julie giggled. "I'd have to call you Oscar!"

Colleen sat up and spread her arms wide. "But all the movie stars would want me!"

"Then I'm glad I'm best friends with you. You could introduce me to Clint Eastwood."

She continued in an Eastwood-esque dialect with finger pointed, gun-like, at Colleen, "Did I fire six or five? Being as this is a 44-magnum finger, and would blow your sunglasses clean off, you've got to ask yourself: 'Do I feel lucky?' Well, do ya, punk?"

Colleen laughed and flipped her sunglasses up onto her bouncy auburn curls, "Lucky enough to have a leprechaun who grants wishes!"

In the distance, the sound of bells wafted across the neighborhood and into the yard. Colleen strained her sight through the rippled haze toward the street, "Good Humor man! That's what we need, ice cream!"

"Nah, I'm feeling too lazy to move."

BEYOND THE BROKEN WINDOW

"Come on, the sugar will give you a little rush. I could go for a Nutty Buddy. Wait . . . I already have one!" She smacked Julie's belly.

"Ha! Very funny. But I'm a Nutty Buddy with no money."

"I do, I'll treat . . . I bet they have your fa-ave, Strawberry Shortcake," Colleen taunted in a singsong voice.

"Okay . . . you talked me into it. I'll drag myself to the street."

That's when life took its turn.

The girls slipped on their flip-flops and ambled around to the street. Seven or eight kids milled around the Good Humor truck three houses down. Six-year-old Lauree, from next door, skipped toward them with a cherry Popsicle in her hand, her arm and chin dripping with sweet sticky red. "It's a new guy!" she hollered to them as they passed her, "He's cool."

"Ha! Cool . . . good way for an ice cream guy to be," Julie said.

As they neared the truck, the children drifted away, one by one, with their faces covered in summer sweat, melted ice cream, and expressions of delight. It was then Julie glimpsed the new guy leaning out of the truck window; a muscular arm and tumble of dark curls against a broad shoulder. He looked up and smiled, and her heart did a little flip. "Whoa," she whispered.

Colleen looked at the ice cream guy and back at Julie. A smile spread across her face. "You really want some sweets, huh?" she teased.

It was their turn at the window. Colleen said, "Hi, you must be New Guy! We've heard about you. I'll have . . . Hmm . . . What do *you* want, Julie, my little Nutty Buddy?"

Julie glanced up under her lashes. "I'm really not that nutty . . . anyway, I'll have a Strawberry Shortcake. My friend *Oscar* here is buying."

Colleen seemed amused by Julie's coyness. Rarely was she so shy, especially around guys.

"I'll have whatever that kid has all over his face," Colleen pointed at the last of the stragglers, "My name is really Colleen, Oscar's just my stage name. What's your name, new guy?"

"Well. I don't have a stage name," he grinned. "Name's Rick. Shortcake and Creamsicle coming up." Then he flashed that perfect smile again and

Julie's *brain* did a little flip—she had a momentary urge to sing out "Nicky Aronstein, Nicky Aronstein!" like Streisand did in Funny Girl.

Julie had a few serious relationships and a string of romances with boys since starting junior high school. In the summer between sixth and seventh grade, she transformed, much like a butterfly. She had been chubby and awkward at Southwood Elementary, always one of the last to be picked for kickball. By September of that year, her legs had grown longer. Her thick, brown hair was sun-kissed with golden highlights to complement her sun-tanned skin and curves appeared where there used to be chub.

A new school, Hampton Junior High, was full of boys who had never seen her as a caterpillar. Thrilled with her newfound popularity, she sampled kisses like flavors at Baskin Robbins, eager to find the sweetest. Through her high school years, she had fallen heart over head in love with several boys, but the relationships ended badly and she was devastated . . . until she met the next one. Despite her free-spirit personality, her dream was traditional. She longed for a happy marriage like those of her parents and brothers, and a house full of kids. She wanted what was in that song about moving to the country, having a lot of children, and feeding them on peaches.

Looking at this new guy Rick sent an electric zap right through her. He's my next, she thought. *This is something special. This could be it. Even if it's not, it's gonna be a helluva ride.*

Chapter 2

JUNE 1977

JULIE AND RICK

Julie, Harry, and Evelyn Fairburn were in the living room tuned into their Tuesday show, "Happy Days," when the phone rang and Julie sprang from the sofa, "I'll get it!"

"Expecting a call?" asked Julie's father.

Harry gave Evie a sideways glance and couldn't help a grin.

"Here we go again," Evie shook her head as she watched her daughter sprint by.

"Hello? Oh, hi . . ." they heard her say. Then the door slid shut.

"Hope this one stays around long enough for me to remember his name," Evie said to the knitting in her lap.

"Now Evie," Harry said, but he saw she was smiling and chuckled.

Julie stretched the phone cord down to the bottom basement step, where she sat, head propped against the wall, far from her parents' ears. At first, the conversation was awkward, Julie unusually shy, Rick unaccustomed to open conversation with a woman.

Julie told Rick about her older brothers, both of whom were married. Russ, 28, lived in Virginia and Will, 23, in South Carolina. She gushed over how cute her nephews and niece were and how she wished they lived closer.

7

Rick told her he had a younger sister named Dawn. She was 15, and he was 24.

Julie had always gone for older guys, so the fact that Rick was six years older was just fine with her.

Rick said his Good Humor stint was just for this summer. He worked as a mechanic at a local service station, went in early in the morning, and painted apartments to pay part of his rent. She marveled at his work ethic and told him she worked at a local store and that she planned to start college in the fall. She was going to major in Hotel Restaurant Management, inspired by her brother, Will, who worked for Marriott.

Rick said he went to the school of hard knocks.

He proudly told her about a '67 Chevy Impala he bought from his neighbor for a song. It was far from being road-ready, but he was hopeful he could take her for a spin real soon.

They talked about music. They both liked Lynyrd Skynyrd, The Who, and Bob Dylan. They talked about books and thought *The Exorcist* was a better book than movie. Julie discovered a softer side under his hard-knock shell, and she liked it.

He invited her to a party—a regular Friday get-together of the people who lived in his apartment complex.

"We call our team the Rough Riders. We play softball when it's warm and football when it's cold," he said, "and we party together all the time."

"Where'd you get the Rough Riders name?"

"Our apartment manager, Butch. Walt saw it first. He's a history major. Anyway, Butch looks just like Teddy Roosevelt."

"Can't wait to see that!" she laughed.

They'd been talking for hours and her mother called through the door, but Julie found it hard to say good night.

Rick found it hard to wait until Friday. *What the hell is wrong with me, getting goofy over a girl?* He vowed to himself not to let his emotions get the better of him.

For their first date, he picked Julie up in a Grey 1970 Chrysler Newport. When he pulled up, she ran out to meet him. Julie wore a gauzy top embroidered in blue and a short denim skirt that hugged her hips, displaying her curves and tanned legs. Turquoise and silver dangled from her ears, neck, and wrist.

Rick watched as she moved lithely across the lawn, and the sight stirred him in ways he hadn't felt in a long time. *That vow ain't gonna last long with her looking like that!* He swiped a hand across his errant grin and got out to open the door for her.

Julie saw him pull up and darted out before her parents could insist he come to the door. She didn't want to hear her mother's usual complaint, "Why can't you find a boy your own age?"

There he was, holding the door for her, just as handsome as she remembered, not in a Robert Redford way, more Eastwood or Burt Reynolds . . . that bad boy look. Maybe a dark James Dean. She could picture him on a motorcycle.

"Meet Jaws," he said. "This monster belongs to my buddy, Walter. Lives in the apartment above me. I totaled my truck in May . . . hit a deer. The reason I took on the Good Humor job. Getting the Impala on the road ain't cheap."

"Big deer, huh?" Julie said. Rick pulled out of Julie's neighborhood and headed toward Goucher Boulevard. As he drove, he finished the story.

"The truck was a pile of shit, anyway. But while I'm wheelless, I wrangled a deal with Walt. I drive Jaws to work, fill the tank at the station, and it's back to him by the time he wakes up . . . usually around noon. Those college boys can sleep! Anyway, whenever he doesn't need it, it's mine to use."

Rick turned into a small apartment complex. There were three brick buildings of apartments, with lawn and parking lots between them. Towson Ridge was near Towson State, so many of the renters were college students. The Rough Riders spent Friday nights at the apartment of Fred and Marilyn Friedman. The gatherings were fondly known as Freaky Friday at Freddie's.

Rick led Julie to the door and pointed to the one next door. "That's where I live."

When they entered the Friedmans, there was music playing—Little Feat—and the group sat in clumps, drinking and talking. The air was sweet with incense, cigarette, and pot smoke. The décor was tasteful goodwill, and a brightly painted crate that served as a coffee table held bags of various snack foods and a bong.

A balding, mustached man in an easy chair called out, "Rick, buddy, join the party! Got some radical smoke today. Come, sit, try!"

"Let 'em get in the door, Freddie." Marilyn, all five foot two of her, waved a dismissive hand at Fred and greeted them with a dimpled smile, "Hey, I'm Marilyn. You must be Julie. Let me get you something to drink."

Marilyn took Julie's hand and led her to the kitchen.

"Help yourself to anything. Mi casa es su casa and everyone else's casa. I seem to be the unofficial mother to all these degenerates," she laughed as she pointed a manicured finger at the counter next to the refrigerator, "There's the bar, so to speak. Everybody usually pitches in with something, so it's a mish-mosh but pick your poison."

Rick joined them, stuck the six-pack he brought in the fridge, and opened a beer. "What do you like to drink, Nutty Buddy?"

Julie smiled at him, "Sorry, only Colleen can call me Nutty Buddy."

"Maybe you can be my Shortcake, then. You do look good enough to eat."

Julie laughed, liking the Shortcake name. She perused the assortment of bottles and pitchers, "How 'bout a vodka and whatever is in that pitcher?"

"Vodka and uh . . ." Rick peered into the pitcher, "lemonade . . . Maybe. Coming right up." Rick found a cup and played bartender. Drinks in hand, they found a couple of dining room chairs off to the side of the main group. Julie handed her drink to Rick to loop her purse on the back of her chair. As she turned back to get it, a tall, athletic-looking guy with a head of blond curls materialized beside her.

"Remember me?" he asked.

"Oh my God! Crazy Randy, what are you doing here?" she cried out and threw her arms around his neck.

"I'm renting an apartment with my brother, Kevin," Randy blustered out, beneath her grasp. "Start at Towson State this fall."

Sensing Rick's stare, she backed away from Randy and took the drink Rick was holding out to her. "Old friends," she said with a nervous smile.

Rick offered a tight half-grin, shook a cigarette out of his pack, and lit it.

She turned back to Randy, keeping her distance this time. "Colleen is going to Towson, too. I can't wait to tell her! You look a bit older and wiser than the last time I saw you."

It thrilled Julie to see Randy. They were close friends back in junior high. She called him Crazy Randy once, back in seventh grade, and the name stuck. She remembered them talking for hours, their subjects meandering from school to music to the meaning of life. Then his family moved when his father, an officer in the Navy, was transferred.

"So, California . . . You get to use that surfboard like you wanted?"

"Caught a few waves . . ." he stopped mid-thought. Someone had changed the record album, and Elton John began his farewell to "Yellow Brick Road." His eyes grew wide.

They looked at each other, smiles growing across their faces, and exclaimed in unison, "Golden showers!"

They'd spent eighth-grade afternoons in Liz Booth's club basement. Both her parents worked, and they could usually pilfer a beer or some liquor from the vast supply in the bar cabinet. Their group consisted of Liz and her boyfriend, Randy and his older brother Kevin, Colleen, and Julie. Much information was shared, some accurate, some not, about teenage subjects—sex, drugs, and rock n roll. They were a ragtag group of friends on the verge of adulthood. Some were ready to jump with both feet, others leery of the bumps in the road ahead. But they felt fearless as long as they were together.

This particular afternoon, Julie remembered as if her thoughts were a snapshot from her old Instamatic camera . . .

The *Yellow Brick Road* album was on the turntable. Liz was stretched out on the brown velour sofa with her head in her boyfriend's lap, her arm extended to touch his hair. Kevin's head was in the liquor cabinet as he tried to figure out which bottle he hadn't already added water to. Julie and Colleen were on the love seat, sharing potato chips and lemonade. Julie was licking greasy salt from her fingertips and singing along with Elton, the song about tender young Alice.

Randy sat cross-legged on the floor facing them, his hair a curly veil over his face as he studied the artwork on the album cover.

"I don't get this song," he said and looked up, a perplexed crease between his brown eyes.

With a bottle in each hand, Kevin pulled his head out and barked, "She's a lez! What don't you get, numb-nuts?"

The look of astonishment on Randy's face threw Colleen and Julie into shrieks of laughter, lemonade spraying from Colleen's mouth.

"Thanks for the shower, Col," Randy said, wiping his arm on his jeans.

"It's a golden shower!" Julie burst out, which caused the girls to slide from the loveseat and collapse in a giggling heap on the floor. They didn't really know what golden shower meant, but they knew the term had something to do with kinky sex. That made it racy and hilarious.

Randy shook his head. The crease turned to smile as he watched them. "And you call me crazy? You two take the crazy award."

Now here was Randy smiling at her again, with that big toothy smile that lit up his whole guileless face.

"Hey, Rick . . . Julie and I were friends since seventh grade. She was like a sister to Kev and me."

"Small world, ain't it?" he said and took a long swig of beer.

"Rick is helping Kevin fix his car. It's a '56 Chevy Nomad."

Rick turned to Julie. "So you know this goof and his goofier brother, huh?"

Julie tried to explain, "It was lemonade . . . I mean the golden, um, shower. Colleen spit lemonade on him. We just made a joke about it, about the golden um, you know . . ."

"Huh, yeah, I get it. Pretty sick humor you got there. Well, let me introduce you to these morons I call friends." he took her hand and walked her away from Randy.

Her fingers did a trill of a wave from the side of her cup, "Catch ya later, CR."

"It's RC, not CR."

It was a private joke of theirs. She called him CR for Crazy Randy, but his name was Randall Christopher, so since seventh grade, when she said CR, he corrected her. She liked that he remembered.

Freddie was sitting back in his chair, beer in hand like the king of the castle. He lifted a baggie of pot from his potbelly and shook it at them.

"Care to imbibe?"

Rick glanced at Julie for her reaction.

"I'm not much of a pot smoker," she told them. "It makes me hungry and sleepy. I'll stick to vodka."

"Exactly how I feel," Rick said. "Candy is dandy, but liquor is quicker!"

"Suit yourself," said Fred, as he reached for the bong.

Rick turned to the guys on the sofa and introduced them to Julie.

Gravy slung back in a relaxed slouch, knees protruding, wore a faded flannel shirt with the sleeves cut off and a baseball cap over his long dark hair. When introduced, he raised the enormous cup in his hand in a toast.

"Grady, aka Gravy, is a cook at Spirits in Towson," Rick said.

"Hence the unfortunate nickname they hung on me," Gravy told her with a crooked grin. He gestured to the man next to him, "My roomie, Cups, here got the better name."

"Yo." Cups said mid-drag of his cigarette. Cups was slick looking, shirt unbuttoned halfway, dark tan, and perfectly layered blond hair. He stood, gestured to the kitchen with his cigarette, and walked away.

"Great conversationalist, Cups is. That's why he gets the big tips when he's behind the bar. Regular Dale Carnegie, aren't you, Cups?" Gravy hollered after him.

Gravy and Rick continued conversing, but the chatter of two girls sitting cross-legged on the floor distracted Julie. She later learned they were Ruth and Valerie, two of three college girls who shared the apartment around the corner. A beautiful, striking contrast to one another, Ruth was short and dark with skin a rich sepia, and Valerie was a tall redhead with skin so pale it was almost translucent. Ruth was relaying a story with gusto to a shocked-looking Valerie. Julie propped herself on the arm of the sofa to listen in.

"So, it was their fifth anniversary and she had the place all romantic, you know, candles and wine, but he just sat reading his paper. She says, 'Honey, what were you thinking five years ago tonight?' He says without looking at her, 'To be honest, I was thinking about screwing your brains out.'"

Valerie's eyes got big, "What did she say to that?"

"She said, 'Oh baby what are you thinking about tonight?'"

"And?"

"And he looks her up and down, over the top of his newspaper and says, 'I think I've succeeded!'"

Valerie had the same look on her face that Randy had all those years ago. Julie was glad she hadn't sipped her drink at that moment or she would have golden showered them with the burst of laughter that sprung from her. Val and Ruth looked up, surprised that someone had been listening in.

"Guess she could have said she *blew* his brains out," Julie said.

The three girls fell into hysterics, and when she recovered her breath, Ruth said, "Hey, Rick! This one's a keeper!"

The third roommate came in the door with a beer in her hand and Fred greeted her with a bawdy, "Joanie!"

She was a pretty blond with a plump figure and a Miss America smile. She sashayed through the living room, saying hi along the way. When she moved past Rick, she pranced her fingers across his back. He gave a brief toss of his head and resumed his conversation.

Joanie plopped down next to Valerie on the floor, "Well, that was a bust!"

"Bummer! What happened?" asked Val, her eyes wide.

"He was a dork, is all. I made an excuse and booked outta there."

Ruth patted her on the back, "Not the first, not the last," she gestured toward Julie. "This slick chick is Julie, she's here with Rick, but we don't hold that against her," she barked out a short "Ha!"

Joanie gave Julie a once-over. "Hey," was all she said.

Val filled Julie in. "Joanie here had a first and, I guess, last date with an assistant professor tonight."

Joanie took a swig from her beer. "I need another. Anybody else while I'm going?"

Val said, "Hold up, I'll go with." The two of them headed to the kitchen and Julie could hear Val retelling the anniversary tale.

Rick's arm slipped around her shoulders, "Need a refill?"

Julie twisted around from her seat on the sofa's arm and looked up at him. There went that brain flip again. She stood, put her hand on his chest, and felt his heartbeat, which quickened hers. "Sure, I'll go with you."

Val and Joanie passed them deep in conversation and Rick told her, "Val went to Hereford High a few years after me. She's from the money side of Hereford. Instead of an 18-wheeler like my pop, her dad has race horses. The guys call Val 'Preakness' and Ruth 'Princess.'"

"What about Joanie?"

"She's 'Predacious,'" he said seriously. "Trust me, I know, I've been her prey." Then he laughed.

In the kitchen, Cups was talking with Hank, a guy with gray-white hair and a three-day growth of beard.

"Cups been telling me his Spirits drink of the week, Gowon, Cups, tell it." Hank said. And as he gazed at Julie, his eyes didn't seem quite focused. "He's a mixolo-agee genius!"

Cups stubbed out his smoke, twitched his head, and answered, "Neutron Bomb. 151 rum, blue Curacao, and Seltzer . . . shaken, not stirred."

"Messy!" Julie said, "and potent."

"Sounds like it'll knock your socks off," added Rick.

"Thaas what the protesters said!" Hank took a large gulp of his beer and chortled to himself.

Rick took Julie by the elbow and moved her to the bottle display. Under his breath, he said, "Hank probably started drinking at noon. Can you believe the guy is only 26? Little over a year older than me."

Julie glanced in Hank's direction.

"Vietnam made him old before his time, man. Helluva thing."

Walter, owner of Jaws, sauntered in around 11:00, folded his lanky frame into a chair next to Fred, and picked up the bong. With him was a rambunctious golden retriever who barreled in ahead, almost knocking a lamp from the table. The dog, Bibbit (named for a character from *One Flew Over the Cuckoo's Nest)*, happily bounded from person to person, nudging and playing cute in hopes of a handout.

When Bibbit drooled on Julie's bare leg, Walt said, "Don't mind the pup." He had a slight drawl to his words, "He slobbers on all the pretty girls."

Rick said, "He learned that from you," and Walt nodded his head in agreement and let out a stream of sweet smoke.

Craig, Walt's roommate, followed in shortly after Walt, guitar case in hand. He'd just played a gig at a local bar. He was a nice-looking guy with a friendly, open face. Judging by his long hair and tie-dye shirt, Julie guessed they had the same taste in music. Rick introduced them.

"What kind of guitar do you have?" Julie asked him.

"This one's a Gibson Hummingbird, got a Les Paul electric I play sometimes with the band."

"I play guitar a little, mostly because I love to sing . . . can't go around just singing a cappella all the time!"

"People look at you weird when you do that," Craig nodded and the corner of his mouth went up, a lopsided grin.

"You play with a band too?"

"We're just getting started. Call ourselves 'Day One.' There are four of us."

Rick said, "They played at the Towson State Coffee House the other night . . . not bad." Craig smiled at the compliment.

"Craig, go get yourself a drink, man. I know you're thirsty." Rick gestured with his beer bottle toward the kitchen.

Craig's smile faltered, "Oh, yeah, sure." He started moving, then turned to Julie and said as he walked backward, "We'll have to catch a tune together sometime."

Julie smiled as he disappeared into the kitchen.

At midnight, Julie told Rick she better get home, parents, and all that, so they headed out to Jaws. Rick opened the door for her. She slid across the bench seat to the middle as Rick went around to the driver's side. When he got in, he was happy to see her right beside him. He gave her cheek a quick peck. She turned and returned a kiss, soft and lingering. They parted and grinned at each other.

"Well, I better get you home, Shortcake." He started the car and turned out of the parking lot.

"Hey, Thursday we're getting a keg to watch the O's play the Red Sox. They gotta make up for the way they got trounced a couple weeks ago. Why don't you come by?"

"Sure! I work till six so I'll be here by the first pitch."

"Bring Colleen, too, if you want. She can reunite with the goof brothers."

"Ha! The goof brothers. Love that!" Julie said. "Yeah, Colleen's a big Orioles fan."

When they pulled up to Julie's house, Rick kissed her again, this time more insistently. His powerful hand grabbed hold of her bare knee, pulled her closer. She would have ended up on his lap had the steering wheel not interceded. Julie's heart was pounding. She broke away to catch her breath, and he buried his face in her hair. Julie kept her arms around him, savoring the heat of him as long as she dared. Then, afraid her parents were watching, slid back over the seat and opened the car door.

"See you Thursday. I'll wear my black and orange."

He watched her as she walked up the driveway. The porch light cast a soft halo around her silhouette. She turned, gave a brief wave, and went in the door. The scent of her lingered around him, something sweet and lemony. He closed his eyes and breathed it in, steeped in it.

"Damn," Rick whispered to himself as he shifted into drive. Then he gunned the engine and headed toward home.

RANDY

Randy wandered back to his own apartment around midnight. He could hear his brother Kevin snoring. Kev must really be sick to miss Friday at Freddie's. Randy was tempted to wake him to tell about Julie, but he'd probably hear a raft of shit about it, so he laid on the lumpy second-hand sofa and just thought about her.

He pictured her and his heart thumped faster; she was so alluring and still had that long hair and hippie style of dressing that he loved.

He was crazy for Julie since the first time he saw her on the school bus. She just had a spark about her, always upbeat, and she'd sing out a song line whenever it came into her weird little brain. She had a habit of touching you when she spoke—a hand on your arm or a poke to the belly—that warmed him and made him want to talk to her forever. He always tried to prolong conversations with anything that came to mind. He had tried to think of something witty to say tonight but was tongue-tied just looking at her.

Rick, on the other hand, was someone Randy and Kevin admired. He was tough, rugged but always friendly to them. While he was under the hood of Kev's car, they'd hand in wrenches and he'd throw out nuggets of wisdom—stuff about life in the real world they couldn't learn in class.

Like the other day, he said, "Think of this engine like your girlfriend. You gotta keep your hands on her if you want her to purr."

Good car advice, but Randy didn't want to think of Rick's hands on Julie.

"Damn! Figures they would be a couple," he said to himself, "The *perfect* couple." He imagined them being crowned king and queen of the Rough Riders and huffed out a dry little chuckle. *Hope that doesn't make me the jester.* He moaned and punched the sofa pillow. His feelings conflicted, a mix of admiration and jealousy. Who was he kidding? Julie was way out of his league.

Kevin said he had tried to call her and Colleen, when he moved here last fall, but never got an answer and kind of forgot about it with classes and everything. Randy had not attempted calling himself. He'd only been in town a few days and was shy about talking to either of them.

He'd done ok with girls in California, mostly surfer girls. That was fine for the sex part, but they didn't get him. He couldn't really hold a conversation with them.

There was one girl he dated junior year that was special, but she moved out of state and he just didn't have it in him to pursue a long-distance relationship. Tonight, when he saw Julie again, he wondered if subconsciously he was waiting for her.

All these years away, he had fooled himself into thinking Julie was a junior high crush, that they were only friends. They had never even kissed, for God's sake! Tonight, when he saw her again, it hit him. No one had ever rocked him the way she did, and he doubted anyone ever could.

Chapter 3

AUGUST 1977

It was a Friday night, and Julie looked forward to "Freaky Friday at Freddie's" and another night with Rick. She had been jittery with excitement all day in anticipation of his smile, his kiss, his strong arms lifting her right off her feet. He looked at her like she was a treasure, and he was her guardian. It was like a fairy tale.

Last week, he made love to her for the first time, with the passion and desire of a man, so different than the boys she'd been with. He took control of her, devoured her, left her weak, trembling, and begging for more. She wanted so much more. When they were with the crowd, he was funny in that sarcastic way of his and he kept his walls secure. But when they were alone, he let the façade slip a little to reveal a peek of the depth within.

She pulled into the parking lot as Rick was coming out his door.

"Mind if we take a little drive? My sister called, asked for a ride to my cousin Leslie's."

"Sure, I'd love to meet her!"

"Slide over, I'll drive."

Rick smoothly backed the car out and started toward the beltway. "My old man is home, and Dawn wants to get outta the house. They don't see eye to eye these days."

"Where does Leslie live?"

"In Wiltondale. Near the college. Dawn and Leslie are a year apart and thick as thieves. Aunt Jo is Mom's older sister, so she never says no to Dawn crashing there. I'll take the scenic route, show you Val's place."

They drove north into Baltimore County. Julie lost track of the twists and turns along the narrow country roads. The windows were open, and the smell of crops ready for harvest and livestock swirled through the car, rich and alive. I'd love to live out here, Julie thought as pastures dotted with Black Angus and fields thick with corn and soy flew by.

"Up on the left is where Val's dad trains his horses."

As they came over the crest of a hill, a white fence came into view and stretched for miles around fields of bright green. There, on the top of a rise, six thoroughbreds grazed, long-legged silhouettes against the sinking sun. Another three stood near the fence and raised their heads as they passed.

"Majestic," Julie said.

"Good word for them. You should see 'em run."

Past the fence, the woods rose around them again and the car rumbled across a one-lane wooden bridge. Beneath, a stream gurgled by, swelled with yesterday's rain. Finally, Rick turned on to a long, rutted driveway that wandered through a crop of trees and came to a rickety split-rail fence. Its gate stood open and grown over with weeds. Ahead was the house, a grayish-green two-story clapboard with a narrow porch across the front. Near the porch, there was a big tree stump with an iron pot of Black-eyed Susans atop.

They pulled to the side next to an old Ford Bronco, a faded blue station wagon, and a rusted-out horse trailer where the driveway gave way to weeds and tall grass. Behind the house was a dilapidated barn and a fenced-in garden, overflowing with August crops: tomatoes, squash, and peppers. Beyond that, fields rolled back to woods again.

Dawn hollered out the second-story window, "I'll be right down."

A muddy yellow lab bounded up to the car from behind the house. Rick got out, and the dog jumped with exuberance. Rick scratched it behind both ears. "This here's Clyde. He's my buddy. Ain't ya boy? Hey, come on, I'll show you Baby."

He led her to the barn. Clyde followed behind, tail wagging. The door was open and as they entered, conflicting smells of gardening and gasoline assaulted Julie's nose. There, among some rusty farm equipment and sacks of fertilizer, was his work of art in the making—the '67 Impala. It was jacked up and various tools were strewn beneath it. The hood was blue and the rest black. One busted headlight gave Baby the unsettling effect of a wink.

"She's a work in progress."

"This is the other woman, huh?"

"Yeah, here's where I spend my time away from you. Aw, you jealous?" He grabbed her and swatted her butt. "Don't be jealous. Once she's running, we can christen her back seat."

Julie blushed at the memory of last weekend's love making and giggled, "I'm gonna take you up on that!"

They walked back toward the house and Rick sighed casually, "May as well go in and meet the 'rents."

"I wasn't expecting to meet your parents. Do I look ok?" Julie asked, running her fingers through her wind-tossed hair.

"You always look great. Don't sweat it, hon, my mom is gonna love you and who cares what the old man thinks. Being how it's Friday night, he's probably well on his way to six sheets. I come by my drinking ability naturally." Rick gave out an ironic chuff.

Julie followed him up the steps of the back porch.

"Watch that second one. It's wobbly. On the list of things to do."

Rick's mom was at the kitchen sink, washing a large pot. Her knobby elbows stuck out and flapped like wings as she worked. She wore a pale-yellow blouse and blue pedal pushers. Probably tall in her youth, she had a bend to her spine that gave her a defeated look. As the screen door screeched open, she turned and brushed a wisp of gray hair from her worry-lined forehead.

"Oh! Ricky! I didn't know you were coming! Should have gotten here sooner, I coulda fed you."

"Hey Mom, this is Julie. Julie, my mom, Beth."

"Hello, Mrs. Madsen. So nice to meet you."

"Nice to meet you, too. Please, call me Beth," As she dried her hands on a frayed dishcloth, Beth smiled, showing straight white teeth, and Julie could see she had been stunning once upon a time.

"Place is a mess," Beth's eyes darted around the room, "Wasn't expecting Ricky to bring anyone."

Julie glanced around the kitchen. Everything was slightly shabby but as neat as a pin, except for the dishes in the drying rack.

"Oh, well, always nice to have company. Come on and have a seat."

"Who's that, Beth? The boy wonder show up?" called a raspy voice from the other room. Rick's 18-wheeling father was between runs.

"It's me alright, Pop," answered Rick. Then to his mother, he said, "We're just giving Dawn a ride to Leslie's. We can't stay."

His father showed up in the doorway and leaned his broad shoulders against the jam, beer in hand. He resembled Rick—same curly dark hair except with gray running through it, same firm jaw, and broad forehead, but hard looking and grizzled from too many miles of rough road. Rick had inherited his mother's blue eyes. His father's were dark—dark and dangerous as black ice.

"You always runnin somewhere, ain't ya," he sneered. Then he noticed Julie. "Hey there, pretty. Introduce me to your girl, Rick." She thought he was attempting charm, but his voice sounded as if he had eaten gravel, all rough—no soft. He was a walking caricature of a hillbilly trucker.

"This is the king of the castle, Julie. I introduce Mr. Floyd Madsen, trucker extraordinaire!" Floyd gave a little bow, lost his balance, recovered and gave her a grin and salute. She noticed a gnarled scar on the back of his hand, running up past the wrist. Just then, Dawn came breezing in, and gave a hurried kiss to her mom.

"I'm staying over. I'll see you tomorrow."

Dawn was skinny, almost to the point of looking malnourished. She wore thick dark makeup on her bright brown eyes and had teased her bleached hair so it fluffed out around her rouge-kissed face. Her attempt to look older hid the natural beauty beneath.

"Don't you go till you give a kiss to the old man!"

Dawn reluctantly retreated to place a peck on her father's cheek. She spun back and headed to the door, and as she passed, she mumbled, "Sombitch stinks."

Julie barely stifled a laugh. This is one spunky chick, she thought. "Nice meeting you," she said, and turned to follow Dawn out the door.

"Gotta run, Momma," Rick said.

His mother grabbed his hand. "Y'all take care now . . . Come have dinner soon. Bring your laundry."

Rick kissed her cheek. "You take care. And call when you need me, hear?" He saluted his father, "Adios, Floyd. Catch you on the flip-flop."

Julie heard Floyd huff as Rick followed her and Dawn. She had an inkling of where Rick's walls got built. As he drove, she scooted over and rested her head on his shoulder. He smiled and took hold of her hand. She sent a telepathic message to him through the breeze from the open windows. *I'm breaking in, mister, one brick at a time.*

Dawn chirped up from the back seat, "You two are too, too sweet together. Kinda make my teeth hurt."

"That's from all the gum you chew," Rick said. Julie peeked up at the rearview mirror and saw Dawn blow a big pink bubble, it's pop an exclamation on his statement. Dawn sucked the gum back into her mouth with a smile. Julie laughed. Then a storm cloud settled over Dawn's face. "I swear, Rick. That sombitch makes life turn to shit."

"He ain't hitting on you again, is he?"

Julie tensed at the thought, and Rick squeezed her hand.

"No. Just bein' a jerk. Wish he'd get back on the road."

"Yeah, it's almost peaceful when he's gone . . . But you'll get out on your own soon. Trust me, distance makes the heart grow . . . less pissed."

"Ha!" Julie said, "Can I use that quote?" she twisted around so she could see Dawn over the seat, "So, what are you doing tonight?"

"Probly up to no good," Rick said and chuckled.

"Hey, *whatever* we do, it'll be *good*," said Dawn as she dug through her purse. "Probly hanging in Towson with some kids that go to school with Leslie."

"Leslie goes to Towson High," Dawn told Julie. "I wish I could get out of Hicksville and go there. I hate living with the cows and chicken shits in Hereford."

Dawn looked out the window.

"How bout we drive them into Towson, Rick, so they wouldn't have to walk?"

"Sure, Rick's taxi service aims to please," Rick said. "But not a bad idea. I could get my eyes on these boys that are sniffing around you two."

"You got nothing to say about who I run with. Like you give a crap," Dawn quipped, but her mouth turned up, a secret grin.

Julie was pretty sure that Dawn was glad Rick gave a crap and thought that Dawn needed some watching over. She seemed like a wild little bird, all ruffled feathers and ready to fly, but fragile. Dawn talked a good game, but Julie thought there was still a lot of little girl under the platform shoes and hot pants. She smiled across the seat and was pleased to see Dawn smile back.

"Well, damned if my girls aren't getting along!" Rick said. He sat a little straighter, as if he was proud of that, as if it was his doing. She patted his knee and gave him a look.

"What?" he asked, all innocent, but he couldn't hide the grin that lit his eyes.

The house was a small, well-kept colonial in a quiet community. As they pulled into the driveway, Leslie rose from her perch on the porch steps. Her ample flesh spilled out of her tight halter top in a way the teenage boys would ogle. Dawn hollered out the car window, "Rick's driving us into Towson! Hop in!"

Leslie shrieked her approval and wobbled across the lawn on her high-heeled sandals.

Julie said, "I'm Julie. Glad to meet you."

"Whatever," Leslie responded in a tone that indicated Julie could shrivel up and die for all she cared. "Rick, drop us at Gino's."

"Yes, Your Highness!"

Gino's was a McDonalds-like fast food place where Julie had hung out when she was in junior high school. There was an old church graveyard across the street that kids used for a make-out and pot-smoking place.

"You aren't hanging in the graveyard, are you guys?" Rick asked.

"Hell, no! I don't party with dead people!" Dawn said. "We're probly just getting Gino's and walking to Four Winds Boutique."

Leslie murmured something to Dawn that made her face light up. Julie guessed it had to do with those ogling teenage boys.

They made their way up York Road to Gino's, and the girls jumped out and slammed the doors.

"Thanks for the ride, Ricky," Leslie said over her shoulder and blew him a sassy little kiss.

"Don't worry, we're cool. See ya around, Julie," said Dawn, and disappeared into the restaurant.

Rick shook his head as he drove out of the parking lot. "Hell on heels . . . I need a drink."

Julie sang out a line from a Kinks song about being a slave to demon alcohol. Then she wrapped her arm around him and kissed his cheek, "Step on it, taxi driver. Far out and Freaky Freddie's awaits!"

Chapter 4

SEPTEMBER 1977

It was the opening day of football season, and Julie picked Colleen up in her beat-up '68 Dodge Dart, a hand-me-down from her parents to her brother Will and finally to her. Colleen and she named it "Old Grandad" like the whiskey.

At the front door of the O'Malley house, she hollered hello. A swarm of redheaded children appeared and surrounded her with chatter and sticky hugs.

Colleen was the oldest of eight. The next down the line was Connor. He waved at her from the sofa and went back to his book as the baby on the floor pulled on his shoelaces. The twins pushed at each other against the open door. Quiet 7-year-old Molly grabbed hold of Julie's hand and gazed up at her with adoring eyes.

Boisterous Finn hollered, "Watch this!" as he attempted a somersault and crashed into her legs.

"Oh, hello, Hon!" Catherine O'Malley, Colleen's mom, called out from the kitchen, "Have fun watching the . . . Now you stop that, Sean! . . . the game. Oh, sweet Jaysus!"

Colleen rolled her eyes as she emerged from the kitchen and shooed the little ones away from the front door. "Sean is using his poop to make art on the kitchen wall. Let's get out of this madhouse!"

Once on the road, Colleen asked, "How'd your date with Mr. Possessive go last night?"

"What do you mean by that?"

"He watches you like a hawk, doesn't let you out of his sight."

"So? He likes to be close to me. I find that charming, don't you?"

"Well, that's not the word I'd choose . . . "

"Hey, growing up, his dad beat on him. Until he got those muscles, that is. He's protective, not possessive. From watching out for his sister, probably."

"Oh, that's sick! I can see the protective angle."

"Yeah, and he's different when we're alone. His edges smooth out. I like to think I have something to do with that."

"I guess it's nice to have a guy crazy over you."

Julie stared at Colleen. "You think he's crazy over me?"

"Duh!"

Julie grinned, "Good, cause I'm crazy over him!"

Truth be told, she was enraptured, electrified in love. When they were apart, she was consumed with thoughts of him. A profound physical ache filled her and threatened to spill over like lava, and she couldn't get enough. Everything that went before had just been a rehearsal for this forever love, and she prayed he felt the same way.

As the girls pulled into the parking lot, a football came flying toward them and careened off the hood. Randy would have gone over the hood as well, but Bibbit the dog tripped him up and he went down hard.

"Good tackle!" Walter called from higher on the lawn, "But he's on our team, ya fleabag!" Bibbit barked back a response that was probably a curse word in dog-speak.

The girls got out of the car. Colleen grabbed Randy's arm and hauled him up as Julie fetched the errant football and tossed it back to Walt.

"You need to work on your passing game," she said.

"Bert Jones, I'm not. But Bibbit is definitely trying out for the Sack Pack."

Walt gave Julie a one-armed hug. "Game day at Rick's . . . Beer in the cooler. Morons on the balcony." He gestured to the balcony above them where Val, Craig, and Cups were flinging bottle caps above their heads, like mini frisbees, a favorite pastime of the apartment dwellers.

Rick pushed the door open and carried out a portable TV with foil flags on its rabbit's ear antennae. "Hey, the cheerleaders are here!" he said and set the TV on a patio crate.

Kevin staggered down the stairs from the second floor, holding a coil of heavy-duty extension cord whose plug end trailed up behind him.

Julie did her Julie thing and sang out the first line of "Wichita Lineman" Julie style, "I am a line-guy from Baltimore County."

Randy joined in from the lawn, ". . . and I drive up York road."

Julie and Randy sang the line about searching for an overload together.

"The next Donnie and Marie, folks!" Walt said, and threw the football at Randy. It bounced off his back and Bibbit nimbly retrieved it.

Rick shook his head, took the cord from Kevin, and plugged the TV into it. "No overload here. Old Kramer is paying for our outside viewing today. Also got the big TV in the living room. We be watching in stereo!"

Kramer was the owner of the apartment buildings. Walt and Hank had been plugging into the outlet in the hallway for months. They rationalized the free electricity was fair compensation for the miserable air conditioning they lived with over the sweltering summer.

Julie kissed Rick's cheek, "Hey there handsome."

Rick squeezed her and said, "You always do this to me . . . Now I've got that stupid song stuck in my head!"

Julie laughed, "I can't help it, I'm a lyrics addict!"

"There are worse things to be addicted to . . . like strawberry shortcake." He released her and handed her a lawn chair. "Now, let's get these chairs set up."

As Julie sat the chair near the screen door, a booming voice captured her attention and she peered in the screen door. Butch, a beefy guy with tattoos on both his bulging biceps, was sitting on the sofa, pontificating on the upcoming game. He had short brown hair, a big bushy mustache, and wore thick-lensed glasses.

"That there is Butch. The one I told you about," Rick told her.

"I finally get to meet Teddy Roosevelt! He looks just like him!" Julie said.

Eddie LeClaire, Craig's musical sidekick, joined the party wearing a blue-banded fedora over his slightly crooked, smudged glasses and shoulder-length hair. Eddie lived down the street with his parents. Marilyn bounced her way over in a blue and white polyester pantsuit, waving a pom-pom and singing the Colts' fight song.

"Christ, now everybody's singing," Rick shook his head in mock dismay.

By 1:00, more than a dozen fans crowded around the two TVs, ready for kick-off. The Colts didn't play until 4:00; the televised 1:00 game featured the Washington "Deadskins" and New York Giants. There were hollers of "*Kill Kilmer!*" referring to the Redskins quarterback.

Cups, words tumbling out a mile a minute, yelled, "Drink of the week, Kill Kilmer. Gin, V-8, with parsley garnish—for the fuckin' turf hanging off his face guard!"

By the way he was bopping, Rick suspected Cups had dipped into some white powder. *Ain't getting tempted with that cocaine shit again.* He took a long swig of beer and put his arm around Julie. Throughout the game, Rick got a weird, warm sensation as she cheered and grabbed his hand.

At halftime, Ken and Suzie, a young couple from the far building, breezed in and announced that they were engaged. A cheer went up around the room, and Suzie blushed as she showed off her new ring.

"Better you than me, man," Rick said as he smacked Ken on the back. "You know you look nervous as shit, right?"

"Yeah, I know . . . but look at her. She's the one and only for me."

Rick looked at Suzie, pretty thing in overalls and a tank top, and damned if she wasn't glowing. Ken was, too. Rick stole a glance at Julie and that Wichita song played in his head, especially the lines about needing and wanting. He felt like she'd lassoed him with an electric wire and he'd be on that line forever.

The Giants pulled it out with a 20–17 win.

By 4:00, spirits were high. There was a joint floating among the group, adding, as Eddie liked to say, "Ambiance" to the alcohol consumption. The decibel level rose when the Colts took the field in Seattle. Most of the gang loved baseball, but they *lived* for football season.

The first half ended as Julie's favorite player scored a touchdown. She jumped up and down yelling, "Go, Rosie!"

"Guy's gotta be tough with a name like Roosevelt Leaks," Rick said.

"How come you know so much about football?" Walt asked Julie.

"Brothers," said Julie. "I grew up tripping over baseball bats and lacrosse sticks and getting tossed around like a football."

Rick smiled. *My woman can hang with the boys.*

By consensus, food was needed. Julie and Colleen volunteered to make a pizza run and collected money.

Walt handed Julie a ten, "Get me an Italian cold cut with extra hots and whatever Eddie there wants. You are going to Maria's, aren't you? Don't go to that Pizza Palace—their subs suck." He sang out, "Maria's! I just had a sub from Maria's!" to the tune of *West Side Story's* "Maria."

"Ok, Walt. No Pizza Palace, I promise."

"Atta girl," Walt said as he chucked her shoulder. Julie chucked him back, which led to a series of fake pummels at each other.

Rick watched, and the depth of the anger that bubbled up inside surprised him. His thoughts raced and tangled red: *They're getting a little too chummy . . . thinks he's Mr. Charming . . . damn that Glen Campbell song!* He stood up and took a step toward them, not sure what he meant to do, but Eddie chimed in with his order, and the camaraderie between Julie and Walt stopped.

"Cheesesteak, fried onions, *man-lays!* Hurry it up! I got a wicked case of the munchies!"

"Ok, ok! We'll hurry!" said Colleen. She grabbed Julie by the arm and pulled her toward the door. "Everybody else happy with pizza?" The rest of the crowd yelled out orders in a cacophony: "Filet Minion!" "Green Eggs and Ham!" "Sophia Loren!" "Deadskins on a platter!"

Colleen and Julie looked at each other, said, "Pizza it is," and danced out the door singing, "Food, glorious food!"

The game ended with a stellar pass from Bert Jones to Roger Carr. Touchdown! There was much hugging, beer spilling, and chaotic celebration.

Rick's mood lifted, with no one being the wiser. Now he was overcome with a kind of elation . . . *The Colts won, I got money in my pocket, and I have the prettiest girl in the room. Damned if I'm not happy!* A picture of *The Grinch who stole Christmas* emerged in his mind. He shook his head and joined his friends in celebration.

Hank, who had passed out in an easy chair during the third quarter, suddenly yelled above the noise, "Body bags! Body bags!" and fell off the chair.

"Oh, shit, he's up to it again," muttered Walt to Rick as they bent to help Hank up from the floor. "I got him . . . Come on buddy, time to shake it off. The jungle is haunting you again."

Hank had been a tunnel rat in Vietnam. He traveled in-country as a brilliant physics student and came back broken. No one knew about PTSD yet. They only knew something happened to soldiers over there that most couldn't even verbalize. Many came home addicts of one substance or another. Hank found his solace in any bottle that had liquor in it. His friends, who were mostly too young for the draft, watched over him like worried parents, thanking God they hadn't had to suffer the atrocities of the Demon called Vietnam.

The night revelry wore down, and the partiers stumbled home to bed, dreading Monday morning's alarm clock calling them to class or work.

Colleen headed to the parking lot as Julie lingered for a kiss at the open door. Rick pulled her against him, wanting to immerse himself in her, but he knew Colleen was watching, so he broke away.

"See you soon?" she asked.

"You know it. Coming over to watch MASH Tuesday, right?"

"Can't wait for the start of the new season . . . but I don't want to watch that show anywhere near Hank. Poor guy gives me the creeps when he screams out like that."

"Yeah, we all got our crosses, but I'm glad that one's not mine. It was a happy day when I tore up that draft card. Well, call after your class tomorrow, hear?" Rick bent down and kissed her cheek, right near her ear, and couldn't stop himself. "Love ya."

His face grew warm, so he swatted her ass and pulled the door shut.

Rick watched Julie through the screen as she walked to the car, and when the dome light blinked on, he saw she was wearing a shit-eating grin.

Chapter 5

SEPTEMBER 1977
COLLEEN

Colleen didn't have a car. She had to rely on rides from her overtaxed parents, or on friends like Julie, who were lucky enough to have a set of wheels. So, she and Julie worked out a plan for Monday mornings. Colleen slept at Julie's on Sunday nights and hitched a ride in Granddad.

Monday mornings at the O'Malley house were pure chaos, with all those kids getting ready for school, but it was always so peaceful at the Fairburn house. She and Jules could snuggle into the twin beds in the guest room and rehash all the events of the weekend before drifting off to sleep.

Colleen had English 101 at Towson State at 9:00. Julie could drop her outside the building at 8:20 and still get to Essex in plenty of time for her English class. Colleen would be one of the first students in the lecture hall and could get her favorite second-row seat like she had done all her life.

Monday, September 19th, was no exception to their routine. Julie, sounding high on love, sang along with the radio, "Wanna be your everything . . . not some puppet on a string . . ."

Colleen smiled as she looked out the window and remembered the day their friendship began.

SEPTEMBER 1973

On the first day of seventh-grade chorus, Colleen entered the room, glanced furtively at the few students already there, and slid into the second seat in the second row—not the first row—she would feel too exposed. In the second row, she could shield herself from scrutiny but still pay attention and keep her A average, undistracted from the losers slouching in the back row. The second seat—not the aisle seat, but close enough so that she could make a hasty retreat at the end of class. Second row, second seat was her safe zone.

Just as the bell rang, the last few kids hurried in the door and someone tumbled into the seat next to her, a whirl of jingling bracelets, flowing hair, and tie-dye.

"Oh, hey, can I sit here? I'm almost late! That crazy Randy . . ." she gasped, pointing toward a tall blond boy settling into the back row. "He's always messing with me, making me late!" She took a breath, "So, we finally have a class together!"

Colleen wasn't sure if the girl meant her or Crazy Randy.

"You remember me from Southwood?" the girl asked.

Southwood Elementary School . . . Colleen finally recognized her, Julie Fairburn. She looked different.

"Oh, yeah, you were in Mrs. Davis's sixth grade," Colleen stammered.

"Right! You're friends with Liz Booth, right? She's in my homeroom this year."

Their teacher, Mrs. Green, tapped her desk loudly from the front of the room. "Quiet down, class! We must take attendance before we can make beautiful noise together!" She started calling out names.

Julie leaned over and whispered, "Hey, you going to Liz's party this Friday? Can I catch a ride? My Dad can drive us home. Maybe you could stay over after."

Thus began a lifelong friendship. Before Julie, Colleen had always been shy and cautious. She preferred to watch life from the sidelines. After their friendship took hold, she rode the waves that Julie left in her wake, enjoying the ride.

SEPTEMBER 1977

Julie pulled the car over. "See you at 3:00. It's gonna be a wonderful day!"

Colleen got out with a wave. She went into the lecture hall and headed down the aisle.

When she approached the second row, she saw a blond head in seat number three. Colleen slowed her pace and hesitated before sliding in.

"I finally got here before you!" said the boy in seat three.

"Uh, yeah . . . Was there a contest or something?" she asked, perplexed.

"You didn't hear about the contest? Whoever got here first got the prize of sitting next to you!" his eyes sparkled, blue sea glass.

Colleen's mouth opened, but nothing came out. She blinked, unsure of what to say.

"I'm joking, I'm joking!" he assured her. "Okay, start over . . . Hi! I'm Pete. I've seen you sitting here the last couple of weeks. I'm usually early to class myself, but you've always got me beat."

"Oh!" was all Colleen could get out before she started laughing. This, she thought, is going to be a great class!

The professor ambled down the aisle. The rest of the students stumbled in and took seats, and class began.

Colleen barely heard Professor Behm droning on about gerund this and adverb that. She kept stealing glances at Pete. He had the nicest blond hair. She liked the way it curled just a little where it met the collar of his oxford shirt. She noticed he was stealing glances her way with a cute little smirk on his face.

" . . . due on the 26th. That's it for today. See you next class." *Oh, shit! I missed the assignment!* She risked a sideways peek at him. *Cool it, don't blush!*

"You got another class now?" he asked.

"No. Not until one."

"Early lunch? . . . With me?"

Colleen smiled, "That sounds good."

"We could walk to Pizza Palace or Harry Littles."

"Oh, not Pizza Palace. I hear their subs suck."

"Really?"

"Probably not. It was a review from a very unreliable critic. Let's just walk and see where we end up."

"Good plan." He agreed and followed her out the door.

It was one of those Maryland fall days that started out chilly enough for a jacket and felt like summer by noon. The sun was bright in a brilliant blue sky and a light breeze had helped dry the dew from the grass. They decided to grab sandwiches at the student center and found a spot on the lawn to picnic. Pete laid his jacket down for Colleen to sit on and eased down beside her.

"So, you're a freshman, right? Are you from Maryland?"

"Yes, I live a few miles away." Colleen unwrapped her sandwich with care and took a bite.

"I grew up in Parkville, went to Calvert Hall. I'm in my second year here." Pete stretched out his long legs, opened a bag of chips, and tilted it toward Colleen.

"Oh, no thanks, I'll stick with the sandwich for now . . . Calvert Hall. My friend Julie dated a guy that went there. Mike Murano?"

"Know the name, but he was a year or two ahead of me."

"She went to prom with him, when she was in tenth grade, but after he graduated, he went off to college."

"Break her heart?"

"Nah, she found somebody else pretty quick."

He ate a couple chips and sat the bag on his books he had piled beside him. "So . . . do you get this assignment?"

Colleen ducked her head and took another bite to delay her answer. *Christ! I can't admit I missed it because I was staring at him!*

After a moment, Pete laughed. "That's what I thought. You weren't paying attention either!"

Colleen glanced up at him. Her cheeks blushed crimson, and she felt something loosening in her. Some warmth dissolving the tension that until now, she hadn't realized she had carried with her for so long.

"Screw the assignment," she said. "I don't have to get an A in *every* class!" and she laughed with him, feeling so light she had to grab onto his arm to keep herself from floating away.

Julie met her after class in their designated meeting place on Allegheny Avenue. Colleen flung open the car door, threw her books into the back seat, and got in.

"I just met the man I'm going to marry," she said.

Julie studied her best friend and saw it—right there on Colleen's flushed face.

"Oh, no!" she said. "You got bit by the love bug too!"

NOVEMBER 1977

JULIE

On the Sunday after Thanksgiving, Julie went to the Colts game against Denver with Rick and some of the gang. Clad in blue and white, six of them piled into Jaws and another group drove down with Ty, a line cook at Spirits. They parked in the lot at Memorial Stadium on 34th Street where the cars were squeezed in, hood to trunk, and pulled out coolers for a couple hours of tailgating.

By 12:45, they were in their seats in section 36, second to the last row, with beers in hand. Rick was filling Val in on Walt's famous flag heist from the year before. He pointed out the team flags on poles all around the top of the stadium.

"During the national anthem, while all eyes were on the American flag, Walt backed himself up to *that* flagpole," he pointed to the one behind them, "which happened to have the Miami Dolphins flag hanging on it. Then he unhooked the rope and pulled that sucker down!"

"You're kidding!" said Val.

"He ain't shittin' you. I was right here when he did it!" Ty said.

"You saw it on the wall, right?" Walt said.

"Oh yeah. It has everyone's signatures! But how did you get it out of here?"

"Folded it up, sat on it through the game, stuffed it under his coat goin' out. Walt didn't look his skinny self that afternoon. He had a belly like Fred's," Rick said.

The national anthem played, and the players took the field. The Broncos got the ball and scored first. By halftime, the score was 14 Broncos–3 Colts.

Rick kept saying, "It's okay, we're a second-half team."

The second half brought more yelling and beer consumption, and Lydell Mitchell ran one in for a touchdown in the third quarter. But in the end, they lost 27–13. By then, much of the upper deck had cleared out, including Val, Julie, and Kevin who left at the two-minute warning to pee while they had the chance. They would all meet up by the bathrooms.

"Muthafucker!" Rick yelled. "What the hell happened?" He kicked the seat-back in front of him. That particular seat was already loose on one side, so it wobbled a little. "Three fuckin' interceptions!" Another kick and the seat gave more.

"Shit! It's coming loose!" said Randy. Another kick.

The remaining fans in Section 36 stopped moving when they heard the banging. They watched the display of anger they were all feeling and started cheering Rick on. The flames were fanned.

Walt grabbed Rick's arm, "Man, cut it out. Let's book!"

Rick pushed Walt backward. He would have tumbled down the entire upper deck had Ty, big as a billboard, not blocked his fall. Rick started kicking with all his strength until one side came loose, then he ripped the metal seat back from its mooring and raised it high over his head.

The fans watching cheered! Rick stalked up to the top of the stadium and threw it over the wall. It clanged loudly against the metal light pole on the way down to the concrete below. As the crowd cheered, Craig and Randy tried to corral Rick, but they were too late.

Julie and Val had finally gotten through the bathroom line and were standing in the promenade with Kevin. They heard cheering from above. Two Baltimore City cops hurried past and up the tunnel ramp. A bad vibe shuddered through Julie, and she started back into the stands. Light streaming down the exit eclipsed as Rick, in handcuffs, was escorted past her by Baltimore's finest. He saw her and offered a diffident grin.

Julie did a double-take, "What the hell?"

Randy hooked her arm as he trailed after Rick, "Come on, Jewel. We got trouble to sort out!" His face was scrunched into a worried scowl.

The rest of the gang fell in behind them, creating a parade of sorts, down the long ramps to the lower level where the police office was located.

Rick had four things going for him. No one was hurt. City cops have more crucial crimes to police. The officer in charge detested paperwork, *and mostly*, the cops were just as devastated by the loss as Rick was. Once they established Walt was semi-sober and driving, they let Rick off with a warning. "But we'll be keeping an eye on section 36," the cop said as he opened the door for them to leave.

The friends piled into the car, and Walt started up Loch Raven Boulevard.

"Well, Rick," Kevin said as he patted Rick's shoulder from the back seat, "You gave us one more story that will live on in infamy!"

"Yeah, add it to the list," Rick said with a mixture of pride and remorse, "and to the list of Lucky-Bastard-Dodged-Another-One!"

Chapter 6

DECEMBER 1977

People are molded and manipulated by their past—each experience adds to who we become. It's how we perceive those events and how we react, what we take from them or leave behind that ultimately makes us who we are.

Tragedy leaves scars.

Some people parade them, martyr-like, for all to see—to solicit attention, or as an excuse for bad behavior. Some hide them beneath layers and layers of insulation, daring not peel it away no matter how much it itches.

Some let their wounds fester, never to become a scar at all, but a parasite that eats their host alive.

They did not have their regular Friday night date. Rick's mother had called and asked him to come stay with her. She wasn't feeling well and Floyd was on a haul. He was vague about details, but Julie understood, "family first."

Saturday morning was a sloppy, gray mix of sleet and freezing rain. Matt called at nine and told her not to bother coming in. Shoppers wouldn't show up in this mess.

Rick called at 1:30, "Hey, just got home from work. Can you come over?" Something in his voice sounded insistent, needy, "The roads are salted, and it's warmed up some."

"Sure! Give me half an hour."

"Great. I still need to wash the grime off. Let yourself in."

When she got to the apartment, she entered with a "Hello." Rick emerged from the bathroom wearing a towel, his thick, dark hair dripping, steam wafting around him. She met him at the bathroom door.

"I like the outfit," she said as she shrugged off her coat.

Without saying a word, he kissed her. Then his hands were in her shirt and at the zipper to her jeans. She helped him slide them down, and he pulled her panties away. As he caressed her bottom, he lifted her to him, shifted her onto the sink ledge and her legs wrapped around him. His wet curls dripped and clung to her face. The heat of him throbbed against her, and then he was in her and she gasped.

Frenzied, he drove into her. The muscles of his back tensed and rippled under her hands with each thrust and she moaned with pleasure. He lifted her again and carried her into the bedroom, laid her on the bed and she raised her hips to meet him. Their rhythm synced but he seemed desperate in his fervor, starved for release.

Now it was late afternoon, and the rain had stopped; it almost seemed time had stopped. Julie lay drowsy and warm in the crook of Rick's arm. The sky outside the frosty window was blushing with sundown, yellow and orange, and rose like peach fuzz. To look at it, you wouldn't think it was an icy winter sky. That moment, before the sun kissed it goodbye and disappeared, the sky looked as warm and content as she felt.

"I had a brother," Rick said, breaking the quiet. "Yesterday would have been his birthday." He wrapped his arm more tightly around her, "Never told anyone that before. Never had anyone I trusted enough."

Julie tilted her chin up closer to his to let him see she was listening, not daring to speak lest she break whatever spell would allow him to go on.

"I was only four, but I remember him . . . a skinny baby. Mom let me watch after him while she was cooking. Just on the floor of the kitchen . . . not really in charge, but I thought I was. She'd lay out a blanket for him. She'd say 'Ricky, watch over your brother,' and I would talk to him and watch his big blue eyes watch me. I'd make funny sounds to make him smile. That little smile made me feel important, ya know? Like I was something special."

She put her lips to his bare chest and held him.

Rick scratched at his head as he continued, "I had a cold. Mom was nursing the baby in her room when I called for her, so she laid him in her bed. Pop was sound asleep; his snores came up the stairs from the sofa, so I knew it was okay to call for her . . . that he wouldn't yell at me to shut up, not be such a momma's boy . . . Mom came in with some Vicks, rubbed it on my chest and laid down with me, and when I could breathe through my nose again, I fell asleep . . . guess she did, too."

His face turned away from her then. "Never even said this out loud before," he wiped at his eye as if some foreign dust mote had gotten in.

"Next thing I knew I woke up, still warm from Momma, but she wasn't there. It was her screaming woke me up. Her screaming his name . . . sometime in the night, old Floyd, damn him, had revived from his stupor enough to stumble his ass to bed . . . laid down, right on that baby. Smothered him with his body and never even knew it till he heard the screaming, too. None of us were ever the same after that . . ."

Julie reached up, put her hand on his cheek, and turned his face to her. She saw the depth of pain in his eyes, swimming up to the surface. He didn't let the tears fall, but they were there, years of them, threatening. He pulled her up and kissed her urgently, and she held tight to him. She wanted to help him peel back the layers, take his pain, and let it heal.

He rolled on top of her and buried his face in the nape of her neck. Then he entered her again, starting slowly and building until he was thrusting with all his strength and he cried out and collapsed. She held him to her breasts and let him pretend his tears were just sweat on her skin. She held him until he fell asleep and prayed he found sweet dreams.

FEBRUARY 1958

BETH

Monday: Beth told herself to be strong for Ricky, for her surviving son, but she kept going under. The waves of grief kept pounding her, washing over her and pulling her down to the dark where she didn't have to remember. Floyd told the doctor it was crib death, but she knew the truth.

Wednesday: The wind woke her, blowing the branches of the oak tree and tapping against the window; whistling through the eaves of the attic, crooning out a mournful moan—or was that her? Someone shoved a bitter pill through her parched lips. She felt the rim of a cool glass and drank. Beth closed her eyes again to the weak light peeking through the curtains, but the wind kept moaning.

Thursday: Jo emerged in her dreams. Talked about Reverend Newel and Palms and lilies of the valley. One of those disjointed dreams that made little sense. She pushed herself under so she wouldn't have to follow its thread.

Saturday: There was a short service at the church—Jo and Marty arranged it—but she remembered nothing except Ricky clinging to her hand.

Monday: She was yanked from her drugged abyss with a slap to the face. Floyd was yelling at her . . . the boy was hungry and she needed to tend to him.

"You better pull yourself together now. Enough of this, you hear me?" He held her firmly by the shoulders and shook her. "I gotta get back on the road, pay the bills. You need to wake up and face the day." She roused enough to mutter something affirmative and pull herself out of bed. Once Beth was standing on her feet, Floyd turned his back to her.

"Can't believe you'd be so stupid to leave a baby in the bed." Then he walked out.

As soon as the door slammed downstairs, she made her body leave the room in search of her son. He was sitting at the kitchen table, hand in a box of Cheerios. He looked up with a hesitant smile.

"Hi, Momma."

She tousled his head and shook her own to clear her thoughts. The doctor gave her pills to calm her, but they only made everything fuzzy. Beth pushed the bottle to the back of the spice cabinet. She needed to see the sharp edges of her life lest they sneak up on her again and steal away her child. She would remain vigilant in her duties as a mother.

Beth set about putting the kitchen to rights, washing the dishes that filled the sink and scrubbing the counters and table. Then she took inventory of the food in the icebox and made a list of what they needed. Through all of this, Ricky followed her like a shadow, helping in his little boy way. He handed her the dishes from the table. He diligently counted the potatoes in the bin, very proud that he was almost five, and he could count all the way to thirteen.

"Momma," he was holding the dustpan as she swept the crumbs from the floor. "Aunt Jo says Baby Gabe is in heaven."

She stopped mid-sweep and gathered him into her arms. "That's right where he is," she murmured into his little ear.

"I shoulda looked after him better, Momma."

Her heart broke wide open then . . . but she held back the tears and arranged her face into something she hoped was reassuring before she set him back on his feet.

"You took the best care any big brother could. Don't you think any other thing," she tried to sound stern. "It's God's turn now to look after him and our turn to look after each another."

"Okay, Momma, I'll look after you. Cross my heart," he said as he picked up the dustpan and dumped its contents in the trash can. "Momma," He turned to her with a stern expression of his own. Beth hoped she could hold on enough to answer his next unanswerable question.

"Can we get Tiger cereal this time? I sure am tired of Cheerios."

A small smile emerged on her face, something Beth thought would never happen again. That was the moment she knew—they would survive.

Chapter 7

CHRISTMAS 1977

Boutique Picasso stayed open every night in December until 8:00, so Colleen was working there for the holidays. Julie and she split the nights and worked together on Saturdays, along with the owner Matteo. The store was closed on Sundays because of Maryland Blue Laws.

They were exhausted after exams and the store's record-breaking holiday sales, not to mention squeezing in time for boyfriends. But the extra hours put enough money in Julie's pocket to get Rick a new winter coat for Christmas.

Finally, Christmas Eve! Julie and Colleen enjoyed the last day of the holiday rush together.

Matt left early to finish his own Christmas shopping. He told them that last year, he waited until the shop closed and had to give his stepfather cheese because the only store still open was the A & P.

Just before closing time, Randy and Kevin barreled in the door, all smiles and good cheer, "How are our favorite soul sisters?" Kevin gave each one a peck on the cheek.

"Exhausted!" said Julie.

"And excited," said Colleen.

"We come bearing gifts," Kevin handed a package to Colleen. "Open it!"

Colleen, never shy around a gift, tore into the paper with vigor. Inside was a 1978 Day-Timer with a tiger on the front, Towson state's mascot.

"You guys know me well. Thanks!"

Randy, who stood with his arm behind him, revealed what he was hiding with a flourish, "Ta-da! This is for you, Jewel, it's a bonsai tree."

"I see, the tiniest tree I ever saw!" as she took it, he kissed her. She wasn't sure if he planned it or if the turn of her head was to blame, but it landed square on her lips.

Julie laughed, "Oh! Is it a mistletoe tree?"

"Banzai!" Randy yelled out. His face colored, and they all laughed.

"But, really, it's a bonsai. There's a booklet on how to take care of it," Kevin said.

"It can live 800 years," Randy told her. "You're all the time talking about fairy dust and magic, so . . . thought this looked like a magic tree." His handsome face was so ardent and unassuming, a rush of affection surged through her. She placed the magic tree on the counter and threw her arms around his neck, "You really do get us, CR"

He beamed and said, "It's RC, not CR." When she let go, he shrugged his shoulders and looked at the floor with a smile.

"We're driving to Richmond from here. Just wanted to see you two before we went," Kevin said. He chucked his brother on the arm, "Got to go, little bro!"

"It's nice your parents moved closer. Here. From us to you two," Colleen pulled out a box of Wockenfuss chocolates and several bow-wearing packages of Berger's cookies. "Treats for the ride. Merry Christmas!"

"I'll give one of these to Mom. Her Balmer roots say, 'Thank youse, hon!'" Kevin laughed.

"Tell them Merry from us, hons!" Julie said as the brothers bustled out the door.

"I love that Kevin still calls him little bro, even though he's five foot ten and Randy's six-three," Julie laughed.

"Once a little bro, always a little bro. I let none of mine forget it!"

"Wish you could come to Fred and Marilyn's tonight," said Julie as she counted out the register.

Colleen's words came in stutters as her head popped in and out of the jewelry case, "I'd love to stop by but . . . I am so excited about meeting . . . the rest of Pete's family tonight!"

She took the trays to their nightly hiding place in the back room at break-neck speed and zipped back out, "Almost done there?"

"You in a hurry?" Julie gave her a sideways smile and shut the register drawer. "Let's get together right after all the hoopla."

"Gotta do that! On the 27th after your brothers go back?"

"Perfect! Men or no men?"

"Men! Definitely men. And dinner. Maybe Bratwursthaus?"

"Rick likes that place. Cool, we got ourselves a plan!"

All the chores done, they gathered their things and turned out the lights. The evening air was frosty against their cheeks as Julie locked the door. It had that crisp Christmas feeling. They wedged their bundles of last-minute gifts around the bonsai in the back seat.

As Julie drove, Colleen held her new Day-Timer on her lap. "You and I make the perfect pair," she said, running her fingers across the raised tiger on its front, "Organized magic."

"Good name for a band," Julie pulled over in front of the O'Malley home. "Tell your parents and the brood, Happy Christmas Eve."

"Same to yours."

"Now go get beautified for your boyfriend!"

Julie peeked over the seat back to be sure her magic tree was secure and drove home, singing about having a merry little Christmas.

Julie's brothers and their families both came for Christmas. Russ, Linda, and the kids stayed at the Fairburn home. Will and Diane stayed at her parents' house in Homeland. Her parents couldn't get enough of her since she was pregnant with their first grandchild.

On Christmas Eve, they all went to Aunt Dorothy's house for an early supper and the 7:30 church service at Providence Methodist. The church was aglow with candles and the altar was draped with evergreens. They sang the old familiar hymns that Julie loved: "Silent Night" and "Little Town of Bethlehem." This is the real Christmas, she thought as she squeezed her father's hand.

Once back home, Julie loved watching the excitement build for the little ones. Not so many years ago, she was the young one who still believed in Santa. They put out cookies and milk and hung their stockings. The adults admonished that Santa couldn't come until everyone was sound asleep. By 10:00, Julie could slip out to see Rick.

When she got to the apartments, a party was in full swing at Freddie's. She made the rounds with hugs and cheer. Marilyn's plump frame was clad from head to toe in red and green with a tinsel scarf wrapped around her neck and Santas hanging from her ears. A large shiny bow perched atop her sleek dark hair.

"Nothing puts you in the mood for the holidays like working retail!" she told Julie. She worked at Hutzler's department store, mainly for her employee discount, judging by her extensive wardrobe. "Well, you know. You're in the business!" Marilyn said, and winked.

Freddie, glassy-eyed and flushed, handed Julie a candy cane. "Welcome to the "Not-Christmas-I'm-a-Jew" celebration! Here's your gift, now lemme feel you up."

Julie laughed and jumped away from his clutches. Marilyn swatted Freddie with her tinsel.

"You are on the naughty list and I don't mean Santa's, mister!"

"Aw, honey, I'll be nice . . . if you'll be naughty!" That's all it took for the two lovebirds to clench in an R-rated embrace.

Rick snuck up behind Julie, wrapped his arms around her, and bit her neck. "Hey, Shortcake, where's the mistletoe?" he whispered in her ear.

"Who needs mistletoe?" She spun in his arms and gave him a smooch.

"Hey, let's go next door. I got something for you." He grabbed her hand and led her into his apartment.

On the table was a small box and a large package wrapped in red paper with a hand-tied gold bow.

"I confess, I'm not so good at wrapping. Dawn helped there. But here . . . Merry Christmas."

The large package was a huge tin of popcorn, with three sections of flavors. Snoopy and the Peanuts gang danced around the tin, "I know you love popcorn . . . and Snoopy. You can keep it here and share it with me. You know, while we watch MASH and stuff."

"So sweet! And salty," she kissed his cheek. He handed her the smaller box, looking sheepish and proud. She unwrapped it, and inside was a pendant on a silver chain. It was about ¾ inch in diameter, a ring of small diamonds and garnets in the shape of a heart.

"Oh! It's beautiful!" She lifted it from the box. "Here, put it on me." While she held it in place, he did the clasp.

"It's shortcake colors . . . You know I love you, Shortcake."

She hugged him, "I love it! I love you."

"I'll be right back," Julie ran out to the car and came back with a big box wrapped in festive print. "Now open yours."

Rick tore the paper off and opened the box. He lifted out a caramel-colored suede coat, lined with shearling. "Wow. This is great!"

"Your love keeps me warm, so I wanted you to have something to keep you warm."

"Darlin', you warm me to the core, come here," He held on to her, his breath soft on her neck, "I love you. Didn't think I could feel this way, but there it is . . . You make me better."

II

Christmas morning, Rick got up at his usual 6:00 am. He had coffee and showered, shaved carefully, dressed, and still had time to sit and worry. He was nervous about spending Christmas with Julie's family. Rick got along fine with the parents, but today he was meeting the brothers. *That's a whole different ball of wax.* He knew how brothers felt about little sisters; he had one.

Even more cause for anxiety, he was throwing her into the fray of Christmas with the Madsens, Ackermans, and Porters. *If this doesn't make her turn and run, I guess she's mine to keep.*

He tried on his new coat, brushing its shearling against his cheek as he slipped his arms in the sleeves. *Almost as soft as her skin.* He slid his hands into the deep warm pockets and felt a folded piece of stationery. He pulled it out and read the words in Julie's quirky left-handed script:

Rick,
The day I met you
You were ringing bells
Jangling a melody, reaching out to me
Through the trees on the summer breeze
Into my heart
You smiled, and I melted (like ice cream in June)
Now it is December
The winter wind dusts the trees with snow
Let it blow
I've got your smile to keep me warm
And your melody etched in my heart.
I love you forever, Julie

Bet she doesn't realize she just ripped a giant chunk of insulation off a grown man's heart.

III

Julie woke to Eliza's tugs. She had shared Julie's bed.

"Wake up! Wake up! It's morning!"

The boys stood at the side of her bed. "I think he came! Hurry, we gotta see."

"Get Gwanma, get Gwandaddy! Come oooon Zhuwie!" Luke chimed in.

The three of them jumped on her in a pajama-clad frenzy.

"Okay, okay, I'm up! Let's go! Hurry up, I'm tired of waiting for you!"

"We were waitin for yoou, silwey!"

She threw Luke on her back and grabbed Eliza and Rusty's hands, and they ran into the guest room.

"Come on! Santa came!" Julie yelled as she jumped on Russ in the twin bed. Luke tumbled onto his father in a fit of giggles.

Linda raised her head as the older two scrambled up onto her bed.

Russ let out a groan and laughed, "Little Julie waking me up on Christmas morning, I remember it well!"

By 10:00, the living room was strewn with torn paper, ribbon, and toys of all shapes and genres. The other adults had traded their pajamas for party attire. Julie was dressing carefully, in anticipation of Rick's arrival. She made three small braids down one side of her hair, the rest loose and wavy. She wore a red velour dress with her new necklace resting just above its scooped neckline—just above her heart. She dabbed a little cinnamon oil on her neck, her holiday scent, and in a swirl of soft and sparkle descended the stairs to join the family.

Evie, in her traditional Christmas sweater, hovered over the table with finishing touches. Harry, electric knife in hand, buzzed over the ham. Russ was on the living room floor with the boys. A partially constructed race track stretched out in front of them, its directions upside-down in front of Luke.

"Might as well read them that way, buddy. They seem to be in Japanese," said Russ.

Julie sat on the couch with Linda and Eliza, surrounded by Barbie and her friends.

"Dis one's Ken," Eliza informed them. "He's her boyfriend. They Kiss!" She smashed Ken's face into Barbie's.

"That's how Julie kisses her boyfriend," Linda said.

"You do?!"

"Well, maybe not that rough!" Julie said, swatting Linda's leg.

As if on cue, the doorbell rang.

"I'll get it!" Julie headed to the door with a gaggle of little bodies following.

It was Rick, right on time.

"Coat looks great! You look like the Marlboro Man. Well, except without the cowboy hat."

"Are you a cowboy?" asked Rusty, his eyes wide.

"Nah, just a country boy."

"Come on in," Julie stood back, holding the door open.

"Come in, come in!" chimed her backup singers.

Rick let Julie pull him along by the hand. There were introductions to Russ, Linda, and the kids, and then Will and Diane arrived and they did it all over again.

"Rick, this is my other brother Will, the obnoxious one!"

"Hey, I thought you wanted him to like me!" Will said, as he gave his sister a squeeze.

"And Diane, she's our math whiz."

Rick said, "Math was my favorite subject right up until algebra. I like to keep my numbers and letters separate."

Diane laughed, "I wasn't great at algebra either. I'm more of a charts and graphs person than a math whiz."

"She's a date whiz, too. She remembers everything I ever did!" Rusty chimed in.

"Seems you have a fan club," said Will. "Glad the obnoxious one did something right."

Russ commandeered Rick and Will to help put the dang-blasted track together. The sisters-in-law moved to the kitchen with Harry to put out food, and Julie sat with Eliza and Barbie on the sofa.

The track was finally ready for a test run. Rick pulled two Matchbox cars out of his pocket.

"Here, these were mine when I was a kid. I didn't wrap 'em or nothin' but Merry Christmas."

"Cool!" Rusty said and Luke echoed, "Coowol!"

"This here is a 1959 Chevy Impala." He handed it to Luke and said, "I got me a '67 Impala."

"And this, this red one here, is a Jaguar."

Rusty took it carefully, as if it were made of glass.

The boys examined their new treasures.

"And I brought one for your sister, too."

Eliza, hearing sister, slid down on the floor, and Rick handed her a cream and peach-colored car. "This is a Ford Thunderbird. My Uncle Marty drove one of these once."

"Thanks, Uncle Rick!" she said and kissed him on the cheek.

"Let's race! You have this one." Rusty handed Rick one of his new Matchbox cars.

"Wets wase!" echoed Luke.

They like me! He smiled up at Julie who was beaming like a Christmas light.

Russ gave Rick a friendly pat on the back. "I think you just made friends for life, man."

Will stood and said, "Think we need some of Dad's Bug Juice," and wandered into the kitchen.

Julie explained to Rick, "It's my father's famous alcoholic concoction—whiskey sour mix, orange juice, and a very light dose of bourbon with cherries and orange slices. He always serves it in the cut glass punch bowl. Harry and Evie aren't big drinkers, but Dad prides himself on the Bug Juice. He makes a virgin one for the kids, too."

"Why's he call it that?"

"That's my doing," said Russ. "When I was a kid, I thought the pulp felt like bugs in my mouth."

Aunt Dorothy and Uncle Jack popped in for a bite, bringing tins of cookies for all, and they were all called in for brunch.

The conversation was light, and music played softly in the background. "I'll Be Home for Christmas," came on, and Evie got teary-eyed. Julie explained to Rick that the song reminded her of the Christmas Harry was away at war.

Then Harry told his story of the same Christmas. "The only cheer us soldiers had was Bing Crosby singing 'White Christmas' over the loudspeaker."

"Don't you just love holidays with family? All the stories and traditions," Dorothy said to Rick, holding her hands to her heart.

Rick couldn't answer that one. He just smiled and took hold of Julie's hand under the table.

There were more gifts to unwrap—Rick gave Harry and Evie a box of gourmet chocolates (thanks to Marilyn's assistance at Hutzler's). In return, they gave him a pair of leather gloves.

Evie said, "To go with your coat, dear."

Harry and Evie opened the gift from their kids. Evie tore off the wrapping and exclaimed, "Oh, my!" and sat back suddenly as if it would grow teeth and bite her. It was a microwave oven.

"Mom!" Will said, "You are going to love this thing . . . Tell her Diane!"

"I couldn't live without mine, right Lynn?"

Lynn said, "Right! Mom, give it a try."

"It's like TV dinners, Mom. You resisted at first, but now you live on 'em," said Russ.

Harry weighed in then, "Now, Ev, we've got to drag ourselves into the future. I sure don't want to be an old fogey!"

Evie relented, "Okay, I'll try it. Julie, will you teach me how this thing works?"

"Sure, Mom." Then she whispered to Will, who was slouched next to her on the couch, "Ya press a button, Knucklehead." They snickered behind their hands.

"Now, Evelyn, enough micro talk! Let's do the big thing."

She looked at him, confused, then it dawned on her. "Oh, yes! Oh, Dorothy, you know, the special gift! Everybody, settle down. Harry?" Everybody settled down in semi-suspense, and Rick glanced around. *Nice* is the word that came to mind.

Harry took a patriarchal stance, and with a gleam in his eye, handed Julie a wrapped box. Inside was an envelope. It contained a note-

This entitles the bearer
matching funds for the purchase
of a NEW CAR!
{Granddad is tired}
Love and Ho, Ho, Ho!
Mom and Dad

Julie hopped up and threw her arms around Harry. "This is so cool! I can choose the car?"

This launched a friendly argument among the family about which cars were best these days. Rusty kept saying, "Jagwire, Jagwire!"

The topic wound down when Harry said, "Rick, you're the car expert. What do you think of that new Dodge Aspen?"

"Well, from what I know it could be the best 6-cylinder engine out there."

"There you go!" Harry said, pleased that Rick backed his choice. "Julie, we'll go test drive one this week!"

"Thanks, Dad. It's a date!"

Her brothers ribbed her; she was the princess, spoiled rotten. She retorted she was spoiled but not rotten.

After all the gifts were gone from under the tree, Luke fell asleep with his head on the car track and Eliza snuggled up on Evie's lap for a nap with Barbie. Rusty, Will, and Russ focused on how to put the Mouse Trap game together.

Julie and Rick bid everyone farewell and headed out the door. They were having dinner with Rick's family at Aunt Jo's.

"Got another surprise for you," Rick swept his arm out toward the street. "Ta-Da!"

There was the Impala, shining like onyx in the sharp winter sun.

"She's beautiful! How did you get her painted?"

"My Uncle Jess ain't good for much, but he knows a guy who owns a body shop. He got me a big discount and threw in a couple bucks for the premium paint. Said it was a Christmas present."

"Wow . . . Beautiful." Julie walked around the car, admiring. "Who's Uncle Jess? Never heard you mention him."

"Pop's oldest brother. You'll meet him today if he shows. They're the only two left of the five brothers."

"What happened to the other three? Or shouldn't I ask?"

"Kelly is dead, wrapped his truck around a tree; killed his girlfriend, too. Rich died in Korea. He's the one I'm named for, and John is in prison, life term. That's a story for another day."

He opened the car door for her, "Are you sure you want to do this? Still time to back out."

Julie slid across the seat to the middle, "Why would I want to back out?"

Rick got in and turned the key. "Well, your family is so normal . . . And then there's mine."

"I wouldn't call us normal. We have our quirks."

"But they're so nice. And proper! No one cursed or threw a tantrum or *even threw up*!"

Julie laughed. "I'm sure you're exaggerating."

"Well, the throwing up doesn't always happen."

"Trust me, I can handle whatever is *thrown* at me."

"Even a stuffed turkey?" Now Rick chuckled himself—until he realized they were pulling up to the house.

Chapter 8

They gathered the gifts from the back seat and bustled up the walk. As they entered, Beth greeted them at the door with nervous chatter, "So glad you made it! Come on in, give me your coats!"

Rick, feeling nervous himself, glanced around for any time bombs. His mom seemed like she was holding it together. She looked pretty, with her hair combed back in a barrette and a nice silky-looking dress. Aunt Jo was in a heated conversation with Uncle Marty's father, sisters, and brother-in-law about politics, nothing new there. Kids and teenagers sat under the tree shaking presents, much to the dismay of Rick's Aunt Meg, Beth's oldest sister.

"Now kids, don't ruin the wrapping. Careful, that there is fragile!" Meg admonished.

Beth's mother, his grandma, sat snoozing in an easy chair. He could hear Marty with his mother in the kitchen, singing along with Bing Crosby on the radio and rattling pots and pans. Marty was the chef of the family.

There was no sign of Floyd.

"Where's Pop?" he tried to sound casual.

"Oh, he and Jess just stepped out back for a cigarette, I think. Haven't seen each other in a while, ya know." Beth attempted casual as well, but Rick knew they were on the same wavelength.

"Jess showed up, huh?"

Beth's eyelids flickered, "Yes, he's here."

Dawn looked up from where she was on the floor. She hopped up and threw her arms around them, "Sure am glad to see you guys. Put some fuckin' sanity in the mix."

Beth took Julie's arm and guided her across the room, "Lemme introduce you to the political debate team."

Dawn said to Rick, under her breath, "Nothin' blew up yet . . . late start." Rick and she had developed a sort of shorthand warning system over the years necessary for survival in their house.

Rick gave her a look that said he understood—their father hadn't started drinking until late in the day. It was a holiday with relatives, so the powder keg had a short fuse, regardless of alcohol consumption.

During the siblings' exchange, Beth introduced Julie to her sisters and Marty's family. Meg explained that two of her children lived out of town and opted not to travel this year, busy with their careers, and the other was presently at her in-laws. Rick interrupted his aunt, who tended to get long-winded about her kids, and led Julie to his grandmother. She was a tiny woman, shriveled and bent with age. She stirred as Rick touched her shoulder and opened eyes that were the same ocean blue as Rick's and Beth's. Her expression seemed clouded and confused, as if she'd journeyed back from some other time or place. When she focused on Rick, her features sharpened.

"Merry Christmas, Grandma," Rick bent and kissed her cheek.

"My Boy!" Her voice was thin and reedy as her body, "Lemme look at ya, ya whippersnapper!" She grabbed his arm in a vice-like grip, "Yer hair's too long."

Rick laughed, "You always say that, Gram."

"Well, I'm right . . . who's this here?"

"This is Julie. The girl I told you about at Thanksgiving."

Grandma took Julie's hand. The strength of the old woman's squeeze surprised her.

"Married yet?"

Julie smiled, and Rick shook his head.

"Well, don't wait! I want some Greats!"

"Cut it out now . . . you'll scare her away!" he said.

59

Julie said, "Don't worry, Grandma, Wild horses couldn't drag me away."

Grandma nodded decisively, as if that answered her question, "Now go see what's takin' that man so long with dinner. I'm hungry!"

"Sure thing, we'll check on that now," Rick said. And as he led Julie into the kitchen, he said, "Wow. You didn't sing it!"

"Huh?"

"Rolling Stones . . . Goats Head Soup," Rick hesitated, then sang, low, " . . . couldn't drag me away."

Julie's mouth dropped open, "You can sing!" Her laughter rang out like jingle bells, and Rick felt some of his tension melt away.

The kitchen was saturated with enticing smells, nutmeg and pumpkin, sage and sauerkraut. Uncle Marty, brow furrowed in concentration beneath his shiny bald head, was stirring a pot while his mother fussed with garnish on some pies. Casseroles and platters of food covered the counters. Next to the stove was a Hallmark plaque trimmed red and gold. It read:

Make it a
December
to
Remember!

"Hey, look what the cold brought in!" Marty turned the heat down on the burner. "That ought to be fine," he said to himself, then he wiped his hands on his apron, stretched to the limit around his rotund belly, and offered his hand to Julie.

"Uncle Martin . . . Not the one with antennas, huh-huh!"

Julie shook his hand. "My Favorite Martian, I loved that show!"

"And my mother, Hazel Porter." Then in a stage whisper, "This is the girl, Mother."

"A pleasure dear." She gave Julie an appraising once over and turned her perfectly coifed bouffant back to the pies. "Now, if you'll excuse me, I've got to get these ready! The natives are restless as always."

"She's a perfectionist." Marty, it seemed, couldn't decide if he was proud or irritated by that trait.

Just then, the back door screeched open and in walked Floyd in a cloud of cigarette smoke.

"Oughta get some Dubya-Dee for that, Marty. That'll set yer teeth on end!"

"Yes, Floyd, I'm aware."

Uncle Jess followed his younger brother through the door. He grinned at the kitchen inhabitants and Julie thought, *it has set his teeth on end!* His left front tooth was half gone, its edge brown with decay, and his right canine was missing entirely. The lowers, crooked and pitted, were tobacco-stained, as was his lower lip. He was taller than Floyd but had none of his broadness. Jess was all jutting bones and sinew. He reminded Julie of jerky in the smoke-house, hung up to dry.

Rick greeted them with trepidation, "Uncle Jess, Pop."

"How's the car lookin'? I was jes sayin to yer Pop, here, you got that engine purrin' like a pussy in heat," he bobbed his head at Floyd. "Ain't that right, Babe?"

Marty, wearing a grimace, glanced at Hazel, but she was oblivious to the raunchy statement. Rick glanced at Julie, who was stifling a giggle behind her hand. Floyd muttered something and pushed his way out of the room.

"Sombitch is hardheaded, ain't 'e." A rhetorical question from Jess.

"Well! Now, dinner is ready. Martin, ring the bell," Hazel gestured to the dishes of food on the kitchen island. "Make yourselves useful and set all that on the dining room buffet."

Martin did, literally, ring a bell—a little silver one with a red ribbon tied around its handle—and the family trooped in, like Pavlov's dogs. One by one, they piled their plates with Turkey and the traditional sides. The adults sat in the dining room. The formal table, not long enough to hold 14, merged with a smaller table. A festive tablecloth covered both. The younger crew crowded around a card table set up within sight through the archway to the living room. Beth was careful to guide Floyd to a seat away from Jess, and Dawn opted to squeeze in at the grown-up table next to Rick. Leslie glared at her and plate in hand, stalked off and sat with her sister and the younger kids, children of Marty's siblings.

Uncle Marty bustled around pouring wine. The political argument continued, getting louder in proportion with the amount of wine poured.

Jo was driving her point home, "Well, don't blame me. I voted for Reagan back in the primary! Carter *and* Ford can kiss my derriere!"

Hazel bellowed, "If I hear the name Jimmy Carter again, I will scream! Now, it's Christmas! No more politics!"

"Thank God for that," said Dawn, around a mouthful of potatoes.

Beth, sitting on Julie's left, said, "My mother, you see, named us for the girls in Little Women. She jest loved that book . . . Hoped to have a fourth daughter, but God wasn't willing."

Meg chimed in, "That's why I named my girl Amy. Works for McCormick in Chicago. They transferred her there."

Floyd picked his glass up and tipped it at her, "Here's to bein' trans-ferred. When's yer turn?"

"Now, Floyd, please . . . be nice," Beth said.

Meg harrumphed and turned away.

Grandma said loudly, "What? What the hell did he say?"

Jess chuckled, "Ya sure got a way with the ladies, Babe."

Dawn told Julie, "Pop was the youngest of the five brothers. So, they jes' called him Babe. Didn't have a Christian name until he was two."

Rick said, hushed so Floyd wouldn't hear, "He hates being called Babe so you just *know* Jess does it to piss him off."

"Think I'll have another," Floyd stood up, knocking Beth's wineglass.

Rick lunged for it and set it right before its contents hit the tablecloth. In the process, he upended his plate, and turkey, gravy, and stuffing flew across the table.

Floyd smirked and took his empty glass into the kitchen for more bourbon.

"Oh, dear!" Beth said.

"No harm done!" said Bob, Marty's brother-in-law. He, being directly across from Rick, bore the brunt of the projectiles.

The kids thought this was wildly funny, adults having a food fight, and started throwing rolls and stuffing at each other with holiday glee.

"Enough of that!" Jo spat at them. She jumped up and whacked the closest child on the back of the head, causing him to cry out. That brought the roll toss to a halt.

The other adults weren't sure whether to laugh or cry, but Julie couldn't help herself. She watched a perfectly cooked slice of turkey slide its way down Bob's tie and plop on the plate in front of him. A swell rose in her and out came a *Ha!* in great force.

Laughing, thank God, is contagious. Soon everyone was chuckling away, including the child with the whacked head.

Everyone except Hazel, "Well, that's it! Clean up this mess! We'll have dessert in the other room!"

Marty scurried to do as he was told, but Jo grabbed his arm. "Hazel, this is MY house! I'll decide where we have desert!"

"Fine, then. YOU deal with this mess!" She rose from the table and strutted out to the powder room. Marty vacillated from his mother to his wife and sat down in a huff.

"What a wuss," whispered Dawn.

Beth, always the peacekeeper, said, "Come on kids, let's clean up so we can have dessert and presents."

The kids cheered and started gathering dishes. Beth looked across the table, "I'm so sorry, Jo. It's all my fault."

"Something like this happens every holiday and you always take the blame, Beth! Cut it out!" Jo retorted. "I'm going to smoke," and she stomped out.

Jess had been sitting back, enjoying the show. He zoomed in on Jo's ass as she left the room. "Think I'll join ya," and followed Jo out.

They cleared the dishes, put away the card table, and brought pies to the buffet. Adults got coffee, the Irish kind. There was a mild scuffle over which kid wanted what pie, but finally, all were sitting, with pie, around the tree.

Jo had calmed down and started the proceedings by handing a gift to each child, youngest to oldest. The young kids ripped into them with wild abandon, throwing paper and ribbons every which way. Jess pulled a chair in from the dining room and stretched out his lanky frame. Acerbic amusement deepened the furrows in his face. Floyd, drink in hand, leaned against the doorway, wearing his signature scowl.

Jo handed a gift to Dawn, "For you, Punkin, from Marty and me."

And one to Leslie, "So you can match."

The cousins tore the packages open and pulled out suede miniskirts—one purple, one fuchsia—with large buttons on one side.

"Cool!" said Leslie.

"And my favorite color!" exclaimed Dawn. She wrapped the skirt around her and did a twirl and a hip shake.

Jess reached out and smacked Dawn on the rear, "Can I get fries with that shake?"

Floyd shot across the room in a flash, grabbed Jess around the neck, and hauled him from the chair, "Fuckin' pervert!" he spat out.

Rick was on his father almost as fast. He seized him, pulled him backward, and Jess sank back down, rubbing his neck.

Beth rushed over and wedged herself between Floyd and his brother, "Now, Floyd, you promised."

Floyd loomed over her shoulder. "Don't ever touch my girl, *Junior!*" he said, punctuating the name he called Jess. Then his aggressive posture slumped, "Lemme go, son. I done made my point." Rick loosened his grip. Floyd stalked off into the kitchen, looking nowhere but the floor in front of him. Beth, wearing a worried frown, followed behind.

Everyone else in the room had frozen like deer in headlights. Now there was a communal sigh, the crisis was averted. As if someone flipped a switch to reanimate them, the gift-giving resumed. Julie moved close to Rick and touched his shoulder. He flinched, body still tense. His eyes bored into Jess, "That was way out of line, Jess. Maybe time for you to go."

Jess stood up and moved closer, "I like yer spunk, kid. You jes remember where you got it from, hear? Yer a Madsen through and through." He let out a short bark of laugh, "You take care a that car," then he pointed a gnarled finger at Julie, still standing behind Rick, "and that perty thing there, too." He turned to the room, "Adios, *family!*"

Julie shuddered with the heat from Jess's glare.

He grabbed his coat from the rack and walked out.

Rick's arm went around her shoulders and Julie refocused on her surroundings. Dawn was sitting on the floor, crying quietly. Leslie, next to her, was leaning in, her posture emphasizing the importance of her low-spoken words. The Porter clan, along with Jo and Meg, were making a gallant effort to resurrect the holiday spirit.

Then, out in the kitchen, there arose such a clatter . . .

Rick sprang into action again. A crazy vision had time to enter her mind as he moved—of Rick, fully dressed in fireman's gear, hauling a huge surging hose toward the flames. Julie followed close behind, pulling along with him.

Beth was bent over, attempting to retrieve a broken casserole dish from the floor. Floyd loomed over her with spittle, like venom, spewing from his lips, "Leave it! Hear me? Don't you dare clean up that mess."

He didn't notice them in the doorway. He grabbed her by the hair and yanked her up to him. Then he slapped her. His open hand raised red stripes on her cheek, "You hear me?"

His backhand swung, and Beth's head snapped back as if it would fly from her body.

Rick lunged and pulled his mother from Floyd's clutches. He flung her toward Julie and almost instantaneously delivered a right hook to Floyd's jaw.

"Why?" He screamed, "Why do you always have to ruin things for her? Damn it, she deserves one fucking Christmas!"

He was interrupted by Floyd's fist against his face. Rick's nose spouted blood as he drove Floyd into the stove. A saucepan clanged against the wall, the gravy remains splattering the plaque about a December to remember. Floyd's fist swung again, connecting with Rick's ear . . .

Jo shrieked from the doorway, "Get out!"

A tear-streaked Dawn was behind her, along with Marty and Bob.

Rick slammed Floyd again against the stove, then lifted him by the front of his shirt and pushed him toward the door.

"Fuck y'all," Floyd gave a dismissive wave, pushed the screechy door open, and stalked off into the frigid night. Two minutes later they heard the cough of his old Ford start up and drive away.

Rick turned and started to say something, but Jo cut him off.

"Get out," her menacing voice turned on her sister. "I mean all a ya. Get the hell outta my house. Take your shit and GO!"

She turned to Dawn and her voice softened, "Sorry Punkin, you, too. At least for tonight. Go on, help your Ma."

Somehow, the four of them got out the door with no conversation from the Porter family. Meg had already herded a protesting Grandma to her car and was getting in the driver's side when they came out. She met them at Rick's Impala and hugged Beth, "Don't think you'll see him tonight. He'll sleep in the rig, as usual, I s'pose. Ricky oughta stay with you just in case."

"Good idea, Aunt Meg," said Rick.

As they pulled away, he said, "I'll drop Julie home and stay at the house tonight."

"I'm staying with you," said Julie.

Rick stared at her, "You nuts?"

"No, I just feel like I can't leave them," she touched his shoulder, "or you. I feel like they're my family, too. I'll call my mom, make up some excuse."

He looked at her again, astounded.

"I'm staying. That's final."

They drove in silence the rest of the way, the December wind pushing them along the narrow country roads toward home.

Chapter 9

They pulled down the rutted driveway into the wood and past the dilapidated fence. Julie noticed Beth had strung lights on it to make the place look festive.

"Those just bring to light how old and tired that fence is, don't think I'll bother next year," Beth said.

"I think they're pretty, Momma," said Dawn. "You better put 'em up next year. Just cause Pop's an asshole don't mean we shouldn't have Christmas."

Rick let a chuckle escape from behind his hand, and Beth's mouth twitched and turned up.

They got in the door amid barks of welcome from Clyde. Beth filled his water bowl and wandered into the living room. Dawn made tea for Beth and opened a bottle of Bailey's someone had given Beth and poured herself some in a jelly glass. She tilted the bottle toward Julie.

"I'd love some," Julie said, then followed Rick into the bathroom and washed the blood from his face. She examined the damage.

"Gonna have a pretty shiner but you'll live."

He grinned up from his patient's perch on the toilet seat, "Told you somebody would throw turkey. Didn't know it would be me." They shared a quiet snicker, "Come on, let's check on the wounds out there," he gestured toward the living room.

Julie called home and then found two dish towels, bundled ice in them, and joined the others. Rick was tending to the woodstove, and smoke tickled her nostrils with a heady redolence. Traces of that smoke stayed on Rick's clothes after his visits here . . . just a whiff of the fire made her warm.

She handed one bundle of ice to Beth for her bruised cheek, and the other she gave to Rick.

"Put this on your eye, babe. It'll help the swelling. You look like Rocky Balboa."

Julie took off her boots, and settled with Rick on the sofa. The four of them just sat, feeling layers of tension and exhaustion rolling over one another in rapid succession.

Dawn spoke first, "Ma, why'd Pop call him Junior?"

"Oh Lordie, is that all that's botherin' you?"

She laughed.

Rick smiled, relieved at the sound.

"Well, the family called him Junior since he was a tot, ya know, bein' how he was Jessie Madsen, Jr. Called him that when I met him. But long about 1951, he decided he didn't wanna be Junior anymore. I guess it was around the time of the fire, can't rightly remember. But he was adamant, and when Jess says a thing, you better listen . . . Now you mention it, what put it in Floyd's head to call him Junior after all this time, I wonder?"

"Maybe because he called Pop Babe," Rick ventured.

"Maybe."

"What fire?" Julie asked.

Beth shot Rick a look and he nodded, "No secrets, here, Mom."

Beth cast her eyes on a black-and-white photograph in a wooden frame that hung on the wall, of a family gathered on the porch of an old farmhouse. A tall, angular man stood holding a small, dark-haired child on his hip. The child, a scowl on her captivating face, pushed away from him with reed-thin arms. Next to the man was an obese woman sitting on a chair, her voluminous dress draped over her knees. A larger version of the held child stood, in overalls, before her, and behind her stood a younger version of the father—it was Uncle Jess. Beside him, were two more boys, broad-shouldered and handsome on the verge of adulthood, and in the center, on the bottom step was a beautiful boy with dark curls, smiling at the camera, his eyes lighting up the whole clan.

"The family house burned down, with Floyd's parents in it. And his sister, too." She gestured toward the photo, and took a sip of her tea, "The hell with tea. Put a little bourbon in this. There's a bottle hiding in the cleaning stuff under the sink."

Rick looked surprised, but got up and found the bottle. He put some in the tea, started to take a swig, but thought better of it. Instead, he poured himself what was left of the coffee in the pot and set some more to brew.

Beth took a sip, shuddered as its burn slid down her throat, and continued her story. "Anyway, this was after Rich had gone to Korea. John and Jess had moved out by then. Kelly was already in the ground. Floyd was asleep and woke to the smoke that was driftin' into his room. Looked for Bonnie, but she wasn't in her bed. Figured Bonnie was in the basement where she liked to go for privacy, all of them brothers around. Floyd heard her yell but couldn't get to her . . . Burnt his hand. That's where the scar came from. He barely got out before the whole place went up. These old houses are like tinderboxes, ya know."

"I'm named after her, my middle name," said Dawn.

"Yep, Dawn Bonnie Madsen, such a pretty name."

"You never talk about her."

"Too painful—Pop's only sister, my best friend. She's the one made that necklace I wear sometimes, the wooden bead with the B burned on it," a dreaminess came over Beth, and just as quickly she shook it away. "There were six. Only two surviving. Bad luck? Cursed? I don't think so . . . My Poppa always said you make your own luck—good or bad. 'Course, then Poppa died and we didn't worry none about luck, just worried about eatin' but that's another story."

She rubbed her finger around the edge of the cup as she spoke.

"They found Floyd's mother's remains where the bedroom woulda been, and Senior's in the back of the house. That's where they think the fire started—that he fell asleep with a cigarette and some of his moonshine. Started moonshine making during prohibition."

Rick smirked, "Pop said they called it Madshine."

Floyd ran to a neighbor for help, but by the time the firemen got there and started pumping water from the pond, wasn't much to be saved. Floyd jest sat and watched his home and family burn to nothing."

"So sad." Julie couldn't wrap her mind around the story. It made her heart hurt.

"Almost makes you feel sorry for the bastard," Rick said. "Okay, enough for tonight. Momma, let's get you to bed."

"There're clean sheets in the linen bin. Make that bed up before ya let Julie sleep in it."

Dawn dragged herself up the steps ahead of the others, used the bathroom, and laid down on her bed fully clothed. Julie tiptoed in, pulled the boots off Dawn's feet, and covered her with a quilt. "Julie," she murmured, but before she could put her thoughts into words, she was asleep.

Julie left the room and softly closed the door.

Rick stood in the doorway to Beth's room, "See you in the morning." He closed her door and took Julie's hand. As he led her down the hall he said, "My mom rarely drinks, I almost fell over when she said she had a bottle hidden."

They entered his childhood bedroom. Everything was pretty much as he left it. Johnny Unitas looked out at them from a poster on the wall, his arm forever cocked in a game-winning throw. There was a small bookshelf and dresser, a bed with a scratched wooden headboard, and a nightstand with a reading lamp, its shade yellowed with age.

The bookshelf held mementos of his younger days: a deer's antler, some paperbacks and comic books, a photo of the Hereford High School Bulls football team, circa 1970. He played linebacker because he was big, tough, and quick to shut down his opponent. Lying alongside it was a wallet size photo of a girl he had dated and a wrinkled notebook page with drawings he had done, quick sketches of a bird on a limb.

On top of the dresser, under a layer of dust, was a football and a framed black and white photograph of a handsome young man in an army uniform. Julie picked it up and brushed the dust off the glass. He resembled Rick, the dark hair and piercing eyes. His expression had the same intensity that she had seen Rick wear when he was deep in contemplation.

"That's my Uncle I was named for. Family got word he was killed in action a few months before I was born." He took the photo from her and looked at it, "From stories I been told, he was the best of the bunch. Maybe God took him so he wouldn't have to live through the shit storm his family left in its wake."

He set the frame back on the dresser, "Let's get this bed made so you can sleep."

Rick folded back the faded quilt. They each took a side of the sheet, spread it open, and watched it billow, then float down and settle on the old double bed.

Julie turned so he could help with her dress. He unzipped it and traced the zipper's descent with his finger down her silky skin to the small of her back. Julie shrugged the fabric from her shoulders and the dress puddled around her feet. She shivered from the night air and the touch of his breath as he kissed the curve of her neck.

Rick wrapped his arms around her, inhaled the cinnamon and woodstove clinging to her. The smell of home. He felt a welling of desire and love and gratitude that he had never experienced before. They stood there a while, not moving, both lost in thoughts too big to comprehend. An owl hooted from the wood and broke the spell.

Rick found a flannel shirt in the dresser drawer and handed it to her.

"Gets cold in this room."

Julie put on the shirt, worn soft from years of washing, and snuggled in under the quilt. He turned off the light and laid down next to her, fully clothed. She nuzzled her head in the crook of his arm. Rick kissed her forehead, and she drifted off to sleep.

The moon peeking through the curtains laid a pattern of silver light across the floor. Rick watched it inch toward him and weaken as the night ticked by. He stayed there, never sleeping, his ears alert for any threatening sound until the pattern was erased by the first cold light of dawn.

It was then he heard Clyde bark.

Chapter 10

DECEMBER 26, 1977

Rick eased himself from the bed and peered between the curtains. Sure enough, there was the beat-up old Bronco and Floyd trying to hush Clyde's greeting. Clyde had played this game before and was having none of Floyd's shushing. Rick slid a box from behind his bookshelf. Inside was a snub-nose .38 pistol he had from his teenage rebel years. He stuck it in the back of his waistband, pulled his shirttail over it, and headed into the hall. It wasn't loaded, but if Floyd was still nuclear, just pointing it would save a lot of trouble.

Beth came out of her room with one sleeve of her robe still dangling beside her.

"It's him?"

"Yep, got a lota balls, don't he?"

"Rick, please . . ."

"Don't worry, Mom, I'm not going to start anything. Let's just see what he has on his mind." Rick bounded down the stairs. Beth stayed on the steps with her ear cocked for trouble.

Floyd had several tactics he used for the day after a blowup. Sometimes, he used the silent treatment, grumbling to himself, acting like he was the injured party. That one pissed Rick off to no end.

The second and easiest to deal with—He went about life as if nothing happened. Sometimes, Rick figured, he didn't remember much of what he'd done. Old Floyd would wake up, find coffee, and look at his knuckles, baffled like he was wondering why his hand hurt. These mornings were easiest to live with, but it was hard for Rick not to rub Floyd's face in his bad behavior.

Door number three was the worst, though. He'd wake up still pissing vinegar and come in cussing and swinging.

Floyd shifted his eyes as Rick entered the kitchen. "Didn't know you were stayin' here last night." It sounded like today Floyd chose door number two.

"Yep. Here I am. And here you are sneakin' in at dawn."

"Gotta change my clothes and get on the road. Got a haul scheduled." He grabbed a mug from the cabinet and poured coffee from the pot Rick had made the night before.

"Well, by all means, get to it." Rick backed from the entranceway to let him pass. Then he followed his father up the stairs.

Floyd said, "Mornin'," as he passed Beth, who had retreated to the landing above. Then he shuffled into the bedroom. Beth went down to the kitchen and Rick stood watch in the hallway. Floyd came out with his old duffle bag, carried it into the bathroom, and Rick heard the toilet flush and water run. Floyd emerged, hair slicked back, fresh shirt on, and smelling of Mennen Skin Bracer.

He brushed by Rick and hustled back down the stairs, a sickening cloud of aftershave wafting behind him. Rick heard toast pop and his mother's voice,

"You want eggs with this toast, Floyd?"

He wanted to go down and shake her. *After what the asshole did to her last night, she still makes him breakfast?* Some things will never change. When he heard the door slam shut, he went back into his room and watched from the window as Floyd drove away.

Julie was sitting up against the headboard. *How does she look so damn beautiful before she's even out of bed?* Rick sat down next to her and slid the .38 under the bed.

"He's come and gone. Likely we won't see him until the end of the week."

"Thank God, your mom can have a little peace and quiet. You think Aunt Jo will get over this?"

"She'll be fine. Jo's been down this road so many times . . . Probly why she married that wimp."

"So Beth married first, huh?"

"Yep. Thanks to me. They got married in December 1952. I was born in March. Beth was 16. Jo was probly jealous at first, till she saw the prize-of-a-husband Mom got." He huffed, "Guess Jo got the best of that contest."

"Well, at least something good came out of it . . . you." Julie gently kissed his bruised cheek.

"You always got something sweet to say. You are my little ray of sunshine, aren't you?" He grinned, pushed her back on the bed, and propped himself over her. "Light my way, darlin'," he dove in for her mouth. 10 minutes later, they were both wearing a grin and catching their breath.

"Nothing like a quickie in the morning," Rick sighed.

"I'll second that."

"What did you say? You want seconds?" Julie let out a squeal as he slid his hand between her legs. "I live to serve."

Beth interrupted their second course by calling up the stairs, "I made y'all some breakfast. Whenever you're ready."

Rick whispered in the ear he had been chewing on, "Damn, nothin' like your mother's voice to wilt a raging hard-on. I promise we will finish this later."

"Oh, I'm not worried a bit." Julie laughed and rolled him over, "But I need nourishment. Feed me!" She hopped up, grabbed the shirt that had been torn from her body, and ran for the bathroom.

Julie came into the kitchen, barefoot, wearing her dress. Rick pulled the chair next to him out for her.

"Coffee, honey? Or tea?" Beth asked as she set a platter of eggs and scrapple in front of them.

"Tea, please, but let me get it myself. You sit and enjoy your breakfast."

Beth started to protest, but Julie was already putting the kettle on. "Well, ok, if you're sure . . ."

"Mom, sit!" Rick said through a bite of eggs, "Julie can handle the tea."

Beth sat down; hands wrapped around her own mug to warm them, "You usually an early riser? Ricky here always has been. No trouble getting him up."

Julie brought her tea to the table and gave Rick a sideways smirk, "No, seems he gets up quite easy."

Rick ducked his head and shoved another bite in to hide his grin.

"Even as a little boy . . ."

"Mom! No embarrassing little Ricky stories!"

"Aw, come on Ricky, lemme hear some stories," Julie teased.

"Well, tell ya what, you and me will have to have ourselves lunch one day while he's at work. Then I'll tell all!" Beth's face lit up with a conspiratorial smile.

Rick looked at Beth. The early morning light from the window behind cast an aura around her uncombed hair. She was different somehow; just for this minute, she looked happy.

Beth stood up and rummaged through the basket she brought home the night before. "Never got to give you yer present last night." She handed Julie a wrapped package, "Go on and open it."

Julie pulled the wrapping off and inside was a V-neck, cable-knit sweater of forest green. She held it up to her cheek, feeling the softness of the yarn, "It's beautiful and so soft!"

"Made it to complement your eyes," Beth said.

"You knit this?"

"Mom knits all the time."

"It's my calming activity, ya know, keeps my mind from wandrin'. Try it on. Wanna see if it fits ok."

. . . the sweater over her head. It was perfect, a loose and . . . blushed.

Clyde, on the rug at the back door, raised his head and let out a short yip. It was a warning of the squall heading their way from above. Dawn stomped in, hair sticking up every which way, makeup smudged beneath her eyes.

"Y'all make a lot of racket for so early in the morning. *Some* people like to sleep, you know." She slammed open the cabinet, pulled out a mug, and poured herself coffee. Then she threw back a chair from the table and sat with a "Humph!"

"Morning Sunshine," Rick said, "wake up on the wrong side, as usual?"

"Shut up! Don't talk to me till I had caffeine," she glared at him and pivoted away.

Beth shook her head and said, "Dawn was probly the wrong name to choose for this one. Stormy mighta been a better choice." She reached over to brush a lock of hair from Dawn's forehead. Dawn growled and batted her hand away.

"So, better get you home, Shortcake, and me to work. Glad the station opened the bays late today."

Julie turned her gaze from Dawn, "Oh, sure!" She stood and hugged Beth, "I love my sweater. I have a gift for you. I think it got left at Jo's, in the, well . . . confusion and all." She turned to Dawn, hesitated, decided to just go for it. She put her arms around the grouch and hugged tight, "Got something special for you, too."

Dawn tensed up at first, ready to give a fight, but her body gave in and she let herself be held. She looked up at Julie, through mascara clumps, "You do?"

"Of course, can't forget my little sister!" Dawn hugged her back then like she'd been pulled in from the storm.

Julie found her purse and took out a small box.

Dawn opened it. Inside was a pair of silver earrings, hummingbirds in flight. Dawn put them on right away. "So pretty, thanks, Julie!"

Julie didn't tell Dawn she reminded her of a little bird. She wasn't ready for her to spread her wings and fly away.

When they pulled up to the Fairburn house, Rick said, "Gotta get to work. Call me later?"

"You got it, Rocky. Now get going before my parents come out and wonder where you got that. That's a story I don't need to share."

"I was hoping you wouldn't. I'm not real proud of my family."

She put her arms around him and said, "Shh, think good thoughts and I'll call you tonight."

She went into the house, hollered hello, and ran upstairs to change into jeans. When Julie came back down, she found Russ in the living room perusing the book about Frank Lloyd Wright she gave him for Christmas. Russ, himself, was an architect by trade. She sat next to him, and he threw his arm around her and continued to read.

"Where is everybody?" she asked.

"Will and Diane are still at her family's. Mom and Linda took the kids to Two Guys to exchange something. Dad is in his study working on something . . . and I . . ." He closed the book and stretched, ". . . am here enjoying the quiet with my favorite sister." He turned to look at her, "What's up, buttercup? How did it go last night with Rick's family?"

"Oh, fine. Like my sweater?" She stood up so he could get the full effect, "Rick's mom made it. Isn't it wonderful?"

"Very nice. Talented lady. Hey, how about we take a walk? I've been eating nonstop since we got here. Gotta work it off."

"Good idea. It's warmer out today. Let's enjoy it while we can. You know Baltimore weather . . ."

" . . . if you don't like it, wait 5 minutes."

They grabbed some jackets and headed out to walk the neighborhood. Julie loved spending time with her brothers. The three of them were very close, regardless of the age difference. Growing up, she always felt safe having two big brothers around. Even now, with them living far away, she could call whenever she required some brotherly love.

"I love having you guys here. Wish you could move back."

"Well, I have to stay where the job is. Right now, that's Charlottesville . . . but you can visit us anytime. We're only a couple hours away."

She linked her arm in his, "Those kids crack me up! Rusty told me he was wearing his taxi pants . . . It took a few for me to figure out he meant khaki! Oh, and I asked Eliza if she slept well. She said her friend Anna came to fly with her."

"Anna, her sleep fwiend," Russ nodded his head.

"She told me Anna always leaves her party shoes next to the bed."

"The girl knows her fashion," Russ said. "She told me you and Rick were quote, In love togever. She's already got you married off." He looked off at the neighbors' lawns, "but, he seems like a good guy . . . nice to the kids. Mom and Dad seem to like him."

"Yeah, I like him, too." Julie could feel herself blushing.

"Maybe a little more than like, huh?"

She thought a minute about how much she wanted to reveal, "Definitely! Definitely more than like . . . more like L-U-V." More blushing going on now.

Russ laughed and sang, "Zhewie's got a boyfriend!"

She punched his arm and laughed with him. They walked a bit in silence.

"He's got a lot going on. Works like crazy. I've never seen anybody take on so many jobs! His home life hasn't been so good. His Dad's a bit of a jerk," she mimed taking a drink, "Sometimes it seems like he's got the entire world on his shoulders, ya know? I wish I could relieve some of that burden."

"Well, all families have their own dysfunction, you know, we are very lucky to have the parents we do."

"I know that, especially seeing how other people were raised."

"You can be there for him, that's great. But you can't fix things for him."

"Wish I had a magic wand."

"Ha! Now you sound like the little sister I know!"

"I know, but," she ran her fingers through her hair. "Oh, I don't know."

He put his arm around her, "Just be happy . . . and let things happen in their own time."

They rounded the last curve, and the house was in sight. Will and Diane were just getting out of their car. Will waved when he caught sight of them.

"So, did Will say anything?" Julie asked.

"About Rick?"

"Yeah, he's more cynical than you."

"Thanks—I think." Russ took a deep breath, "He is cautious, not cynical. And he's like a mother hen about you."

"He's not sold, huh?"

She turned and walked backward so she could see his face.

"Let's just say the verdict's still out. He worries. He remembers you being hurt before. I wasn't here to live through that drama, he was."

"This is different."

"Ok, so like I said let things happen."

"In their own time, right."

Not wanting to think about previous drama, she turned back around and said, "Race ya!" and took off toward home.

Chapter 11

JANUARY 1974

Colleen, Liz, and Julie stood in line, their skates slung over their shoulders, waiting for the doors of Orchard Ice Rink to open. Liz tugged on Colleen's sleeve and whispered, "Check out the dudes behind us."

Colleen did her best to look without the dudes noticing, "Cute . . ." She elbowed Julie, who was digging in her purse for her membership card. Colleen shifted her eyes in the direction of the group behind them.

There were four of them: the tall skinny one kept bopping up and down to some internal song, the blond-haired one kept punching him in the arm and telling him to quit being such a spaz, the other two were huddled in conversation, throwing furtive glances at the chicks in front of them.

The girls sent Morse code looks to one another and began a routine to get the guys to notice them. Liz said loudly, "You are freaking me out, Chickie!" as she pushed Colleen into Julie.

Colleen glanced behind her and tried to think of a cool reply. Nothing witty came to mind, so she just burst out in laughter and grabbed hold of Julie's arm, which caused her skates to fall to the pavement with a clang. It worked like a charm. The tall guy stopped bopping and stared as one of the conversation guys pushed by him and bent to pick up the skates. Julie reached down at the same time, and they bumped into each other. They came up laughing and rubbing their heads.

The proverbial ice was broken and the seven of them skated and hung out on the bleachers together until the Zamboni rumbled out at 9:00 to smooth the rink's surface. During the break, they went to the snack bar, all but two of them. Liz and cool dude number four disappeared.

Joey, the tall one, said, "Jimmy's got a doobie. They're probably out getting high somewhere."

Colleen said through a mouth full of hot dog, "Sounds like Liz."

The lights went low, and the DJ came on the loudspeaker, "For the next 10 minutes, it's couples only, so don't be lonely. All you righteous dudes find a foxy mama and get your groove on, down on the ice. Here are the soulful sounds of Chicago!"

As the opening chords of 'Color My World' sang out, the blond, Mike, asked Colleen to skate with him.

"Get it on, you two!" said Joey.

"You are such a spaz!" Mike said as he led Colleen to the ice.

The boy who bumped heads with Julie put out his hand and said to her, "I'll try not to hit you in the head again."

"Maybe you knocked some sense into me." Julie took his hand, and they glided around the rink together under the silver sparkles of the disco ball. He was a better skater, but she was holding her own until Mike and Colleen sped by them hand in hand, oblivious to the world around them. Startled by their near collision, Julie lost her footing and almost fell, but his arms slipped around her waist and pulled her upright. Their eyes met and suddenly Julie didn't feel the cold. A break in the wall at the back of the rink was right beside them. He stepped off the ice and pulled her with him into the darkened bleachers. He kissed her, and her knees went weak.

His name was Sam and he was 17. He lived in Ednor Gardens in the city with his mother and his younger brother. He was sweet and funny and had the greenest eyes she had ever seen. That winter and into spring, they spent every possible moment together. By April, she knew. He was her first *true* love. He never rushed her, but he told her he loved her and she knew this was it—she was ready to give herself to him willingly and totally.

She was drowning in love and didn't want to come up for air.

She thought they would go on forever, until Evie caught them, literally, with their pants down. She and Harry forbid Julie to see him—after all, she had just turned 15; he was almost 18 and out of school. He was worldly in ways she was not. They thought he had coerced her into sex. No matter how much she insisted it was her decision, and sang his virtues, they would not give in.

Sam and she snuck phone calls, wrote letters professing undying love, planning a life together after she turned 18. Sam camouflaged his envelopes with Liz's address (her family had moved to Philadelphia). Julie felt broken as if she would never take a normal breath again.

Sam's father, divorced from his mother, came down hard on him for flunking school. Sam decided he would earn their parents' respect by joining the Navy.

As summer loomed, the calls and letters dwindled.

Colleen slept over the first Saturday of summer. They spread their sleeping bags on the floor to prepare for a night of junk food and TV—Midnight Special and Night Gallery.

"I haven't talked to Sam in over a week, I'm going through withdraw!" Julie said, "He's never home when I call."

"Julie, I talked to Mike today and . . . oh God, I hate this." Colleen put her hand on Julie's shoulder, "He said Sam was going out with some girl from their neighborhood."

Julie stared at Colleen. Her lip quivered, "No."

"I'm so sorry to be the one to tell you but sounds like he wants to move on."

"No," Julie said again. She took a deep breath in and let it out in shudders. Then she fell apart.

All the following week, she cried and pored over every minute she had spent with him. She was hurt and angry, then angry at herself for understanding where he was coming from. Their relationship had become stressful and difficult, so she really couldn't blame him—still, she was miserable. A blanket of depression wrapped around and smothered her. A darkness descended that she had never known before. She needed to struggle out from under it.

Maybe a breather is what we need. He'll realize that this is real and we can start fresh.

A couple weeks later, Julie and her parents went to Ocean City for a week and stayed in Aunt Dorothy's apartment. Colleen couldn't go, so Julie invited Liz.

Evie and Harry let up on restrictions. It was vacation, and they were far from Baltimore, so they gave the girls some freedom. The first night, the girls went up to the arcade on the boardwalk at Ninth Street. They met a group of guys playing Skee-Ball and goofed around with them, flirting and being silly, and Julie felt free again. When their 11:00 curfew came, Liz promised the boys they would return the next day, and they skipped back to the apartment, giggling and feeling fine.

The next day was spent at the beach. After dinner at Phillips Seafood restaurant with Evie and Harry, the teenagers escaped again to the boardwalk. The same boys were there. One had his eye on Liz and said he had procured a couple bottles of Boone's Farm wine.

Liz took Julie's arm and whispered, "I really like Bruce, let's go on the beach with them!"

Why not? I need a diversion. "Ok, just keep an eye on the time."

The group moved down the beach, close to the ocean, away from the lights. Bottles were passed around, and Julie was a little tipsy. She noticed Liz was sucking face with Bruce. The boy next to her, Josh, pulled out a joint, lit it, then handed it to her. She had tried pot before, but it didn't do a thing for her. *No harm in taking a toke.*

Josh was talking about dolphins or sharks . . . maybe dolphins eating sharks, she couldn't follow. She looked up at the vast night sky . . . interesting how the stars were realigning, multiplying . . . into a canopy of neon, a circus sign.

"Far out, look at the colors!" She whispered, and she began to float. She grabbed hold of Josh's arm. He looked at her and laughed, but it sounded like pinball bells.

"Woah," she said.

"PCP, Freakadelic, huh?" Josh said, and he started kissing her. His mouth tasted like wine, peachy, fuzzy, juicy . . . another toke on the joint . . .

and she was lying on the sand. The earth was alive beneath her and Josh's body was above her, keeping her from floating away. They were kissing again. His hand was in her shirt, and her skin tingled. His hand was in her pants and she was exploding. The salty breeze caressed her face—she could taste and smell and feel it—and the world was perfect.

Liz's voice drifted in from somewhere. "Time . . ." she said, with bells attached to her words, "Time . . ."

Julie pushed Josh away and sat up. "Time . . . Oh!" She pulled down her shirt and buttoned her shorts. *How did they come undone?* How long had they been here? Liz pulled her up, and she watched traces of herself detach from Josh.

Laughing manically, they stumbled up the beach and down the boardwalk to the apartment, all the while shaking sand from hair and clothing.

They tripped up the back stairs and hollered, "We're here!" to her parents, closed the door to their room, and collapsed on the beds. The world had come back in focus, but grins were still plastered on their faces.

"Where has that stuff been all this time?" Julie asked.

"Never had it before?"

"No. I tried pot, but I never got high."

"That's normal," said Liz, like she was an authority on the subject, "It usually takes a few times for most people to get a buzz."

"But that wasn't just pot."

"No, that was primo. PCP laced."

"I want more."

The rest of the week went by in a blur. And then the rest of the summer. Julie visited Liz in Philly for a week. Every night they got high. A boy Liz knew gave them Quaaludes. *After all, it's 7/14, Quaalude Day.* Then Liz came to Towson for a week. Julie existed in a world of extreme escape.

Jimmy told Liz that Sam was screwing the girl from the neighborhood.

"You tell Sam that Julie was with a guy in Ocean City, so he can shove it," Liz told Jimmy.

Sam called Julie, and they fought about it. She told him he was all she wanted. She cried. Then she told herself that being a party girl was more fun than crying, she enjoyed being numb.

The O'Malleys went to Ireland to visit relatives for a month, so Colleen was not witness to Julie's drug infatuation.

Will, home from college for the summer, caught wind of what was going on and gave her a lecture. "Look, I'm no prude. I've done my share of partying, but you are self-destructing."

"Pound sand, Will, it's my life and I like being high! Sure beats the misery I've been living."

"There is a happy medium, Jules."

"Medium's for sissies, I've never felt so free."

Harry and Evelyn went away one weekend in August, leaving Julie and Will at home. They allowed Liz to spend the weekend with strict instructions that no one else be allowed in the house.

"We don't need anyone else," Liz said, "because I've got our party right here!"

She opened her hand to reveal a small square of what looked like Scotch-Tape with a tiny square inside. "Windowpane, Acid, amazing LSD!"

Liz cut it in half, handed her one and put the other in her mouth.

Julie hesitated, looked at the miniscule see-through rectangle in her hand. *What can this little thing do?* She shrugged her shoulders and popped it into her mouth. Nothing.

"Where's the liquor cabinet? I want to do a Kevin-style recon!" Liz said.

Julie led her to the dining room to peruse the bottles. Will was out until later and he wouldn't care about a few swigs of liquor, anyway. Still nothing on the LSD front. She reached into the cabinet and pulled out a bottle of . . .

"Woah, starssss."

They floated out around her arm, big yellow stars! She gaped at Liz who was wearing a Cheshire Cat grin and looked like a Peter Max painting, and felt the grin on her own face.

"Freakadelic!"

"Let's go look at the sky." Liz grabbed her hand and led her out the back door. Sure enough, that circus sign was in the sky again.

They spent the next couple of hours exploring and sharing stories. The TV was on and Liz was chatting away about something when Julie's ears started ringing and world folded in, Liz and the TV and the furniture all whooshed together as if they were being sucked into a giant funnel!

Julie grasped Liz's arm, "I'm freaking out!"

Everything whooshed back but flat like a poster and the colors were so intense they seared into her brain like a light saber. She closed her eyes, but that made it worse. She couldn't feel her body, except where Liz was holding her arm. Panic set in; what if she stayed this way forever? She tried to explain—couldn't find the words—but Liz figured it out somehow.

"Here, just look at the TV." It was a black and white rerun of "Twilight Zone." "No color."

Julie sat and stared at the screen, afraid to look away. She heard Will come in and Liz telling him about the Acid and the bad trip.

Julie kept staring at the no-color TV, and then Will's hand was rubbing her back, bringing her back, bit by bit. His voice was soothing, soft and velvet, "I'm here. Just breathe. It will be over soon."

Hours later, she fell asleep and when she woke, Will was sleeping on the floor next to her. She sent a prayer up, "Thank you, God. No more drugs for me."

In September, High school began, and she was swept up in the excitement of something new. Sam wrote a letter from boot camp, saying he missed her. She sent him a letter, saying maybe they could get together when he came back to Baltimore. That didn't happen. They both had new lives, and looking back would have been painful. Besides, she had started dating a really nice boy in her science class.

Chapter 12

MARCH 1978

March came in like a lion roaring; wind gusts tore at the trees and sent branches skittering down the street. Julie, Rick, and Butch sprinted through the freezing rain with drop cloths and paint to the empty apartment. Rick unlocked the door with his master set of keys and they hurried inside.

"Glad I didn't leave the ladder on the porch, mighta got warshed away!" said Butch as he wiped his glasses with a bandana.

"Rainy Sundays are good days to paint," said Rick. He unfolded the drop cloth and popped open a paint can.

"Guess I'll leave youse to it. Come have a beer after, if youse don't drown."

"Might take you up on that."

Butch pulled his baseball cap down tight on his head and hurried back across the lawn. Julie closed the door behind him.

"Alone at last," he waggled his eyebrows at Julie.

"Get painting, mister," she said with a grin. He dabbed her nose with his brush.

"The ceiling, not me!"

Her laugh was music. He hoisted the roller above his head and painted a fresh white swath.

Julie got busy on the ladder, painting the edges with a brush. They fell into a familiar rhythm as the lion's breath rattled the door and drove rain against the window. Once the ceiling was done, they took a break. They sat with their backs against the wall and shared a bottle of coke.

"What do you want to do next Sunday to celebrate your birthday?" Julie asked.

"Stay in bed all day with you."

"No, really! 25 is big! We should do something special!"

"Darlin', I ain't special."

"You are to me."

"There you go, being sweet again . . . Look, as long as I'm with you it'll be fine. No special party, hear?" He stood, took her hand, and pulled her up, "Now you better get painting because I got a hankering to take you right here on this floor."

Rick didn't want to celebrate this birthday. He was disappointed in himself. 25 years old and still living in a dinky apartment. No credit, no insurance, none of that stuff that made you a responsible citizen. No money in the bank to speak of. He worked his ass off, yet had nothing to show for it except his car, and Baby cost a fortune to keep running. The thought of it put him in a funk all week.

II

It was St. Patrick's Day, so the green beer flowed at the Friday party. Freddie deemed it, "Not-Irish-I'm-a-Jew-but-I'll-Drink-To-Anything Day."

"Anything" included Midori sours Kevin whipped up in a pitcher. He brought it into the kitchen where Julie and Val were making green dip.

Kevin poured a cup of his concoction, "My version of drink of the week. Hey, Preakness, want to be the taste-tester?"

"Sure, why not?"

He handed her the cup. Val took a sip, pursed her lips, and took another. "Yum!"

Kevin's face lit up, "Like it?"

"I like the way the flavors clash: sweet and sour. Makes the taste exciting."

"Not bad for a car head, huh? Wait till you taste my pineapple pancakes."

Julie sent Val a Morse code nod. *That's a breakfast invitation!*

Val batted her eyes at him and said, "In horse country we prefer blueberry. Let's make both."

Julie left the kitchen to look for Rick. He was counseling Randy on his recent woman woes, so it was a good time to talk to Craig about her plan.

"Hey, I want to do something for Rick's 25th birthday. Are you playing at Spirits on Sunday evening?"

"Yeah, what did you have in mind?"

"Rick wants nothing, so we have to . . . well, act casual. I was thinking a Marilyn Monroe-style happy birthday song. He, well you know how he is about drawing attention... but the sexy angle would make him happy."

"I'm catching your vibe. Eddie and I could follow with the Beatles 'Birthday' song."

"That'd be far out. We think alike, don't we?"

"Yep."

"Anyway, Rick acts all 'no big deal' but I know he'd be disappointed if I did nothing. He's a tough shell, but there's marshmallow in there somewhere."

"You get how he thinks, I like that. My last girlfriend had no clue. Broke my heart and poured lemon juice on it. Ah well, music understands me."

"If all else fails, there's music."

He smiled and gave her a quick eye signal as Rick approached. She winked and turned to hand Rick a beer.

III

Saturday night, they got together with Colleen and Pete to watch *Saturday Night Live*. They roared at the weekend update segment and from then on "you ignorant slut" became Rick's and Pete's tag for each other. Rick thought Pete was an ok guy, even though he acted like he knew everything sometimes. Billy Joel sang "Only the Good Die Young," and in true form, Colleen and Julie got up and danced and sang along.

The only birthday gift Rick wanted was an entire night with her, so Julie told the parents she was sleeping at Colleen's. As soon as Col and Pete were out the door, he picked Julie up, carried her to bed, and gave her a night to remember.

When Sunday morning rolled around, March showed off its lamb side. Birds chirped out a conversation from the budding trees and sun streamed in the window. Bob Turk, the weatherman said temperatures would be in the 70s. Julie served Rick breakfast in bed with more shortcake for dessert.

Rick was just pulling on his jeans when he heard a commotion on the terrace, and he looked out the door.

"Softball weather!" bellowed Kevin. "Get your lazy asses up!"

Randy's feet thundered up the stairs, followed by a pounding on the doors, "Time to swing the bats, boys!"

On Sundays, the guys played pickup games at Towson High School against other local teams. The games were usually spontaneous, nothing planned but high-caliber athleticism.

The Rough Riders all assembled their gear with mania—gloves, bats, and coolers—and headed to the field. Somehow, Ty had wrangled the day off, and the guys were happy to see him. He wasn't fast but that didn't matter because he usually hit a home run. It wasn't long before the Wiltondale Wombats showed up to take them on and softball season officially began.

The women folk spread blankets near the team benches where they cheered and gossiped. Colleen and Pete arrived around 3:00, and the guys had Pete sub in on the field. Dawn and Leslie showed up to show off their shorts and drink beer.

After the game, both teams headed up to Spirits for dinner and bragging rights. Julie and Rick loaded bats and balls into the trunk of her new Silver Aspen and gave Leslie and Dawn a ride home.

When they got to Spirits, they parked in the back lot.

Rick tossed her the keys and said, "I gotta take a major piss and it's gonna be a madhouse in there."

Julie leaned on the passenger side as he relieved himself between the Aspen and the car next to it. Two college guys came around the corner. They saw Rick's back and the stream running beneath the car.

"Hey, asshole! You pissin' on my tire?" said the bigger of them. The other posed tough behind him.

Rick zipped up and turned around. "Just beatin' the rush at the urinal," he said, attempting friendly banter.

"My car ain't a urinal, you fuckin' asshole."

Rick sized them up for a minute. One was bigger than him and wearing a football jersey but looked like he had half a bag on. Guy number two was scrappy and looked like he was itching for a fight. Jersey Guy swaggered closer, pumping his fist with his minion flanking him. *May as well give 'em what they want.*

Rick charged forward, the old linebacker kicking in, and swung, connecting with Jersey's jaw. Jersey was knocked back into the lot. Scrappy jumped on Rick's back and tried to hold him as Jersey cocked his arm back to punch. Rick was a moving target even with a guy on his back. That's when a voice hollered, "Hey, boys!"

They stopped mid-battle and turned to the sound.

Julie stood at the open trunk of her car, brandishing an aluminum baseball bat. The light of the street lamp showed the words emblazoned up its side, BALL BUSTER.

"Can I play, too?"

Scrappy let go of Rick; his mouth slack-jawed. Jersey stepped back, confused.

The bat undulated in Julie's grip, its words beaming out a threat to their manhood.

Jersey dropped his arm, mumbled, "Hey man, it's cool," and pushed past Rick to get in his car.

Rick raised his fist at Scrappy. His mouth slammed shut. He scurried to the passenger side and got in. The door wasn't even closed when Jersey backed up. As they drove off, he yelled, "Get you later, fucker."

Rick watched them peel out and turned to Julie. He was still feeding on the sweet power he felt when his fist connected with that face. Julie's face looked so tough, so battle-ready—he let out a bark of laughter, "Darlin' you're the best wingman I ever had."

Julie put the bat away, closed the trunk, and they joined their friends inside.

Craig announced a special song by a special lady. Julie sang an exceptionally racy Happy Birthday. Rick watched, spellbound by his woman. *She makes me feel...* He found it difficult to put a word to it . . . *like I'm not a loser—like I'm worthy!* At the end of the song, he enveloped her in his embrace, unabashed at being the center of attention, and whispered, "You make me better, best birthday present I ever had."

The crowd cheered.

Ty hollered, "Get a room!"

Pete yelled, "Do it here!" Colleen smacked his arm, which prompted him to say, "We'll do it here!" and she squealed as he grabbed her.

Craig and Eddie launched into their birthday tribute and everyone started buying Rick drinks, smacking him on the back, and singing along. A drunken Kevin threw his arm around Rick's shoulders, "Man, you are the best buddy!"

Rick ducked his head, speechless.

"I mean it, man, you would do anything for your friends," he tapped Walt's back. "Am I right or am I right? Did he have to pick me up at 2:00 am. when my car broke down? No!"

"Rick sure bailed me out of trouble a time or two. Give the man a drink!" Walt said.

IV

Julie hung back and watched Rick bask in the glow of his buddies' admiration. She ordered them some food and struck up a conversation with Ty about how he braised pork.

"For pork, I like to use beer and a little fresh grated ginger."

"I love the smell of fresh ginger!"

"Yeah, me, too. My momma puts ginger in her chitlins."

"I don't think I like chitlins."

"Lawd, you just never tried 'em," he waved his big dark hand at her. "I have you over next time my momma makes them, Gawgia style. Y'all gonna love 'em! Turn you into a southern girl . . ."

Joanie sauntered over to Rick who was leaning back against the bar. She gave him a grinding hug, told him she wanted to give him an 'Orgasm' for his birthday and signaled to Cups over Rick's shoulder.

"Two O shooters, Cups, for me and the birthday boy." She ran her red nails down his chest to his belt and grabbed hold.

Cups, knowing when trouble was looking for a place to happen, whipped up a batch of 'Orgasm' shooters—Irish cream, Grand Marnier, and Triple sec—and to quell that trouble, hollered over the bar noise, "Orgasms for all!"

Julie watched Joanie grind against Rick and a twang of jealousy bit at her. She could have kissed Cups when he set shot glasses down along the bar. She drank hers down, stood, and wedged her arm between Joanie and Rick, "This man's mine, back off."

Then she pulled glassy-eyed Rick away and kissed him deeply, the sweet drink still on her tongue.

Rick drank every birthday drink they sat in front of him. By 11:00, he was feeling no pain, and the crowd had dwindled. Rick picked up Julie's keys from the bar and said, "Letch fly, wingman." He grabbed hold of her arm and stumbled toward the door.

"Oh, no, baby. I think I should do the driving," Julie said, attempting to take the keys from him.

"I'm fine, fine." Rick pulled his hand away from her. "Now lesz'plit."

Craig, who was still sitting at the bar, put his hand on Rick's shoulder, "Hey, buddy, let your lady drive tonight."

"That," answered Rick, "is no lady! Shoulda seen 'er with that bat."

Walt was sitting next to Craig, "Yeah, Rick, we heard the story. Now give her the keys."

"Nope, I'm drivin'."

"Rick, please, you are not driving my car!" Julie tried again to take the keys to no avail.

Cups came out from behind the bar, "Rick, man, you'll get me in trouble if you drive like this . . . come on, give 'em up."

"Fuck you, man," said Rick.

Walt tried again, "Hey, it's your birthday, you allowed to be shitfaced, just not behind the wheel."

Walt and Craig were behind him and Cups was in front. So, he threw the keys, hard, at Julie. The keys just missed hitting her in the face. Instead, they careened off her raised hand and clattered to the floor. She bent and picked them up, "Thanks, baby, now let's get home."

Walt escorted him out to the car. "See you in the morning."

Rick retorted, "Fuck you very much" and got in. Julie drove them home.

When they got to the apartment, Rick opened the car door before she even had it in park. He stomped up the terrace and threw open the door, nearly ripping it off its hinges. Julie followed him inside and reached out for him. He turned and swatted her hand away.

"Don't you ever . . ." he pointed a finger in her face, "EVER! talk to me that way in front of my friends!" His finger poked her cheek.

"I wasn't . . . I just . . ." She reached for him again, and he shoved her against the door.

"Don't." He raised his fist and cocked it back, his eyes burned holes in her.

Julie stood, back against the door, panic-stricken. Rick stood, fist high, fury distorting his face; a freeze-frame from some B movie. Then, in slow motion, he lowered his arm, turned away, and stumbled down the hall.

Julie held on to the doorknob, trembling, trying to move. Finally, she fled to her car and drove as far as the corner before the tears came. She sat there and cried, wondering what had happened. Had she said something to set him off this way? It was almost midnight. She had to get home.

The house was quiet when she tiptoed in. Thank God her parents weren't night owls. She used the bathroom, undressed, and climbed into bed, but it would be a long time before she slept.

Why? The night played over and over in her mind with no solution.

Rick called her the next evening. "Hey, Shortcake. How d'you feel this morning? I haven't had a hangover like that in years."

Julie mumbled something about being ok.

"Walt said I was wasted. Must have been all them shooters! I should know better on a work night." After a pause, his voice softened, "Hey, come over?"

She didn't know what to say to him. Didn't he remember? Should she bring it up and cause more trouble or just let it lie? "Well, I have a paper due."

"You can do it here; I promise I won't bug you . . . I'm feeling like I need to see you."

When she said nothing, he said, "Hey, I feel like I was kinda shitty to you about driving. I don't remember it all, but I'm sorry."

"It's okay," she attempted a laugh. "You were pretty out of it, all right."

"No more shooters for me!" he said with false bravado.

"So . . . come over? You know I love you." soft again.

"Yeah, the paper can wait a day. See you in an hour." She hung up the phone. *Okay . . . He was drunk. He didn't even remember. He said he was sorry and besides, he didn't hurt her, he was just messing around with that fist thing* . . . She was flooded with relief. After all, they had argued before, and he never acted like that. This was a fluke that they could put behind them. She needed to see him, too.

95

V

Rick hung up the phone, immensely relieved. His day had begun at 6:00 am when the alarm slammed into his skull like a jackhammer.

He had just made it to the toilet before throwing up a fowl mix of last night's spoils. He choked down a couple aspirin and stood in the shower until he was stable enough to dress without falling over, then dragged himself to work. All day he had been tossing thoughts around his aching head, trying to string together the pieces of the night.

Rick remembered vividly, the charge that surged through him when he punched that college boy, and he smiled when he remembered Julie holding that bat . . . damn, she was hot.

Joanie flirting with him, he remembered that. Screwing her last year turned out to be something he regretted. He thought they were on the same wavelength; it was a onetime drunken lay. But she kept acting like they were a thing. Rick did like Julie's reaction . . . she was fucking jealous! Guess that meant she really *did* love him. The rest was foggy . . .

Walt and Cups ganged up on him about driving. That pissed him off, and Julie was in that mix, too. She said some stuff he didn't like, but now he couldn't remember what. When they got home, he remembered yelling at her. He kept seeing flashes of the look on her face. Did he dream that? He couldn't remember her leaving. A feeling of dread gnawed at him all day; that he'd screwed things up and she wasn't coming back. It scared the hell out of him—that she was gone—but worse, that he couldn't live without her.

She was coming over, so it couldn't have been too bad. Rick got out of his dirty work clothes, showered, and shaved. When he saw his own face in the mirror, half-covered with shaving cream, some other memory tried to surface. He pushed it away. Better to forget about it and move on.

Chapter 13

MAY 1978

Ken and Suzie's wedding was held at Hunt Valley Golf Club. It was an outdoor ceremony with 80 in attendance, including many of the Towson Ridge gang. The bride and groom would move to Ohio, shortly after the wedding, so it was also a farewell party.

Suzie was stunning in her white wedding gown. Val and Ruth were bridesmaids (Joanie was no longer their roommate. She had moved in with the assistant professor at the end of March). They bitched about the dresses, but they looked pretty in fluffy pink chiffon.

Walt announced to their table that after graduation, he was taking a job in his hometown of Charlottesville, Virginia. He'd told Rick beforehand, but hearing it announced made it real. Walt was the closest thing to a best friend he had. The guys he ran with in high school were in jail, junkies, or just plain losers. He'd been fine as a loner, but he sure had gotten used to having the moron around. Julie sensed his melancholy and tried to cheer him.

"My brother lives in Charlottesville. We could go visit Walt and Russ at the same time!"

He smiled as she chirped on, Miss Optimist. She had a way of making things better, even if sometimes it irritated the hell out of him.

The music was provided by "Day One." Eddie played keyboard; Craig, guitar; a guy named Amir played bass; and a drummer rounded out the group. Val and Ruth asked to sing a tribute to the bride. They introduced themselves as Preakness and Princess and did a funny rendition of "Runaround Sue" that made Suzie (and her parents) blush.

Then Craig asked Julie to sing a duet with him. Julie acted demure, but when Rick cheered her on, she grabbed the mike like a pro. They sang "I'm Gonna Make You Love Me" and got a standing ovation. Rick was astounded. First because they sounded good, second because this guy was singing with his girl and he didn't want to punch his teeth in! *I have become the fuckin' Grinch!* He felt his heart grow, right there in his chest.

It was time to throw the bouquet. The single ladies and little girls gathered on the dance floor. Ruth and Val dragged Colleen and Julie into the mix and then stood in front of them, a pink chiffon wall in a mock basketball block. Eddie pushed his glasses up on his nose and counted down, three, two, one!

Suzie tossed the bouquet of blossoms high and hard. Tall Val stretched; short Ruth jumped. They collided and almost fell on top of the flower girl. The bouquet descended and careened off Val's head, right between Julie and Colleen. The best friends, to their surprise, caught it together!

Pete and Rick stared at each other with panicked expressions and then had a good laugh at each other's faces.

"Well," Craig said into the microphone, "a double wedding will save you some bread!"

"Ahh, no, no, no!" answered Pete. "Right there, is what you call a forfeit! You can't have a double catch."

Rick, still laughing, said, "Pete, you ignorant slut! Come on, I'll buy you a drink. What are the fuckin' odds, man?" The two of them bellied up to the bar and watched the gaggle of women hugging and squealing like little girls.

The night was ending. Eddie crooned into the microphone, "Everybody find a partner for one last slow dance. A song called "Where Away" written by our own Craig Wellington."

Julie ran to the bar and pulled Rick to the dance floor, "Come on, baby, dance with me!"

Rick put his arms around her, and they swayed together as the music began. He could feel Julie's breath against his neck as she softly sang along . . .

> . . . every time you leave
> You steal a piece of me
> I hoard our every moment
> In my memory
> To warm this solitary life
> To light my way
> Let me hold you, have you, keep you—stay.

Rick closed his eyes. He was mesmerized. The room seemed to melt away . . .

> Wear away my empty soul
> Without you, I'm diminished
> Where away our love becomes
> A life together—finished.
> Weary of this lonely life
> Help me find my way
> Let me hold you, have you, keep you—stay.

The last lines lingered in his head long after the band said good night.

The wedding was officially over. The bride and groom ran off to their car that had been adorned with witty sayings and trailing tin cans.

Colleen was staying at Pete's new apartment on Walker Avenue. Julie insisted they take the bouquet with them as a housewarming gift. Julie, Rick, and Walt piled into Jaws and headed home in great spirits.

After they said good night, Julie and Rick hurried up the walk and in the door.

Rick tossed the sports jacket he had borrowed on the back of a chair and kicked off his shoes, "Alone at last."

Julie kicked off her own shoes. "And I'm staying aaall night." She rested her arms around his neck, and he caressed her back. "Can't believe that bouquet. I thought Pete was gonna throw it again, right at me, when I told him to take it home."

Rick let out a light huff of air, "Well, will you?" He pulled back to look at her face.

"Will I what? Let him keep it?"

He smiled, "You caught the damn thing . . . so now," softer, "will you marry me?"

Her lips parted and she stared up at him like she was searching for the punch line.

"I mean it. It hit me like a sledgehammer, there on the dance floor. I want to have forever with you."

Julie's eyes moistened and a shimmer of tear rolled down her cheek.

"Oh God," he said. "Please be happy tears."

"Yes." She whispered, "Yes, y . . ." her words were cut off by the kiss.

The next morning, early as she dared, she rang Pete's apartment. No answer . . . waited ten minutes . . . called again. This time Pete answered, "Where's the fire?"

"It's Julie. I need to talk to Colleen, it's urgent! Oh, no one died or anything, it's good . . . just please!"

After a muffled pass off, a groggy Colleen said, "This better be good."

"I'm the next bride!"

"Huh?"

"Rick. Me. Getting married!"

"Holy shit! Wait. Let me get coffee! I'll call you back in five to hear the whole thing! (muffled movement) Holy Shit!"

Rick, lying next to her on the bed, heard Colleen's outburst and snickered.

"Let's get dressed. After you're done talking to Colleen," he glanced at the clock. It read 7:46, "Should be noon by then."

She smacked him with a pillow and that dazzling smile of hers.

"You know I'm right! Anyway, after . . . we can go pound on Walt's door and shock him, too."

"Really? You want to?"

"He's MY best friend . . . gotta get all sobby and sappy, you know, that's what us guys do!"

Julie went to start the coffee. Reflecting, Rick laid back on the bed. He felt so wonderful! If someone had told him two days ago that he would be engaged this morning, he would have said they were smoking some wacky shit! He may have had a fleeting thought or two of the possibility . . . but always pushed them away before they had time to sink in. Last night, on that dance floor, it all came together like a revelation. He *loved* her—*needed* her to be his forever—it felt *good*!

After Colleen called back and got the skinny on the proposal (it was now 9:47, not noon), they pounded on Walter's door. Walt, still half asleep, opened it. He saw the two of them standing there, beaming like summer came early.

He was pleasantly surprised at their news. He had seen Rick transform over the last few months—lose some of that melancholy that was always hanging on him—so he wasn't surprised by his desire. Walt was surprised that Rick could pull the trigger. Rick had a heart of gold. He'd do anything for his friends, but figuring out what he should do for himself was a different story.

Walt offered him this advice—Rick needed to ask Harry for her hand *before* she broke the news.

Chapter 14

SUMMER 1978
EVIE

Harry gave his consent after he grilled Rick on some basics, like insurance and savings. Rick had gotten a job at a lumber company and was eligible for benefits after three months, so that was a step in the right direction. Harry's primary concern was that she was too young, but he knew his daughter—she was hard-headed! She would run off and elope if they stood in her way.

Evelyn agreed with that assessment but had deeper concerns. Julie had been self-sufficient at a young age. She had no doubts she could manage a household and earn a living. But—Julie had a strong tendency to be love blind. She'd seen it with that boy, Sam, and with the next one that went off to college. Evie couldn't even remember the poor boy's name, which was remarkable considering the rate at which it sprang from the lips of her daughter!

Rick was a nice boy. Evie had no doubt his intentions were noble. She worried about his background; family roots run deep. Beth seemed just lovely. The woman had grown up in poverty, lost her father in WWII. Lord knew many from their generation lost loved ones. Harry, himself, had been in Germany, and she thanked God he came home safe. Evie was sure Beth had done her best for her children with what she had. Why, Beth herself was still a child when Rick was born! No, Beth was lovely.

The father was her worry . . . they met Floyd once, briefly. He was coarse and poor-mannered and . . . Evelyn hated to be a snob. He couldn't help his own background, and he had done nothing out of line. Even so, he made the hair on the back of Evie's neck bristle.

Evelyn prayed the apple fell far, far from the tree.

The boys and their wives were supportive. They all had such busy lives, with children, work, and corporate ladders, so had visited little since Christmas. Their only source of enlightenment was long-distance phone calls. Russ broached the wedding with his typical optimism and assuredness. Of course, he wasn't the one who had to worry about wedding plans. Will, though himself skeptical of the marriage, told Evie that Julie sent sunshine and rainbow vibes through the telephone line. If he didn't know better, he'd say she was tripping on some happy pill. Will always had an interesting way of putting things!

Beth called Evie about having a wedding shower.

"Dawn, my sisters and I are over the moon at the news! We jest love Julie!"

What's not to love? Evie thought to herself. Instead, she asked what Floyd thought about his son getting married.

"Floyd seems to think the same as us, but who knows what Floyd ever thinks about such things. He ain't one to show a lot of mushy emotion."

II

The school year ended. Walt bid farewell with promises to uphold his duties as best man.

He and Rick had Colts season tickets together, so he bequeathed his seat to Julie as a wedding gift. At $100 a season, it was a generous gift.

The couple wanted an outdoor reception and didn't want to wait until spring. The Colts played an away game on the last weekend in September, so they chose September 30th for the big day. The ceremony would be at the Providence Methodist Church and reception in the Fairburn's backyard.

Rick suggested Julie take fewer classes in the fall, so she'd have less on her mind. She agreed it was a good idea. So she only registered for Psychology 101 and English 102. It would push her AA degree back a semester, but she had reordered her priorities. Education had slipped way down on the list.

The Towson Ridge Apartments went through changes, like every summer. Fred and Marilyn bought a small Cape Cod-style house in Lutherville. They were expecting their first child in October. After Walt moved out, Craig rented a house in Timonium on Willow Haven Court with Eddie. He said having another musician as a roommate was great—no more complaints about late-night practices.

Randy got a phenomenal summer job at Padonia Pool as a swimming and diving instructor. He loved working with kids and got to be in the pool most of the day.

Hank went into rehab at the VA and gave his cats to Julie to look after. Hanoi was a gray tabby, who Rick called Annoy, and Flea Bag was all black and fluffy. Julie amended her name to Phoebe.

Butch and Honey moved and a new apartment manager took Butch's place.

Rick was outraged when he heard the news, "Son of a bitch Kramer better keep our deal going. This new guy better get word of it."

"All these empty apartments . . . I mean . . . he couldn't paint them all," Julie rubbed his shoulders as she spoke, "well, not alone, anyway. I'm sure he'll be happy to hand over the brushes." She sure had a calming effect over him!

"Damn straight. But he's not gonna paint any of 'em. I'll make sure of that. We've got a honeymoon to pay for!"

When they met the new super, Rick didn't think there would be too much trouble. He was a mild-mannered bachelor, around 45, with a receding hairline and a gaunt face reminiscent of a field mouse. Rick made sure the guy knew they were the official apartment painters. If he respected that, they would get along just fine. The man cowered at Rick's aggressive introduction and agreed. From then on, Rick referred to him as Milktoast.

Rick's heart seemed to beat faster as September approached; the wedding preparations were coming down to the wire. He couldn't concentrate and was all fidgety. How was he going to take care of her? He had his mother and Dawn to watch out for—now he had Julie to worry about. How was he going to keep her happy? She was used to a cushy life; he had squat to give her. By the end of August, Rick was feeling full out panic.

Walt came up Labor Day weekend and stayed with Rick. Saturday night after Julie went home, Rick did something he had never done before: spilled his guts to his friend.

"Man, I'm a wreck . . . can't sleep, my heart's ticking like a time bomb. How the hell am I gonna take care of her? Along with all the other shit I got on my plate?"

"Don't be so hard on yourself. You do not need to carry the world on your shoulders," Walt said, "besides, you now have *a partner* to help with all life's shit."

"I'll never know why she wants to marry me in the first place. How can I keep her happy? I'm nothing."

"Not true, Amigo. Julie knows what she's getting with you. She *chose* you, man. Just keep being the good guy you are."

He felt a little better—until Baby broke down. How was he going to get to work?. Julie offered to drive him, but her classes started right after Labor Day. He hated the thought of depending on her or anyone, but what could he do?

Rick got the bus routes and figured out a compromise. Julie could drop him at the bus depot in Parkville on the way to her 8:30 class. A co-worker offered to give him a lift home Monday, Tuesday, and Thursday and Julie said she loved an excuse to see him every Wednesday and Friday evening.

III

The first week worked out fine. The second Wednesday Julie's class ran late, and then there was a horrible backup on the beltway, an accident had closed all three lanes. She thought about pulling off and calling, but that would make her later. Finally, she got to the Belair Road exit. Now she had to figure out the fastest route across to Harford Road.

More traffic! Julie sent up a silent prayer. *Please, God, let me get there!*

She pulled up to Harbor Lumber at 6:40, almost an hour late, and the place was dark. No sign of Rick. A stab of panic went through her.

Then she remembered the neighborhood bar up the street. There he was, sitting at the bar with a draft beer and a bowl of nuts in front of him. As the light from the open door spread across the floor, he looked up.

"How's your day goin'?" He said to her and turned back to watch the TV over the bar.

"I am so sorry! Class ran late and then there was this accident . . . well, I wasn't in the accident but . . . oh, you should have seen the traffic! And . . ." She sucked in air and raked her fingers through her hair.

"You're gonna pass out one of these days, the way you talk without breathing."

Rick turned to the bartender. "Get her a vodka-tonic and I'll have a bourbon-ginger, heavy on the bourbon."

"Oh, um, sure. Vodka tonic sounds good. Anyway . . ."

"Save it, darlin'. Let's get dinner." He handed her a menu. They ordered. They ate and all the while he stared at the TV. She didn't want to babble on again, so she just ate. He ordered them another round.

Julie was getting a little drunk—*no, scratch the word little.*

Rick asked for the keys, and she gladly gave them over. On the way up Harford Road, a car cut them off and she yelled, "Watch out!"

"I saw it, for Christ's sake!" He reached over and twisted the radio on with such vehemence she thought the knob would pop off. She suddenly felt very sober and didn't say another word until they pulled into the parking lot.

Rick turned the car off and removed the keys from the ignition.

"Thanks for driving, I'm feeling clearer now," she said. "I better get going. 7:00 comes early, but I'll be here. Promise."

"*You* are the one who offered. I never asked you to get your sleepy ass out of bed for me."

"I know. I don't mind . . . just . . . I got class and . . ." she shut up before she started babbling again.

"And maybe," he slammed his hand against the steering wheel. "MAYBE . . ." slammed again, "your CLASSES are overwhelming you!"

"But they're not!" she yelled back.

The keys flew from his hand and smashed hard against her chest. Rick got out, slammed the door, and smacked the hood on his way by. As he stormed up the terrace, she flashed back to the last time he had thrown keys.

That night, as she lay awake praying for sleep, she replayed the night. She vacillated from anger at him to anger at herself.

He had a right to be mad. After all, you made him wait an hour. But that wasn't your fault.

He thought you forgot him.

You are both so uptight about the wedding.

He hates being criticized about his driving. You know that, stupid!

He shouldn't have yelled. You shouldn't have yelled.

She must have fallen asleep because she saw herself dressed in her beautiful wedding gown—organza skirts and lace bodice—off the shoulder neckline framing her décolletage. Her hair in ringlets flowed down her back and was crowned with daisies.

She walks up the aisle to Rick, standing there so handsome, his dark hair, ocean blue eyes, and exquisite smile. People in the pews are throwing rice . . . wait, not rice, *they're throwing keys.*

Julie woke with a start—her alarm was ringing. She hurried through her morning preparations and ran to the car without breakfast. *Get there, get there! Almost 6:45!*

Rick was pouring coffee when she came in. He handed a to-go cup to her. It was warm in her hands, and the cats wound warm around her legs, purring. He put his arms around her, "Morning Sunshine," he kissed her forehead, her nose, her mouth. "Wish I could take you back to bed," he murmured into her hair.

His arms dropped, and he picked up his own to-go cup from the counter, "But the day waits." The two of them walked hand in hand to the car . . .

Their wedding was three weeks away.

Part Two

Chapter 15

SEPTEMBER 1978

The honeymoon plan was to drive down the Skyline Drive and Blueridge Parkway through the mountains, with stops along the way—final destination, Nashville. On Sunday, they drove to Harper's Ferry and had lunch, then went south to pick up the scenic route. Rick drove, so Julie was free to enjoy the scenery.

It was the kind of perfect day when the sky goes on forever, the air crisp and clear, making the world brighter and sharper. The trees stood tall around them to show off their full fall finery, a bright collage of red, gold, and orange rustling in the breeze; autumn's song. Julie said she loved driving in the mountains, chugging up, up, up, and then flying down, daring Rick to stay off the brakes. The windows were open, and the wind tossed and tangled her hair into knots till she tamed it into a braid.

"The birds are gonna fly in to nest in that hair," Rick teased.

They toured Luray Caverns. The echoes and mirrored pools were fascinating; it was sheer wonder that water had the power to reform rock. Rick noticed a pointed correlation to what Julie had done to his heart. He used to be the rock, but now he felt all spikey and drippy and—could he truly be thinking this?—melting.

Their reservation that night was at a historic Inn in Luray, Virginia, that looked like an old southern mansion. After checking in, they dressed for dinner. Julie wore her new floral sundress, and Rick rose to the occasion and wore a button-down shirt and khakis instead of his customary jeans and tee shirt.

The formal dining room was elegant, with candles glowing on the tables and the lights low and soft music playing—what he assumed they called dinner music. It made him feel awkward, in a bull and china shop kind of way. The guy who showed them to the table even pulled Julie's chair out for her. He'd have to remember to do that himself sometime. As they perused the menu, Rick gazed at Julie and felt a surge of love for her. These emotions, so intense and uncontrollable, often crept up and overwhelmed him, threw him off balance.

"The candlelight turns your eyes to emeralds," he told her. "You look more amazing than your usual amazing self."

Julie smiled up from the menu, "And you look pretty wonderful yourself, Husband. I like saying that word, husband."

He had to admit, he liked hearing it, liked knowing she belonged to him for real.

"Now feed me, I'm hungry!"

Rick laughed, "What looks good? Besides you."

"Ha! I can be your last course. Oh, yum, they have broiled salmon. That's what I want. Daddy always called it candy fish, on account of the vertebrae you can eat. They look like candy."

"Yuck, I'll skip the bones," Rick said with a mock shudder.

The waiter approached with a bottle of wine, "Compliments of the house for our newlyweds," he said as he uncorked the bottle. "Would you like to sample it, sir?"

"Nah, let the lady sample. I don't know much about wine tasting. I'll have a Bourbon and ginger."

"Of course, sir." The waiter poured chardonnay into Julie's glass.

She lifted it to her lips and sipped; her eyes closed as she swallowed and a drop stayed on her lower lip, glistened there. Rick wanted to lean over and lick it off.

"This is wonderful! You've got to try this, Rick!"

"Okay, I'll have some to toast the night, go ahead and pour me a glass. Now let's feed you. I think the lady here will have salmon and I'll have this Seafood Newburg."

"Yes, the salmon, please, with asparagus and a house salad with blue cheese."

"Same salad for me, and bread if you got it, the lady is hungry," Rick told the waiter.

"Very well, sir. Freshly baked bread is on its way."

"I like being called sir . . . almost as much as husband," Rick said when the waiter was gone.

The bread came and then the meal. Julie said the salmon was cooked perfectly, but the Newburg was a little thick for Rick's taste.

"Am I supposed to eat this or lay bricks with it?" he asked Julie.

Her head jerked up, brows raised in alarm, but Rick laughed and declared he was just kidding. Julie smiled, and her eyes returned to her plate. He watched his slender wife as she attacked her meal with gusto.

"Where do you put all this food? Ah, that's alright. We're gonna work it off when I get you back to the room."

After the dinner and wine were gone, Rick signed the check, and they continued to the bar for another round or two. They struck up a conversation with the bartender and traded anecdotes about small towns and big cities. At 11:00 they staggered to the room, joking about last courses. Rick hung the "do not disturb" sign on the door, and they undressed each other and made love with drunken abandon, then fell asleep wrapped in a tangle of sheets and each other.

II

It all went downhill, or more appropriately, down a mountain from there.

Julie woke the next morning and looked at the clock, "10:30? Wow, we did some sleeping!"

She snuggled into her pillow and smiled at the thought of how wonderful last night had been. *My dreams came true—I'm really married!*

Rick was already up and in the bathroom. He came out with just his jeans on and pointed to a little sign on the side table, "We missed breakfast, says there served until ten. What the fuck? People like to sleep in on vacation!"

"I'm sure we can find something on the way out."

"That's beside the point, Julie, a place shouldn't expect people to get up so God-damn early on vacation!"

"You're right," Julie patted the pillow. "You wanna come wallow in bed with me awhile?"

"We got an eight-hour drive to Nashville, better quit your wallowin'." He said, and started throwing clothes into his suitcase.

Julie got up and slipped her arms around him, but he said his head ached. "Let's save it for tonight," he said as he squeezed a handful of her ass. "Now go get dressed, darlin' and until my head feels better, you can drive."

Once the car was loaded, Rick slammed the trunk shut, and then his door, and settled in the passenger seat. Julie drove to a gas station where they bought donuts, coffee, and a full tank. They headed south and Julie kept the tape deck playing her favorite music while Rick slept. She softly sang along with Joan Baez about diamonds and rust, and Judy Collins about sending in the clowns.

Then Rick woke up and changed the tape to Bad Company, which was better driving music, anyway. Rick liked to tease her about their age difference, and they both sang along to "Young Blood."

Rick howled at the end.

The sun set orange and turned the world to fire. The orange faded into lavender, lavender to indigo. A curtain of night brought a sky full of stars and an enormous yellow moon. Julie thought the moon grinned like he had a secret he wasn't willing to share.

The weary couple finally pulled into a motel within the city limits of Nashville. They checked in and walked down the block to a package goods store. Rick grabbed a six-pack of ginger-ale, a bottle of Jack Daniels, and some Fritos and headed to the cashier. Julie threw a couple Moon Pies on the counter and Rick paid.

"Now let's get horizontal, I'm bushed."

They wandered back to their room, chatting about their plans for tomorrow. Julie unlocked the door and pulled her shoes and jacket off. Rick got ice from the motel's ancient ice machine and made them drinks. Then he laid down on the bed with his head propped against the backboard, drink and cigarette in hand, ashtray on his lap. Julie turned on the TV and snuggled in beside him, and the next thing she knew it was morning.

Rick asked at the front desk about a breakfast place. The chubby girl behind the counter suggested a diner not too far from the motel. They enjoyed a southern breakfast of eggs, sausage, and grits and the rest of the day was spent sightseeing. By 6:00 they were ready for happy hour and food and found a great little bar with authentic Nashville honky-tonk charm. The greasy smell of fried food and popcorn hung in the air. It went well with the jukebox music and wagon wheel chandeliers.

A band was setting up, so they lingered over drinks at the bar, then moved to a table near the dance floor for dinner. People started drifting in, in twos and threes and most seemed to be locals. Rick heard snippets of conversation about a long day's work and babysitter woes. The band started around 9:00 and played some good southern rock: Lynyrd Skynyrd, Charlie Daniels, Willie Nelson. The newlyweds sang along to the familiar songs and socialized with the crowd.

As the night wore on, the atmosphere got rowdier. The air was thick with smoke and heavy guitar riffs, the dance floor sticky with spilled drinks. Rick wasn't much of a dancer, but enjoyed watching Julie dance with a couple of girls from the next table. *That girl can move to anything.*

Around midnight, Rick was ready to call it a night—his head was aching from the loud music and he'd had his fill of Bourbon. He tried to get Julie's attention, but she was droning on and on about her college classes with some guy that had joined the girls next to them. Rick overheard some bull crap about Psych 101. *Yeah, that guy looks psycho.*

"Hey, Julie," he yelled over the band. "Come on, time to go home with your husband!"

She spun toward him, her hair flying out, her face flushed from dancing, and desire slammed him like a right hook.

"Okay, babe, I'm ready."

"Gotta pay the bartender, gimme some cash. I'm out."

She pulled out some bills from her pocket and handed it over to him.

Rick looked at the money, a crumpled ten and several ones. He had already paid the waitress, so this covered the bar but, what the hell? Indignation bubbled up as he grimaced at the bills. *Does she think she can dole money out like I'm some low-life? If she thinks she's gonna be in charge of the finances, she's got another thing coming!* He threw the money on the bar and grabbed her arm.

"Come on, bedtime," he growled and pulled her toward the door. Julie let out a little squeak of surprise and let him drag her along. A mask of malevolence had slammed down on his features, but she tripped along beside him all the way to the car. He drove the few blocks to the hotel, feeling steam coming out of his ears like a mad bull in a cartoon, maybe the one in that china shop.

Rick didn't say a word, and she didn't dare. She shot a furtive look his way and quickly looked down again. They got in the door and he grabbed her arm, swung her around, and pushed her against the wall. Her eyes went big.

"You getting a big head, aren't you, college girl?"

"What? I . . ." He slammed his powerful hand over her mouth, crushing her lip against her teeth.

"Don't you *EVER* withhold money from me!"

Julie looked confused, but tried to nod her head. His vice-like constraint prevented movement, and a whimper escaped her.

"I work harder than any two men. I sweat and bleed for a living, unlike those pencil-neck muthafuckers from college!" He took his hand away, saw her blood on it, and stalked over to the whiskey, took a hefty swig.

Julie slunk down the wall and snagged a hand towel that had been discarded on the floor. She held it to her damaged lip.

Rick turned back to face her with a sneer, "You think you're so smart because you're a college girl. I never needed college. I learned from the school of hard knocks, and lemme tell you it was quite a lesson."

She looked so pathetic huddled there. The sight infuriated him, caused conflicting thoughts to tumble through his brain. He pushed away the fear that was creeping in—fear of what he could do to her with his strength and fear of the weakness she made him feel. He took another drink. Its burn helped fan the wildfire of rage and squelch the rest. Yes, he thought, I can give in to the anger. Anger, I understand.

"Aw, poor baby. Is your lip bleeding?" he said with a sarcastic slur.

Julie stood up and moved toward the bathroom, never taking her eyes from him, "I don't know what I did," she mumbled into the towel.

"Better figure it out, darlin', cause it ain't gonna happen again."

Julie made it to the sink. The salty blood taste made her sick to her stomach. She wet the towel, and the cold felt soothing against her mouth. In the mirror, she saw his reflection leer in at her, bottle dangling from his hand.

"So, you asked for money and I gave it," she told his reflection as she wiped tears from her eyes, "that's all I had in my pocket, the rest was here in the room." He kept staring, his eyes boring holes into the mirror.

Julie imagined she could feel his heat radiate from the cold glass as she puzzled through the course of the evening. Her ability to connect the dots was impaired by too many drinks. It was as if her mind was sifting through mud—and he kept staring.

Finally, she turned to face him.

"You're pissed because I was talking to that guy!"

"I could give a shit about that pencil-neck asshole!"

"That's it, isn't it? The money's just the fucking topper!" Julie raised her voice, triumphant that she figured him out.

Before she could blink, he was on her, lifting her off her feet. The sink's sharp edge dug into the backs of her thighs and her head slammed against the mirror. His palm slapped savagely against her face, and his wedding ring struck just under her eye.

A loud banging followed the crack of her head. Someone in the next room yelled through the wall, "Keep it down in there, or I'll call the management!"

Rick backed off and watched Julie slump down from the sink. "Get away," she whispered, "just get away from me."

Julie felt her eye puff up, making a matched set with her mouth. Rick backed out of the bathroom, took one last belt from the bottle, and lay face down on the bed.

Julie soon heard snoring and knew he was down for the count. She moved with caution into the room and stood for a minute. Her hands were shaking; her body swayed. A pillow had fallen to the floor. She snatched it up and took it back in the bathroom. After she locked the door, Julie pulled towels from the rack, made a nest of sorts in the bathtub, and gingerly lowered her aching body into it. She let the tears come. Too wrung out to think, she told herself, "Breathe . . . breathe and sleep."

That became her mantra as she drifted off . . .

Breathe and sleep, breathe . . . and sleep . . .

Chapter 16

OCTOBER 1978

Rick woke with a moan, head pounding, and vision blurry. He smelled coffee. With puffy eyes, he scanned his surroundings. Julie sat next to the room's credenza; she turned to him and the light from the window fell across her swollen eye and lip. His heart seized up, gripped in a vice, then sunk, a leaden weight, into his stomach. Rick slid from the bed and knelt in front of her. He reached to touch her bruised cheek, and she flinched.

"Oh, Julie . . . I, oh God." pieces of the night blew through him with a horrifying realization. He did this. Tears sprang to his eyes, "I'm sorry."

She lifted her hand from where it rested on the chair arm and touched the curl that always fell across his brow. "I've got coffee . . ."

Rick buried his face in her lap to hide his shame, "This was . . . I don't . . ."

She laid her hands on his head.

He looked up, face distorted with anguish, "Please, forgive me. This will never happen again."

They got home on Thursday evening, after a long day of driving. Annoy and Phoebe greeted them at the door. Backs arched, they wound around legs and purred. As they unpacked the car, Julie suggested Rick drive to work Friday and Saturday.

"I won't need the car. I'm going to play hooky one more day—do laundry and unpack my boxes."

Julie looked at the tower of cardboard in the living room with her guitar beside it and her magic bonsai sitting on top.

"I live here." The reality of it took hold, and the corners of her mouth turned up, "I really live here with you!"

"Wait! There's something I wanted to do! Ahh, shoot! I screwed it up."

"What?"

"Okay, pretend we haven't come in yet." He pulled her back out the door, picked her up, and cradled her, "I want to carry you over the threshold!" and he did.

Julie avoided seeing anyone for the next couple of days. Her lip healed quickly, but she still had remnants of a black eye. She told her parents they would come over Sunday, that she had to catch up with schoolwork. When Colleen called, she begged off a visit.

Cups and Gravy had been her cat sitters. Knowing they would be at work, she slipped their thank you gifts inside the screen door, then she walked around the block, enjoying the warmth of an Indian Summer.

She stopped short when she got back to the apartment. Colleen was getting out of her car. She saw Julie and waved, "There you are! I came by to bring a wedding gift. I was going to stick it in your door."

"What a co-inky-dink! I was just putting gifts in Gravy and Cups' door!" Julie started walking again, to where Colleen was standing.

"Liz sent it to me because she realized you would be away."

"Typical Liz, always making things harder than they should be . . ."

"And always late! She said sorry she couldn't . . ." Julie walked out of the shadow and the sun shone on her face, "What happened to your eye?"

"Oh, barroom brawl in Nashville."

Colleen's shoulders raised, and a hand flew up to her mouth.

Julie, glad for quick thinking, chuckled, "No, just kidding! Some guy's elbow got me on the dance floor. He was boogieing down as I was spinning around. Crash!"

Colleen's shoulders relaxed as she let out her breath, "Those dance floors sometimes feel like a barroom brawl!"

"For real! Look, don't tell my folks. Don't want them lecturing about us drinking too much, you know. I'm hoping it'll be gone by Sunday."

"Got it. Little white parent lies save everybody gray hairs."

Marilyn gave birth to a baby girl on October 21st. They named her Abigail. Colleen and Julie visited the happy family bearing gifts and casseroles.

"Abigail means 'joy of the father' in Hebrew," Marilyn said. There was no doubt she was her father's joy. Freddie was glowing! He held his precious bundle out for them to see.

"Is she the most beautiful, or what? Nothing is too good for my girl. I've even given up the weed for her." He cooed, "Yes, I have, my sweet bundle of joy!"

"Let the girls hold her, Freddie."

"Okay," he said and handed the baby to Colleen as if she was made of fine china. "Careful now, hold her head."

"For God's sake, Freddie. Colleen has held seven siblings. She knows how to hold a baby!"

"Oh, right, forgot you were Catholic."

Colleen and Julie got a laugh out of that one.

"What? What do I know from having eight kids? I'm a spoiled only child of affluent suburbia."

It was Julie's turn to hold her. Colleen passed her over, "Now I know you're not Catholic, but you do know how, right?"

Julie gazed at the cherubic little being in her arms, and her heart swelled. She couldn't wait to have one of her own and would happily have eight of them. "Doesn't it just make you want to throw away the pill and get started?"

"I think I'll get married first, and I am not quite ready to stop our trips to Planned Parenthood," Colleen said. "Until then, you can have one for me to play with."

"Should I call Rick and tell him to be ready for you?" Fred rubbed his hands together, "Don't think he'd mind that chore!"

"Oh, Freddie, really! You are such a perv!" laughed Marilyn.

COLLEEN

Colleen suggested that since Freaky Freddie would not be hosting the annual Halloween party this year, they should throw one together. The Friedman's apartment was still vacant, so they put up some folding chairs and tables, and Pete set up a sound system with speakers wired in both apartments. Milktoast was invited, and it thrilled him to be included. Rick said he figured it gave the guy a charge, being in on something without the boss's knowledge, like a double agent or something. Sure enough, he came dressed as James Bond and kept saying 'shaken, not stirred' every five minutes.

There was a box set up to cast votes for best costume. As usual, the partiers had gotten creative. Kevin came as a horse with Val, aka Preakness, as his rider. Randy's latest girlfriend, Kim, and Ruth came as astronauts in honor of the first woman astronaut. Ruth announced herself as the first *gay black* female astronaut. Randy was their alien friend. Gravy wore a diaper and wrapped himself with clear plastic. He was a test-tube baby. Eddie, in smudged sunglasses, and Craig came as the Blues Brothers, and said they'd give a joint to anyone with a destroyed disco record.

Julie and Rick dressed as Bonnie and Clyde. Pete and Colleen dressed as old-time FBI agents. The girls got plastic Tommy guns at Woolworth's, and they had fun shooting each other all night.

Joanie showed up, out of the blue, with a couple of friends from Towson State's soccer team. Val saw her and nudged Colleen, "Who invited the troublemaker?"

Colleen knew about Joanie's reputation; she had a taste for other women's men, "She goes near Pete and I'll knock her perfect teeth out!"

Joanie, costumed as Marilyn Monroe and a little too plump for the dress, sashayed over. Her friends, who wore their uniforms, followed.

Val said, "Look what the Halloween cat dragged in!"

"I was planning on the Friedman party, but I guess Ricky is throwing the gala this year! Where is that handsome hunk?"

"The Friedman's moved, and I guess you know Rick and Julie are married," said Colleen.

"I heard. Shame, he was bangin, if you catch my drift. And I know bangin," Joanie turned to her companions. "Billy, Tony . . . This is my old roommate, Val, and this is . . . Connie, right?"

"Colleen," Val said.

Tony mumbled a hello and Billy asked where the beer was. Colleen pointed, too angry to speak, and the guys made a B-Line for the keg on the porch next door.

"Catch you later, girlies." Joanie trilled her fingers and sauntered off.

Julie was heading toward Colleen, Tommy gun raised and did a double-take as Joanie passed her.

"Can you believe it?" Val said. "Hope she doesn't start anything."

Julie laughed when she saw Colleen's face, "You don't need a Tommy Gun, that's a look that could kill!"

Colleen sneered and pointed her gun toward Joanie.

"I know how you feel, honey, I've tangled with Miss Predacious before! Come on, let's go find our men."

Julie told Rick they were going to tally the votes, then met Colleen and Pete in the bedroom to count. Colleen wasn't letting Pete out of her sight while Joanie was around. Gravy aka test-tube baby was the winner. They were returning to the party when a ruckus began on the porch.

Rick had one of Joanie's friends by the front of his shirt. By the blood coming from the guy's nose, he'd already punched him once or twice. Tony, the guy's friend, stood near, twitching and bouncing from one foot to the other. Cups and Ty, dressed as Han Solo and Chewbacca, were behind Rick, ready to back him up. Kevin attempted to break it up, "Rick, man, the guy's not worth the effort!"

Pete said, "Oh shit, here we go again."

Randy said to Pete, "You said it, dude. Rick's temper to the max is getting out of hand."

Colleen saw the fire in Rick's eyes and Julie said to her, "Gonna be a bad one, better get the hose."

Colleen half expected Julie to pull out a garden hose and spray everybody down, but she rushed to his side, put a light hand on his pumped-up chest, "Baby, chill . . ." she said, under her breath.

Randy gave Colleen a nervous sideways look. She took hold of his arm in case he had thoughts of jumping in there himself to protect Julie. Julie could handle herself.

Rick's eyes flicked toward Julie and he deflated some, then pushed instead of punched, "Get lost, Punk! Before *I really* get mad!"

The punk stumbled, fell, got himself upright again, and hightailed it to the parking lot. His buddy followed. They got to the lot and he turned, "This ain't over, I'll get even."

"You're gonna have to wait in line, jerk face," Rick said and turned away.

Colleen watched as Joanie sauntered up to Rick, "You are such a bully, Rick," she winked. "It makes me so hot!" she reached out to touch him.

He slapped her hand away, "Get the fuck outa here, bitch."

Pete squeezed Colleen's hand and she felt him shake with quiet laughter.

Joanie stepped back, looking flustered. She glanced around, saw them watching, then drew herself up, and stomped away.

The show was over, and the crowd returned to partying. Julie took Rick's hand in hers, "What started all that, anyway?"

"Son of a bitch spilled beer all over those throw pillows you love."

Julie's tough-guy face emerged, "I'll kill him!"

Rick smiled, "That's my wingman!"

Chapter 17

NOVEMBER 1978

The brothers and their families were coming for Thanksgiving, so Julie's mother was in a dither. Evelyn called Julie on the weekend to ask for help with preparations, "I'm just so thrilled that both the boys are staying here. I've already changed sheets but I need help with the crib and, let's see . . ."

Will's son, Tyler Harry Fairburn, was born in April, and he was the spitting image of his father.

"Of course, we need to get things together for the bigger kids . . . and now you're sure you can come Wednesday?"

"Yes Mom, I told you, my classes are canceled on Wednesday."

"Well, if you are sure . . . I was thinking we should invite Rick's . . . well, what will the Madsens be doing for . . . don't want to steal him away."

"Mom, take a breath!" *Guess I come by it, naturally!* She chuckled to herself and glanced at Rick on the sofa next to her to see if he'd heard her. He was chuckling too. "Rick's dad will be on the road, so Beth and Dawn may enjoy coming. I'll talk to Rick and get back to you."

"And I'll see you on Wednesday, bright and early?"

"Yes, Mom, Mellow out! Bye."

Rick looked up from the football pool in his hand. Freddie had a new lucrative side business as the neighborhood bookie, and it gave Rick pleasure to be on a 3-week winning streak.

"You heard?"

"Uh-huh, apple falling from the tree, right?"

"Yep, I didn't fall far! But anyway . . . did you hear the part about your mom and . . . well, my mom . . . I'll take a breath."

Rick threw his arm around her and tickled her ribs. She laughed and swatted at him, and they both ended up on the floor in a heap. Julie was laughing so hard, she could hardly breathe. "Breath . . . let me catch it!" He let up on the tickling. "Woman dies from laughing!" she said as she wiped the tears from her eyes.

"You are one twisted chick." He bit her neck and sat up to let her recover before he said, "Yeah, good idea. They were probably going to Jo's, but the 'normal family' Thanksgiving would be a nice change for them."

"Oh, stop with the normal . . . We are weird, too, just nice weird."

"And that's why I love you."

Thanksgiving Day was chilly, but the sky was clear and bright. The trees still had a few colorful leaves clinging to them, reluctant to succumb to the song of winter winds. The family gathered in the living room with the football game on; the volume low so they could chat. It had been a while since they were all together. Dawn had opted to go to Jo's—Julie figured her new boyfriend, who lived close to the Porters, had something to do with it—but Beth was thrilled by her invitation. Rick picked her up because she didn't like to drive any farther from home than Hunt Valley.

She and Julie were in the kitchen with Evie. Beth had insisted on helping, and Evie put her in charge of table settings, "Thank you so much for inviting me. Your decorations are just lovely."

"Why, thank you, Beth. I'm glad you could join us." She looked at the turkey in the oven, "Almost done! I suspect we'll be sharing grandchildren someday. So, good to be with you."

"Mo-om!" Julie swatted her with the dishtowel she was holding, but secretly she was thrilled at the idea.

Beth and Evie smiled at one another, an unspoken language between mothers.

Rick came into the kitchen and went to the Bug Juice bowl, "Mom, did you try this? Don't worry, it's G-rated."

"I did, it's real good." She turned to Evie, "Your family is so nice, and the little ones, so cute! I remember my little ones like it was yesterday."

Rick refilled his mother's punch cup and handed it to her, "Eliza just told me she watched the ponies last week on TV. I thought she meant horse races until Russ told me it was the Colts game."

"Ponies . . . oh, that's a good one!" Beth said and went back to counting out silverware from the silver chest.

Dinner was ready, and everyone chipped in on the transfer to the table. They were all able to squeeze in, nice and cozy, with the baby in a high chair next to Diane. The meal was delicious and the conversation drifted from sports to parades to Christmas plans.

They were finishing up dessert when the phone rang. Harry answered it.

"Happy Thanksgiving!" he said merrily into the receiver. "Yes, he's here . . . well, sure, just hold a moment." Harry laid the phone on the table and stuck his head into the dining room. "Rick, I think it's your sister."

Rick stood, patted Beth on the shoulder, and took the call into the hallway out of earshot. When he returned, he beckoned Julie into the kitchen.

"Something's going on with Dawn. She wants me to pick her up. I'll run over, get her, and come back."

"Is she okay?"

"I think it's just teenage drama. Anyway, she's boohooing about that Brice guy."

"I knew he figured in somewhere! Okay, go ahead, I'll make sure your Mom doesn't worry."

"Love you, Darlin, you're my wingman!" He kissed her and went out the door.

They all pitched in again to get the dishes in the kitchen and the left-overs put away. Evie made a package for Beth to take home. "Floyd will want a turkey dinner, won't he? Poor fellow, working on Thanksgiving."

"I suspect that's the nature of the profession, right Beth?" said Harry.

"Oh, heavens yes, he is on the road all crazy times. I don't mind though, I'm used to it, and a course, I have Dawn with me. She doesn't roam far when Floyd's on the road."

"Daughters are good that way. Well, let's leave the rest of this mess and go sit and enjoy the company," said Evie.

"Good idea!" Harry put his arm around his daughter and she smiled up at him as he guided her into the living room.

The kids had their crayons out and were making turkey pictures for everyone. Rusty gave 'his best one' to Beth. "I will cherish this!" she told him. "I remember when Ricky was your age, he liked to color, too. His teacher told us he had artistic talent."

"He did?" Rusty asked, eyes wide. He thought Rick was the coolest guy he knew, "I'm gonna make him a pitcher next." He got busy again with his colors.

Beth turned to Linda, "I s'pose Ricky got that from me, I've always been told I had a *flair* for things. You nurture that talent, hear?"

"I will. When he's not playing cars, he's drawing."

Julie chimed in, "He gets it from his father, the great architect."

"I'm sorry I didn't push Ricky in that direction. He coulda been an architect," she waved her hand dismissively, "Floyd always told him that art class was for sissies. Men should put their hands to work in shop class."

Evie said, "Our generation thought that way to a great extent, but the world has changed. I like to think society is becoming more accepting of all kinds of things!"

"I'll drink to that!" Will raised his coffee cup in a toast.

The front door opened and Rick and Dawn came in with a gust of wintery wind.

"Gettin' cold out there," he said with a shiver.

"Come have some coffee, Hon!" Evie fluttered around them. "Dawn, would you like some pie?"

"No thanks, I had dinner at Aunt Jo's." She plopped down on the floor next to the kids and started coloring with them. Julie could tell she had been crying but looked like she had been able to pull her shit together, except for the black crayon digging trenches in the paper.

WILL

Will raised his cup and said, "Come on, Rick, I'll give you some of my special brew."

Rick followed him into the kitchen. Will poured a nice-sized dollop of Bailey's into a coffee and handed it to him, "Only way to get through the holidays, Man."

Rick had grown on Will since last Christmas. They'd only been together a few times, but he seemed okay. Will sat next to him at dinner and they conversed on several subjects. Rick was rough around the edges, but he was sure smart enough. His mind flashed on that old Sunday school song about hiding your light under a bushel.

Diane thought Will was too hard on people, especially when it came to Julie's guys, but Diane hadn't seen the fallout from Julie's past mistakes. His baby sister had been pretty messed up for a while. Will was home from college at the time and had a front-row seat.

He was pulled out of his reverie when Rick said, "Thanks for the warm-up, I needed it after my sister's drama."

"Hey, I know about sister drama! You should have seen Julie when she was 15."

"Oh, Yeah? She's told me some, but I guess not all. Drama, huh?"

"Oh, shit, man, well, you know, teenage girls . . ." Will felt sheepish, maybe he shouldn't be sharing information like that, "Nothing over the top, but you know, girl stuff." He was mighty thankful when Diane came in with Tyler, "Oh, hey, babe . . . and baby! Ha! Say hi to Uncle Ricky!"

Diane eyed him up, "How much Bailey's did you drink?" She picked up the bottle. It was just about empty. "Just what I thought. You are mine tonight," Diane jostled Tyler. "This one's going to bed. And then we are." She chucked his chin and sashayed out with a naughty grin.

Will felt even more sheepish, "What can I say? The woman owns me."

Rick laughed out loud, "Buddy, you are funny! Let's have a drink or two before you go. Without our owners, that is."

"Ha-ha! You got it, Bro! Wait . . . You *are* my Bro!"

II

They walked out to the living room together, Will's arm around Rick's neck. Rick sat on a hassock near Julie who was on the floor with the kids.

Will sat down heavily on the sofa next to Russ. "Are we not men? We are Devo!" he announced and cracked up. Russ just looked at him.

Julie said to Russ, "Saturday Night Live, numb-nuts."

The parents looked confused, and the under-thirty crowd laughed.

Luke began chanting, "Numb-nut, numb-nut!"

Rick sat with his coffee and watched this family he was now a part of. He noticed how they touched each other with open affection, and how that affection showed on each face. He glanced at his mother, swept up among them, unfeigned pleasure radiating from her. Even his ornery sister seemed content to be amid them. He let the warmth wash over him and relished a calmness that he rarely knew.

"Will wins the obscure quote award," said Russ. "And I win the old fart award for not knowing Devo."

Luke and Rusty began a chant of "Fart! Fart!" and the older brothers made fart noises. Harry laughed and swept Eliza up in his arms.

Rick put his arm around Julie, who had laughter tears on her cheeks, and kissed the top of her head. She smiled up at him, and the world was right.

Rick stood and took Evie's hand, "Thanks for having us. It was the best Thanksgiving in . . . well, I don't know when," he turned to Beth. "Now it's getting cold. I better get Mom home before those back roads get icy."

Everyone kissed and hugged, holiday spirit overflowing. Rick got his women to the car.

"Julie, your family is so nice!" Beth said once they were buckled in.

"They're the normal family," Rick smirked.

Julie poked him.

"Normal . . . Is that what it looks like? Never lived with normal." Beth said and let out a short tinkle of sound. "Whatever it was, it sure was good to have a holiday with no hollerin' or fightin'."

Julie said, "Oh, we argue some, don't think we don't."

"Y'all argue, but you don't fight. There's a difference."

"Does anybody wanna know what happened to me?" Dawn whined and puffed out her lips.

"Sure, Honey, I want to hear all about it," Julie tried to soothe her. "Soon as we get Momma home, you and I can talk," she looked at Rick.

"Hey," Rick said, "these roads are getting slick. Maybe we should stay up home."

Beth and Dawn smiled, each looking out their own window.

Rick took Julie's hand and whispered, "Surprised she wants anybody to know."

Hours earlier, when Rick pulled up to Jo's, Dawn came rushing out the door and jumped in the car. Jo followed her and came around to the driver's window. "Found this one and Leslie in the back bushes with two boys, one with her shirt up around her neck. Other one pants undone! Don't know how far it woulda gone if it weren't interrupted." Jo looked back at the house, "Leslie's gettin' chained to 'er bed if I have to. Dawn, here, decided it was time to go home."

Rick said, "Sorry Aunt Jo. I'm sure Mom'll call you tomorrow."

"And on Thanksgiving, too. Thank God Hazel didn't get wind."

"I'll take care of this one. Go on and enjoy the rest of your holiday. Thanks, Aunt Jo." He rolled the window up and they drove away.

III

Julie sat on Dawn's bed, patting her back as she cried.

"I don't know if he'll even talk to me again. It was humiliating. I told him we shouldn't do it there. But you know boys once their pecker gets hard there's no stoppin' um."

"Well, Dawn, there is a time and place . . . But that's beside the point. Have you . . . you know . . . not stopped?"

"Yes, we been doing it since October. God, it's all I think about!" She threw herself down and buried her head in her pillow. Suddenly, she sat back up. "Don't tell Momma! Please, Jules, don't tell. She might tell Floyd and I'd get beat black and blue all over!"

"I won't tell, but we have some talking to do. Do you use any protection?"

Dawn's brow formed a V between her eyes.

"You know, rubbers? The pill?"

"How am I sposed to get the pill? An' no about the rubbers. I jest keep track, you know, of my periods."

"Well, rhythm, sweetie, does not work so well. Just ask Colleen's Mom. We'll see about getting you the pill."

"Ain't my first you know, I'm not ignorant. He's just the nicest."

Julie stood up. "Get some sleep and we'll sort things out in the morning."

"I don't think I'll ever sleep again if I can't see him," but she laid back down and closed her eyes. Julie remembered feeling the same way at the same age, and her sister-in-law Linda talking to her about birth control, unbeknownst to Russ. Two truths crossed her mind—*Boys can turn your world upside down, and sometimes family secrets are okay.* She closed the door and went to find Rick.

They were at the kitchen table with Beth's hidden bottle and some mugs. "You learn anything I need to know?" he asked as she sat down and poured herself some whiskey. She took a sip, a sweet burn going down.

"She's in love," Julie looked down at her mug.

Beth's worry lines had deepened, "Thank Jesus Floyd weren't here. Can you imagine?" She put her hand up to her mouth as if to keep the words from forming—as if not saying would keep the vision from her mind.

"Welcome to holidays with the Madsen clan," Rick shook his head. "I thought with Floyd not here, it may be uneventful," he let out a chortle, what Julie came to think of as his sarcastic laugh. "Nobody's telling Floyd nothing, hear?"

Beth looked at him as if she couldn't believe he even had to say it. "Less he knows about, the better's what I always think."

Clyde barked from outside. "Lord, the poor dog! Been out all day."

"I'll go wrastle with him. Give him some attention," Rick said. He grabbed his coat and went out, and they could hear yelps of delight as the door closed.

Beth glanced around the kitchen, "Could use a coat of paint in here, use some of my artistic *flair*—well, maybe in spring." She waved her hand dismissively, at the cabinets, "You know I've never lived anywhere but here. This was my family's home."

"I didn't know that." Julie said and leaned in closer to Beth. "How did you and Floyd come to live here?"

"Sure you wanna hear that ancient history?"

"If you don't mind telling me, I'd love to hear."

Beth took a sip of her bourbon laced tea, "After my Poppa died, 'twas Momma and us girls. Poppa'd paid off the mortgage, before he went overseas. He was a smart man . . . where Rick gets his brains.

Anyway, Floyd and me started up together when I was just fourteen and he was sixteen. His sister was in my class at school. Bonnie was quiet, kept to herself, and so was I. We were friends. I'd known him all along, but Floyd came to fetch her from here one day, just before school started up again, and over that summer, he grew into a man. Took one look at him and I was sunk. Lord, he was handsome! And sweet and gentle. Wouldn't believe that now, would ya?" She took another sip. Julie stayed quiet.

"Then the fire . . . Nobody cried over Floyd's parents too much. Both were meaner than junkyard dogs, but poor Bonnie . . ." Beth touched her necklace, the one Bonnie had made her, "Jess—this was after he put a halt to the Junior name—rented a house up the road and took Floyd in. *That* was like putting two wildcats in the same sack.

But Floyd and me started spending all our time together and, well," a blush rose from her neck to her cheeks, "we made Ricky. Meg had got hitched, moved out and Momma thought it'd be good to have a man around this house again, so when we got married, he moved in here. We made ourselves a room in the parlor there," she gestured to the room off the kitchen, "for privacy, and he got his class A license.

Then, not too long after Ricky was born, Jo married Marty, and Meg's husband left her with three under three. Momma moved in with her to watch the babies so she could work. Floyd and me had the whole house, and Floyd thought he'd made a silk purse out of a sow's ear! Then he talked Momma into cosigning a loan to get his rig, and off he went on the road. But that's when he started drinking too much. Too much time in that truck to mull over his woes is what I think. 'Course, after Gabe died . . ." she hitched like something was caught in her throat.

Julie put her hand on Beth's arm, and her eyes brimmed as she thought of the pain of losing a child.

"After that, Floyd changed. We all did."

"Why, sorry to ask this but why didn't you leave him?"

"For years, I was such a wreck, I couldn't see the forest for the trees . . . thought I deserved it, letting my baby die. Then Dawn was born . . . If he weren't away so much, I mighta seen fit to leave, but I loved him . . . still do.

And he needed me. Us women, we walk through fire for the man we love, don't we?" Beth looked at Julie with a twist of a smile, "Floyd and me still got our good times when he's home. You gotta weigh the good and bad. When the scales tip big for the bad, then you gotta go."

The back door swung open. Rick and Clyde tumbled in with a rush of cold air.

"You ladies talked the legs off the table yet?"

"I believe we have." Beth set her mug down decisively and stood, "I'm goin' ta bed. Julie, thank you for a nice day." She looked at Rick and said with a wry grin, "You are a lucky man gettin' in with the Normals." The music of her laughter followed her up the stairs.

Chapter 18

DECEMBER 1978

Julie was used to a chaotic December. The store was mobbed, and she worked extra hours. She had exams and final papers due. 'Twas the season to decorate and Christmas shop. Rick wasn't accustomed to December differing from any other month, and it grated on him.

Rick had to admit, her Christmas spirit was contagious when they went to Towson Plaza to buy gifts for Dawn, Beth, and Grandma. In years past, he just gave something utilitarian to Beth; like the time he replaced the toaster Floyd had thrown through the window. He re-glazed the window, too. He usually got Dawn a stuffed animal or something, but she was too old for that now. Julie suggested jewelry.

"Will gave me this ring when I was 13," she twirled the turquoise ring she always wore. "You should get her something that'll remind her you'll always be there for her."

Rick liked the idea. "I'll get something from your store. She's been dressing more, whaddya call, bohemian. Wonder why?" he looked Julie up and down and grinned.

At first, his Grinch heart grew large. He watched Julie skip around with Christmas lights twinkling in her eyes, singing carols, baking cookies, decorating.

By December 17th, though, his patience had worn thin. He was holidayed out. He woke to find Julie at the dining room table working on a paper.

"Gotta get this done! I haven't had a minute all week," she said as he poured himself some coffee.

"You didn't forget the game today, did ya?"

"Course not! That's why I dragged my butt out of bed." She slid her fingers through her hair and said distractedly, "I left the bread and stuff out for you. Oh, and can you pack the cooler?"

Rick mumbled an affirmative and got ready for the game. The Colts were playing Buffalo. They had a worse record than Baltimore this year, but Bert Jones was still on the injured reserve, so Rick's weekly bet with Fred was gnawing at him. He should just stick to the pool this week and skip the $25 he usually put on the Colts, but wouldn't that be bad karma? Rick picked up the phone and dialed Freddie's number.

The wind whipped around the upper deck like a banshee. It tore off hats and tossed programs, cups, and anything that wasn't nailed down. Parents held tight to their children, fearing they would be lifted skyward. Cheeks were red and raw and so were emotions. Baltimore lost. Rick was feeling like a banshee himself, wanting to blow something up.

II

As soon as they got home, Julie ran to the bathroom and took off a few layers of clothing. Then she poured a drink and sat at the dining room table where her papers and typewriter were. "I'm sorry, babe, but my final paper is due for English. I haven't had time to get it done."

"Too much on your plate," said Rick. He took his football pool out of his pocket, ripped it to shreds, and let it fly like confetti, "Another loser."

He stomped past her, beer in hand, and turned on the TV to catch scores of the late games.

Julie tried to concentrate, but the TV was loud, and she could tell Rick was stewing, "Hey, how 'bout some spaghetti? I've got that leftover sauce in there."

"I believe I'll drink my dinner," he made a snorting sound. "Leftovers. I just fuckin' *love* leftovers."

"Want to get Maria's?" she sang Walt's famous Maria song, trying to get a smile out of him . . . No luck.

Maybe he'd snooze a little, she hoped. That would help his mood. "I just gotta read through and type it for tomorrow. Won't take long."

He turned the volume up.

She sighed and gathered her things.

"Okay, I get it! I'll finish this in the other room!" She moved everything into the bedroom where the typing and TV wouldn't clash. *Jesus! I just gotta get one thing done. Is that too much to ask?* She set up the typewriter on the bed and spread her papers to organize them. The cats leaped up, wound around each other, and rubbed against her. Phoebe kneaded the pillow to her liking and curled up for a nap. Annoy settled in next to Julie and expressed his pleasure with a loud purr. She stroked him absently as she began to read and edit.

A crash rang out from the living room. Julie jumped in alarm, causing the cats to dive under the bed. Papers fluttered as she sprang down the hall to investigate. Rick was still sitting on the sofa, but his beer was dripping down the wall, its amber bottle shattered on the floor, its yeasty smell hanging in the air.

"What the hell?" came out of her mouth before she thought about it. Then she saw the look . . . A fist of fear squeezed her insides and she couldn't move.

Rick rose from the sofa, "Looks like I spilled my dinner." He stalked toward her, "I don't like eating *ALONE!*"

Her legs grew rubbery. She trembled. He cupped her elbow in a tight grip, and her body obeyed as he pulled her to the kitchen.

"Now . . . *WHAT* are we having for *DINNER?*"

Before she could speak, his finger flew up to her lips, "Shh, no talking."

Julie nodded and opened the refrigerator. *What should I do? He already made it clear about the leftover sauce.* She racked her brain for a solution before it was too late . . . Everything was frozen, her *and* the food. *You stupid woman, why didn't you defrost something? Think!* Too late . . .

Rick reached in and grabbed the Tupperware that held spaghetti sauce, pulled the top off, and sneered, "How many nights do you expect I want to eat spaghetti?"

She stayed silent. Suddenly, the container smashed against her face. Red sauce dripped down her like blood. Rick took hold of her arm, pulled her to the bedroom, and scooped up a handful of papers, "This has got to go!"

He slammed them against her chest and rubbed them into the sauce that clung to her shirt, "I've told you and told you!"

The ruined papers fell as he picked up the typewriter and threw it against the wall. It bounced off and clattered to the floor with a final *DING!* She stood there, tears carving rivulets in the sauce on her cheeks.

Hands encircled her wrists and yanked her to him. Rick leered down; his breath torrid on her face, and held her there, against his body; reveling in his power over her. Then he released and shoved her viciously. Julie crashed against the doorjamb and pain shot up her back.

"Now clean this shit up, hear? I don't want to see another fucking paper."

As he walked past her, he screamed in her face, "*GOT IT*?" Then he stalked down the hall. The front door slammed, and she let herself dissolve into a puddle on the floor.

She got it . . .

Rick's violence came from a current of emotion that ran much deeper than he could deal with—consumed him, transformed him. She understood the underlying reasons, at least some of them—she got all that, but didn't know how to help him. She needed to heal his wounds and make him the man she knew he could be.

Julie kept thinking their love was strong enough to overcome anything. If he could only see that, too. She wished for some magic healing potion. Isn't that what love is, though? *And marriage is forever, unconditional love. I've got to fix this! I will not quit this marriage!*

She sat there on the floor amid the mess and prayed through her tears, "Please God, help me figure this out."

She thought about what Beth said . . . *Us women walk through fire for the man we love* . . . she could walk through fire. If that's what it took to extinguish his torment, she would walk through anything.

She gathered up her ruined papers and shoved them deep into the trashcan. School could wait another year.

Chapter 19

FEBRUARY 1979

February is the shortest month, but it feels like the longest. If it weren't for Valentine's Day, Julie thought, she'd just as soon wipe it off the calendar. Valentine's Day was on a Wednesday. Julie took the day off to make Rick's favorite dinner—roast beef, mashed potatoes, green beans, and homemade biscuits. She made strawberry shortcake for dessert, and as always, he would joke about how she, his Shortcake, was his favorite dessert.

At 6:00, everything was ready. Julie had the table set and candles lit, both on the table and in the living room, with the lights down low. She had soft music playing, Roberta Flack. All that was left was to carve the beef. When Rick came in the door, she was waiting, wearing a sexy black velour dress and her heart necklace with red lace panties underneath.

"Happy Valentine's Day, Handsome."

"Well, don't you look good enough to eat?" Rick tossed his coat aside, and kissed her.

She handed him the drink she had waiting. "Such service! I like it when my wife has off from work!"

Julie had been working full time at the store since January. She'd decided to take a sabbatical from school, mainly because it caused so much friction between them. Now that she wasn't tied to classes and homework, their marriage had been much happier.

This Valentine's celebration felt like turning a corner in their lives. They had gotten through a bad patch, a tense Christmas season, and a January that had a tentative, tender feel. Now the future looked good. They were going to be okay.

Rick had not lost his temper with her since before Christmas. That horrible night of the Buffalo game seemed to be a catharsis for him. He never said he was sorry. They never even spoke about it, but since then, he kept his anger in check, with her and the rest of the world. A couple times she had seen trouble brewing, but he had been able to step back and rein it in.

Maybe, she prayed, that was the so-called rock bottom he had to hit before he could see clearly. That would make the December incident worth it.

She told herself back then, she would get through Christmas and then suggest counseling. But really, she no longer felt the need. Rick seemed content and in control. When he was happy, she was happy.

II

Rick walked in the door on Valentine's Day to a gorgeous wife, a perfectly made drink, and his favorite dinner. He was a happy man! Their lives were suddenly what he had always imagined marriage to be. Julie had quit school. It had been her decision. He didn't demand it, but she had less on her plate and that made for smoother sailing. He tried not to think about that night in December. He knew he had been out of control, but he never hit her. He had been mean—had taken the Colts loss out on her when she got snotty about that school paper. Yes, he had pushed her, but he never *ever* hit her. He always caught himself before the fist showed up.

He was *not* his father.

Since then, he made a concerted effort to swallow his anger before it got him in trouble. He was pretty proud of his efforts!

Now here he was, spending a perfect Valentine's Day with the woman he loved more than anything. He had gotten her some caramels and a pair of post earrings, little cupids. She usually wore those dangly kinds, but he thought these were a good Valentine's present. He put a lot of thought into the gift. She always seemed to appreciate that more than what was in the box. Yeah, she was a keeper alright.

They had finished their meal and dessert, and he had just given her the earrings when the phone rang.

It was Dawn, and she was crying hysterically.

"Slow down, Hon. I can't get what you're saying."

He heard her breathe in, "That sombitch blacked my eye!"

"Who did?"

"Somebody told him I was screwing around. I told him I wasn't, but he called me trash. I got all kinds of pissed at that, so I pushed him. Then he hauled off and hit me."

"Brice—you talking about Brice?" Rick's knuckles turned white on the receiver, his ears whooshed and his vision clouded, "Where are you?"

"Towson. Spirits. He's at Gino's, at least he was."

"Cups there with you?"

"Yeah."

"You stay put, hear? I'll come get you."

He hung up so hard the ringer chimed.

"I gotta take care of something," he said as he grabbed his coat. "That fucking preppie asshole hit my sister! I'm gonna kill him."

Julie grabbed his arm, "Rick, please don't. Get Dawn and deal with him later. You may really *kill him* in this frame of mind!"

"Damn straight!"

"I don't want a husband in jail for murder. Please!"

He shook her off. He knew she was right, damn it! "Alright, alright. Lemme go get Dawn. Poor kid doesn't deserve this shit." He went out and started up Baby's engine.

At York Road, he couldn't help himself, turned right instead of left, and into Gino's lot. He cruised around, looking in the windows, his body thrumming with adrenaline. There was a group of kids, but he didn't see Asshole. *I should just go get Dawn, but . . .* He threw the car in park, cut the engine, and went in. There was a kid he recognized, another preppie with David Cassidy hair, in a booth with another guy and 2 girls. Rick stormed over and hauled him out of the booth by his coat collar.

"Where the hell is Brice, asshole?" The kid gaped at him, terror in his eyes. "I know you're his buddy, now *SPEAK*!"

Cassidy look alike mumbled something. Rick shook him, "Speak up!"

The rest of the group at the table sat back, afraid but mesmerized by the show going on in front of them.

"He left, Man! With Dawn. They were goin' to the graveyard. They never came back. I swear!"

Rick threw the kid into the booth. A soda knocked over and spilled everywhere, but nobody moved.

"You give him a message from me, hear? You tell him if he ever lays a hand on my sister again, I'll kill him." The guy nodded. "Look in my eyes, muthafucker! You think I'm kidding?"

They all knew he wasn't kidding by the look in his eyes. This guy *was* crazy enough to kill.

"Yeah, yes, sir. I'll tell him."

Rick turned and walked out. He was shaking, electrified. I really would have . . . nobody touches my sister. Even Floyd knew better.

The last time Pop hit Dawn, she was about 12. She called Rick crying, and he went hunting.

In the past, he'd handled Floyd in many ways: talked him down, got his Mom to safety, taken his licks so Momma and Dawn didn't have to. But that was the first time he used his fist on Floyd.

He found him on a barstool at the Pioneer House, a dive bar close to their house. Rick pulled Floyd off that stool and when he started swinging, he couldn't stop. When the bartender and two others finally pulled him off, Floyd was a bloody mess. He never hit Dawn again and only struck Mom when nobody was around to see.

Rick walked into Spirits and a packed bar. Cups, who was busy pouring, nodded, and pointed to the kitchen's door.

Dawn was sitting in the kitchen watching Gravy spin his Valentine magic on the customer's plates as waiters bustled through and the expediter hollered out orders. Ty waved a spatula at him from his post at the grill. She had a bruise under her eye, but not as bad as he expected, thank God.

"Hey Gravy, thanks for standing in," Rick said.

"No problemo, bro. She helped me out here." Gravy put a final swirl of sauce on a plate, and Dawn placed a raspberry in the center, "You'd make a fine prep cook, Dawnie. Let us know if you need a summer job."

"Let's get you home, punk."

"I don't wanna go to school tomorrow. Let me stay with you tonight."

"No way! Mom can decide about school, but you can't stay with us. Julie and me need a holiday alone for a change." Dawn pouted, but didn't keep at it.

"Gravy, gotta ask to use the phone to call Julie."

"Over there." He pointed past the dish station.

When Julie answered, he said, "Darlin' I got Dawn. She's ok. Gonna run her home and come right back to you."

Julie said, "You do what you have to do."

"What I have to do is to be alone with you. I won't even go in. See you in an hour."

"I'll be here."

"I love you, Shortcake." He heard the dial tone before he finished his words.

III

After Rick stormed out, Julie blew out the candles and poured herself a tall glass of wine. *Another holiday with the Madsens.* She took off her dress and threw on her robe. It may be awhile before Rick returned, so she may as well snuggle in.

Stretched out on the sofa, she thought about Rick's words—*Hit my sister, poor kid doesn't deserve this shit.* When she heard him say it, she had such a visceral reaction—her pulse quickened, her body tensed with a vibration that caused a buzzing in her ears.

Why would he rush to punish this boy when Rick himself had done worse to her? Could he not see the comparison—the irony? The more she thought about it the more pissed off she got! *Poor Dawn, but... What about me?!*

The phone rang. She heard his voice, and venom ran through her veins.

It was all she could do to keep from screaming at him, but she said, "You do what you have to do."

"What I have to do is to be alone with you. I won't even go in. See you in an hour."

"I'll be here."

"I love ..."

She hung up, mad at him, mad at herself for feeling so hateful. She threw her emotions into cleaning up the kitchen. By the time he got back, she had calmed down some, but still ...

Then he threw his arms around her and whispered in her ear, "I'm so grateful I have you to come home to. You know I couldn't live without you."

... And all those bad feelings flew away.

BETH

On the next Saturday, President's Day weekend, Ricky and Julie came by with valentine chocolates and were greeted by Clyde and the new long-legged shaggy-haired mutt. Floyd had given Dawn a stray he found on the road, an early birthday present and a friend for Clyde, he rationalized to Beth. At first, Dawn tried not to like the mangy bitch, all tangles, with one ear flopping down. Then it looked at her, eyes full of love and a tongue hanging out sideways, and she couldn't help herself. She named her Valentine.

Rick and the dogs went out to help Floyd spread salt on the steps and driveway. Oprah on "People Are Talking" had predicted up to 6 inches of snow for Sunday. Beth jest loved Oprah and Richard Sher on that show! She watched it every morning.

Julie and Beth sat at the kitchen table with cups of tea and Julie cast her eyes to the vase of roses between them.

Floyd had brought them home on Valentine's and after supper, he surprised Beth again by making love to her right proper. Their sex life had disappeared completely for a few years after Gabe. She suspected Floyd was finding his release elsewhere, but she didn't have the heart to care. Eventually, he started in again with her, mostly a few sweaty grunts when he was soused, but sometimes he took the time to cater to *her* needs, like he had in their early years, when he took her right to heaven.

Julie leaned her nose into the red velvet petals and inhaled. "Love the smell of roses."

"Floyd gave em to me." Beth told her and winked, "part of the good."

Julie showed off her new earrings, "My 'part of the good.'"

Beth blinked, taking in Julie's echo. It caused an uneasy feeling to settle on her. She brushed it from her mind as if it was a dust bunny, and waved her hand dismissively, "Lord, honey, you got years of good ahead of you. I am so happy Rick has found you. You raise him up, ya know."

Julie smiled and placed her hand tenderly on Beth's.

"Til high school he was such a good boy, and smart? His teachers told me he was brilliant! I still got some of his papers and art in a folder somewhere. I'll have ta show em to you some time."

"I'd love to see them."

"Then he got in with that bunch of hoodlums and school fell by the wayside. Barely graduated. Thank the Lord, those Wilder boys got locked up ..." her gaze drifted with her thoughts a moment; more dust bunnies to sweep. "He moved away from living with his Pop, found his way off whatever drugs he'd been taking and started a new path. But I never saw him lookin' happy again, till you. You give him *reason* to be good."

Julie rose from her chair and hugged Beth tight, "I love you, Momma."

Beth's eyebrows raised, thrilled by her affection. She smiled and patted Julie's back, "Love you right back."

A commotion of dogs and men bust through the door, interrupting the quiet. At the same time, Dawn clattered down the stairs, dragging her overnight bag and Parka.

"Can you ride me down to Leslie's?" she asked. "Don't wanna get snowed in here." Her eyes furtively shot to Floyd.

"Sure, let's saddle up," Rick turned to Beth and kissed her cheek. "Love you Momma, Happy Valentine's."

Beth took Rick's hand, "You're my angel, ya know," then gave it a playful tug, "Now go have fun in all that snow we're getting. Oprah said we're getting six inches, at least! It's gonna be a marshmallow world!"

"Momma, take good care of Vallie for me," Dawn said. The dog leapt up and put her paws on Dawn's chest. Dawn scratched her head, "I'll be back soon, Mutt Face, now quit droolin' on me!"

"I'll watch her. You have fun with Leslie, yer my snow angel number two!"

Dawn smiled at her mother, "Ain't neither one of us is angels, Momma, but glad you love me, anyway."

Beth looked at her children and swelled with love. *I should've done better by them, but they are turning out okay after all.*

"Thanks, fer the help, son," Floyd said. "Hope ta see you soon." He put out his gnarled hand.

Rick shook it, "Take care of that sore back, Pop. If the snow hits, I'll come shovel. Get Ed's Garage to plow the drive."

Father and son getting along, 'part of the good,' Beth thought and smiled at Julie who was thinking the same thing.

V

Julie and Rick were sharing a lazy Sunday morning together: no work, no football, no painting, and no family allowed. They had the Sunday paper spread around them on the bed, two cats curled up at their feet and a bowl of fruit on the bedside table. Julie held the Funnies in her left hand. Her right hand was casually tracing circles around Rick's propped-up knee, her legs were tucked beneath his under the sheet. She turned toward him and he fed her a grape. He ate one himself and pretended to read the sports pages, but really, he was enjoying watching her. She chuckled and held up the page for him to see.

"Look what my buddy Snoopy is up to."

"Curses, Red Baron!" he said.

She stretched and looked out the window. The clouds hung low, promising snow. She sat up with sudden inspiration, "Let's have a snow party!"

His finger reached out and helped the strap of her satin nightgown slide down her arm and reveal her nipple. He leaned over and kissed it. "Good idea . . . if it snows. Presidents' Day's a holiday for most of our crew and I get to go in late."

"We can call everybody when we see the first flakes."

"You are a flake."

"That's why you love me, now, kiss me some more!" She pulled her arms free of their satin restraints, raised up to her knees, and pulled his face to her breasts. For the next hour, the newspaper and party plans were forgotten.

The phone rang and they looked at each other with dread.

Julie reached for the receiver.

Rick said, "If it's family, we're not home."

"Hello, we're not home," she said.

"My turn!" Colleen sang out.

"What? Wait . . . you mean . . . *REALLY*?!" Rick looked at her quizzically. "Go make coffee or something, Colleen's got big news!" Rick took his cue and left the room, shaking his head in amazement at the girls' bond.

"Now, continue. When did he ask?"

"This morning. He was going to ask last night at our Valentine dinner but we ran into some Calvert Hall friends and had drinks with them and then he was too drunk, he thought, and then this morning I found a ring on the pillow when I came back from the bathroom!"

Julie glanced down at the pretty sapphire ring and diamond band on her finger that she and Rick had picked out together. She wanted a sapphire instead of a diamond—to match his eyes, she told him.

"Of course, you said 'Yes.'"

"Then I said, yes, yes, *yes!*"

"So, you consummated the marriage ahead of time, then."

"Yes, yes, yes," Colleen said, and they both giggled.

"Hey, come over tonight! No classes tomorrow. We're having a snow party!"

"Yea! We'll bring some food and booze. Oh, and PJs in case we get that six inches."

"You already got your six inches!"

"No, 12 inches . . ." pause for effect, "we did it twice!"

The first flakes started falling late that afternoon. Gravy and Ty arrived with wings and ribs they wrangled from the Owner of Spirits, and Cups promised his arrival as soon as the bar closed. Val, Ruth, Randy, and Kevin arrived together from their respective apartments on the other side of the building. Val and Kevin were in a heated discussion about barometer readings.

"Don't mind them, it's how they make love," Randy said. He handed over the beer and chips in his hands and pulled off his boots.

Milktoast bustled in with a grocery bag full of goodies, followed by Colleen and Pete.

"The future Mrs. McDonald!" said Julie.

"Pete, you ignorant slut! Congratulations, buddy," said Rick.

"Rick, you ignorant son of a slut! Thanks . . . that fuckin' bouquet, right?"

"Who knew that shit really worked?"

The men looked at their women who were jumping up and down and screaming and shook their heads at the spectacle before them.

"Come on, I'll buy you a beer."

The snow continued to fall. The friends had snowball fights and used cardboard boxes as makeshift sleds to career down the unplowed road.

By 8:00, the temperature had plummeted to a frigid three degrees, and the partiers moved inside for the duration. At midnight, the snow stopped falling.

"Looks a bit shy of the six they promised," Val said.

"Sometimes that happens with men," Colleen said.

Ruth said, "That's why I've switched sides," and all the girls laughed hysterically.

Rick thought Ruth was pretty brave coming out of the closet, but he was glad she didn't talk about it much. He looked around at his buddies. *Yeah, they're all thinking of that two-girl thing.* He chuckled to himself.

By 2:00 am, the crowd had wandered home. Colleen and Pete, Julie and Rick settled in for a last celebratory toast, and the snowfall outside began in earnest.

When they awoke, almost three feet of the white stuff lay on the ground. Rick got a call that Harbor Lumber was not opening. Matt called Julie with the same news.

"Good thing we have supplies!" Rick said and held up a full bottle of vodka. "Anyone for a screwdriver?"

"Rick, you ignorant slut, I believe I will," Pete responded.

The girls threw together some breakfast, and they fueled up for warmth. Bundled in parkas and boots, they went out the door and found a world transformed. Everything—cars, roads, bushes, houses—was covered beneath a puffy blanket, white and sparkling. The ice-covered power lines looked like tinsel. Rick could almost hear his mother singing along with Dean Martin like when he was a kid. *It's a Marshmallow World in the winter . . .*

He hoped she was out enjoying this, "Hey, I think I should call up home."

Julie returned his worried look, "Sure, go ahead."

Rick called and let it ring 10 times. No answer. They must be out in the marshmallows. He would try again later.

He rejoined the group that had grown in size. Everyone wanted to experience the snow phenomenon. Milktoast brought a few shovels out of the supply locker, and Kevin and Randy, fitness freaks, were happily getting a snow shovel workout.

At 5:00, Rick called his mother again and got an out-of-service message—the phone lines were down in Northern Baltimore County. He called Dawn at Jo's. She had talked to Beth on Sunday night and all was well. Nothing more he could do until the roads were plowed. Up home, that could take a week.

The phone rang Tuesday afternoon . . .

Chapter 20

"Is this Mr. Madsen?"

"Yes, who's this?"

"This is Dr. Lou Craig at Greater Baltimore Medical Center. I am calling about your mother. There's been an accident . . . Coma . . . Intensive care . . ."

Rick heard little after that, or maybe he just couldn't comprehend. The world folded in. Beads of sweat broke out along his brow, and he collapsed into the nearest chair. All his life, he expected this call and here it was, in a marshmallow world. Julie took the phone from his hand and listened to details.

They made their way through the snow in Pete's Chevy Blazer. Rick sat in the back, gripping Julie's hand, his lifeline. "I should have been there. I promised . . ."

"Shh. Let's just get there and assess." She touched his chest, his pounding heart.

"Mrs. Madsen is in a coma," the Nurse said. "On Monday, she took a tumble down the stairs and suffered multiple fractures, wrist, rib, and clavicle. A blow to the head caused a subdural hematoma—brain bleed. I believe her husband . . . Is that your father? Told us the dog was responsible for the fall."

Rick stood beside his mother and held her hand. The other arm was in a sling, and there were bandages on her head and tubes everywhere. "I'm so sorry," he said, "I promised to take care of you."

The nurse said, "I'll notify the doctor the family is here."

She retreated on hushed feet, leaving only the sounds of beeping machines. Julie followed her to the corridor outside the room.

As she stood, wiping tears from her cheeks, she saw Floyd shuffling toward her, carrying a coffee cup. Julie placed a warning hand on his arm, "Rick's in there. Give him a minute."

Floyd looked like something blown in from battle. Instead of the usual greaser style, his hair flopped down across his brow, uncombed, and his craggy face and posture had lost their defiance. Now he just looked worn out, shoulders rounded forward, expression sagging. Under his jacket, he wore a scrub shirt and there was a stain on the knee of his jeans.

"The nurse gave me this," he gestured to his shirt. "Mine had blood on it . . . didn't even notice till they said." He held up the cup, "They got coffee down there if . . ."

"What happened?" Julie asked, dreading the answer.

"Damn dog, the new one, got er off balance and there she went. No phone, no way out the drive . . . sun came up and I started walking to the fire station . . . the Hereford boys plowed in. Thank God for them." He stopped as if he ran out of words.

The door slid open and Rick looked out. "Has the doctor . . ." his eyes fell on his father, his speech faltered as he focused, "You."

As if in slow motion, Julie watched his expression transform from grief to rage. Her body reacted and shifted between them. Rick sprang.

In his efforts to reach Floyd, Rick shoved Julie against him. Caught unaware, Floyd was propelled into the opposite wall. Coffee splashed up and rained down. People came running.

"You did this!" Rick barked. A beefy orderly encircled Rick from behind, and he went limp, grief enveloping him once again.

Beth was on life support. The doctors agreed she had no brain activity. Floyd would not allow the removal of the ventilator, could not pull the plug. Attached to lines and tubes, she withered there for weeks while they watched. The Beth they knew was already gone. Only a shell remained until her body, too, let go, and the music of the beeps became a high-pitched monotone.

The doctors saw the evidence—Beth's X-rays told the story—old fractures, testimony to atrocities suffered in silence, mended but never healed.

They arrested Floyd on charges of second-degree murder. Jess posted bail and took Floyd in. Trial was set for April.

Rick, Julie, and the cats moved into the house with Dawn until the dust settled. The cats weren't fond of the situation, but Dawn doted on them, so they adjusted. Beth's sisters attempted assistance, advice, and admonishment. Rick was in no condition to make decisions about anything. Julie begged them to give it time, nothing could be done until after the trial.

Floyd was not welcome at the house, so Rick and Julie packed the old duffle with clothes and toiletries for Jess to retrieve. Items were thrown in willy-nilly as they packed: razor, comb, deodorant. From the dresser, Rick pulled out jeans, tees, boxers . . . In the top drawer, along with the socks, was a battered shoebox with the trade name PETERMAN across the top. Rick pulled it out and sat on the bed to look through it.

"Come look at this," he called to Julie. "My Uncle Rich's dog tags and Gabriel's baby bracelet."

Julie threw a bottle of Mennen skin bracer into the Dopp kit and wandered in. Rick was looking through some letters, yellowed with age. The first was from Uncle Rich, dated November 1951 on Marine Corps stationary.

Hello Floyd—I hope everybody's well up home.
It's hell here but a differnt kind than there.
First it was hot as hell here. Now It's dam cold, lots of frostbite going around.
We whooped some commie ass in Seoul. Now we're in the mountains whoopin ass!
I told some funny stories' bout bootlegging to the guys. They think having a still at the house is a good thing. Ha-Ha. I told em you don't wanna mess with drinking my Pa's Madshine, makes you mean and crazy. We seen that with Pa, right?
Give Bonnie a hug from me. Hope your lookin out for her now I'm gone.
Your brother, Richard

Next, he found a piece of construction paper with a child's scrawl—a picture of two figures, one smaller than the other, with sticks in their hands.

The caption read—*My DaD anD ME FisH RICKY*

"Huh, forgot about fishing," Rick's head gave a lopsided nod, "huh," he laid the picture on the bed with care, "that kinda stopped after Gabe died."

Rick envisioned his battered six-year-old body being flung against the wall. Before Gabe died, Floyd had taken him fishing. After, he used him for a punching bag.

There were a couple of report cards from Fifth District Elementary for Richard Madsen.

Grade two reported all good grades, effort, and conduct.

A note from the teacher read:

Ricky does well with mathematics. He seems to have a good number sense. He excels in his reading ability and shows great talent in artistic endeavors.

Grade three was similar in content—the teacher's comments read:

Rick has great promise as an artist! His reading level is above standard. He is thoughtful and has a tendency to 'stick up' for our smaller students. I suspect that is because of his new baby sister, whom he delights me with stories about! Miss Anderson.

"I remember her. Had a major crush on her, she was pretty hot for a teacher."

Julie smiled and poked him, glad to see his grin, "Ladies man even at nine, huh?"

On a piece of lavender-colored stationery, folded small and shaped as if carried in a wallet for a long time, a note in Beth's precise handwriting:

> *My Dearest,*
> *I am looking at our boy and see you in him—the goodness of you made him. I miss you so much when you're on the road. I pray those roads will lead you back to me soon. I miss your arms around me at night. I miss our specal mornings when Ricky is napping in his cradle and I crawl back in with you.*
> *I tell you- take me to heaven.*
> *And You really do, you know. Heaven.*
> *Come home safe.*
> *Yours always and forever, Beth*

Rick touched the paper where his name was written in his mother's perfect script. That jagged thing inside him shifted.

The next bundle of letters was tied together with a rubber band, hard and crumbled with age. Still in envelopes, they were addressed to a Mr. Chris Robin, Box 341 Hereford, Maryland. The first was dated January 1952.

> *Dear Floyd,*
> *I have settled in. I paid my rent for this month but I might be writin from another address come next. We'll see. Thank you from my heart* ♥ *for helping with my plan.*
> *I know you were scared it would back<u>fire</u> HA! That is a good joke!*
> *I know you will be ok now they're gone. No more strap.*
> *And I will, too. No more you know what.*
> *But ill miss you and the brothers, even Junior!*
> *Love, Bonnie*
> *PS. Hope you are still courting Beth. You should marry her, she is the best friend I ever had. Maybe the only.*

The next was dated April 1952.

Dear Floyd,

I am doing good here. I got a job as a maid at a motel. It keeps me fed and they pay in cash. Mostly the other workers are ok but I keep to myself

I still get nightmares of Senior's ugly, sweaty face up over me. I can smell his tobacco even — but when I wake up, I remember he is gone and won't be gettin at me no more.

I will be happy if a man never touches me again!

I need to say thank you again. I know you said in your letter you done it for selfish reasons but I talked you into it so . . .

Yes—The money is safe. I keep it well hidden. Who knew they woulda had so much stashed away? Good thing Mom was a sound sleeping drunk so you could get to it.

Well, I got to go make beds and throw away used rubbers YUK I will write soon.

Bonnie

PS: I found a stray cat and they are letting me keep it in my room. I named him Clyde. Get it? PSS Notice how we are all named after criminals? xcept for Rich.

Guess we come by it natural

Letter number three was dated December 26, 1952.

Dear Floyd,

Merry Christmas Sorry I wasnt with you- I spent mine with Clyde and some people I work with that also don't have no family here. We got drunk and sang carols. I am writing this with a wicked hangover Kinda makes me understand why Ma was such a bitch in the morning- Ha-Ha!

On to your news—

So sad about Richard. Wished I coulda told him how much he meant to me. He is surely in heaven.

Cant say I'm surprised about John's sentence — his heart started going bad long ago. Too much Senior in him. The dead guy probly had it coming if he was STUPID enough to tangle with John anyhow.

I'm going to be a AUNT! Best Present I ever got! Wish I could hold that baby when it comes! You are right about not tellin Beth but I wish I could tell her. I am so happy about you 2—about you 3!

You sound like it is __TRUE LOVE__ the way your letter goes on about her!

Send me a picture when it gets born, Love Bonnie

"Holy shit!" Rick gaped at the letters.

"Yeah, Holy shit alright!" Julie's mind was whirring with dates and names, "Floyd and Bonnie set the fire?"

"Sounds like . . . how do you think she got out?" Rick, too, puzzled through the facts, "Wonder if she's still alive? Last letter here was long ago."

"Sounds like she was being . . ." Julie couldn't say the words, "By her own father." She shuddered. "I guess Floyd knew and did something about it. It puts a whole other layer on him, huh?"

"Last Christmas . . ." Rick said.

Understanding dawned upon Julie's face. "That's why he called Jess Junior . . . When Jess smacked Dawn's butt, he was comparing him to Senior! So, Jess knew what his father was up to," she shuttered, "or was doing it, too."

"Holy fuckin' shit!"

Rick went to work every morning and found a house project every evening: the loose step on the porch, squeaky doors, dripping faucets. He said he needed to get the house ready to sell. Julie knew he was also keeping his mind occupied. His mood swung wildly and with no apparent pattern or provocation: guilt, anger, grief.

Dawn withdrew into her own private hell. When the sun rose, she burrowed beneath her blankets, refusing to go to school. Julie would return from work to find her wandering the fields with the dogs and cats trailing behind, scratching at bug bites until she bled.

In the wee hours, the creaking floorboards would wake Julie, as one or the other of Beth's children paced away the sleepless night. Were they searching for ghosts or trying to bury them?

Julie just kept running in frantic circles to keep her herd alive. Beth's presence was everywhere: tea bags in the kitchen, laundry in the dryer, soap that smelled of her—lavender and linen.

Julie loved living in the country, but maybe Dawn would cope better away from constant reminders of her mother and father. Julie suggested the idea to Rick; his response was noncommittal. So she broached the subject with Dawn, who fell into hysterical sobs at the thought of leaving her home.

The first day of spring came and went unnoticed . . .

Chapter 21

MAY 1979

COLLEEN

Colleen was concerned about Julie. Her ability to deal with all this turmoil was commendable: Beth's lengthy demise, the funeral, the trial. She was still dealing with the aftermath. Dawn and Rick were a mess—who could blame them? The home they grew up in was being sold. Their father was convicted of killing their mother, for God's sake! Then there were the letters. Colleen was sworn to secrecy about that. At least they were back in the apartment and had talked Dawn into living at Leslie's. Julie said the thought of going to Towson High clinched it.

Yes, Julie handled all that and to everyone else, she seemed fine, but Colleen knew her better. She always put up a positive façade, but she was not fine. The friends hadn't spent a lot of time together lately. She and Pete had been hanging with his Calvert Hall friends. Colleen knew she needed to get Julie alone to let her vent.

When she entered Boutique Picasso, the door's little bell tinkled. Matt stuck his head out of the backroom and shouted, "Hello!"

Julie popped up from behind the counter, "Boo!"

"Aaaah!" Colleen jumped, "you sure are perky!"

"Caffeine is amazing and I've been living on it!"

"Uh, yeah . . . so, Nutty Buddy, I need some Julie time, these exams are stressing me out."

"Oh, that sounds like just what the Doc ordered!" Julie agreed, then stopped, reconsidering. "Well, I need to check with Rick."

"Sure, call him. We can walk across the street when you close up."

Matt called from the back, "Ladies, go." His signature laugh rang out like a jazz riff on a piano, "Go do your thing, I'll close."

Julie smiled and picked up the phone. Colleen watched her body tense, her grip was so tight, her knuckles were white. "Hey, Colleen's here. She needs some Julie time. Can you spare some?" a nervous giggle. "Oh, I won't be late, we'll just go across to the Crease or something," she listened. "Ok. See you at home. Love you." Julie hung up and visibly relaxed, "Let's do it."

It was happy hour, so they ordered a couple of appetizer specials and 2 for 1 drinks. "Anything new on the house sale?" Colleen asked between nacho bites.

"I still have some cleaning out. Dawn can't bear to do it, and Rick has no clue about kitchen stuff or Beth's clothing and all."

"That's got to be hard."

"It makes me feel close to her . . . she was a . . . sweet, well, special to me, ya know? A kindred spirit." Julie teared up.

Colleen handed her a bar napkin. "Find any more family secrets?"

Julie took a long swallow of her vodka tonic. "Funny you should ask," she pulled a plastic bag out of her purse. "I found the folders Beth kept, one for each child. Rick's had artwork in it. Some little boy stuff, but the ones he did later, maybe junior high?—some charcoal, some pen and ink, and they are really . . . I mean *really* good. His use of shadow and . . . well, here."

Julie pulled a bag out of her purse and carefully unfolded a couple sheets of drawing paper, "I have them to see if I can get them copied." A girl's face appeared in charcoal. Colleen held it under the light. It was so lifelike, she felt she knew her.

"Wow! I'm no art person but, yeah, this is wonderful!"

"Some of the landscapes seem like Rick was in an oak tree that used to grow in front of his house. The intricacy of the crosshatch must've taken hours. And the perspective, well . . ." She unfolded the next drawing, a pen and ink.

Again, Colleen held it to the light. Part of a house was in the forefront and at the top were tree branches. Then the world unfolded, a fence, a garden with a figure bent to its rows of plants, rolling fields and way back, a line of trees. Colleen felt like she was in that tree herself. Julie started her second drink as she watched Colleen fall into the drawing.

"Look there," Julie pointed to the window of the house. There was a ghostlike figure of a young man Colleen hadn't noticed. Julie continued, "His dead brother, you think? Or maybe his absent father?"

"Or maybe himself," Colleen said and shivered a little.

Julie hadn't thought of that possibility. She nodded her head. "I am just stunned by his talent. *And* . . . there were essays and reports he wrote. Most had D's for grammar—*ain't* no surprise there."

Colleen barked out a "Ha!"

"—but A's for content . . . a character study of William Caulfield, one about Steinbeck, and one about The Great Gatsby. They were deep, I tell ya!" She drank and rattled the ice that remained, "I was impressed . . . and pissed! He coulda helped me write my own damn papers instead of bitching about them. I failed English 102 because I didn't turn in my final paper."

"How come?"

Another rattle of ice before she answered, "Oh, spaghetti sauce spilled on it and I gave up."

She signaled the bartender for another round, "He should have gone to college. School of Hard Knocks, my ass! And why did he make me quit?"

"Wait, he made you quit? I thought that you decided . . ."

"I did." She started drink number three, "Because he resented the time I spent on school so much." Another sip, "It *was* my decision, but done for him."

"He doesn't deserve you, you know." Colleen placed the drawings back in the bag with care.

Julie shoved a cheesy nacho in her mouth and took her time chewing. She dabbed her mouth with a napkin and said, "So, enough about Rick and me. How are you? Let's talk wedding!"

By the end of happy hour, Julie was loose, giggly, and drunk. Colleen suggested she drive and they could get Julie's car in the morning.

"Ok, and you can schleep over! In the Pete and Col schweet!"

They sang their way to the car and got to the apartment safely. Rick had mentioned to Julie he would eat at Spirits and was not home yet, so they cozied up on the sofa with the cats and Clyde, for a few games of Gin Rummy and girl talk.

Julie told her Valentine moved with Dawn. She said Uncle Marty finally grew a pair when Hazel fussed about a dog in the house. They had old-time giggles over Julie's rendition of him.

She stood with a pillow under her shirt, "Mother! You do not live here. This child needs her dog, and by God, she will have her dog! I put my foot down!" She stomped her foot and the pillow fell out, so she added, "And I shall diet!"

Colleen added Hazel's part, "I'll get you for this, my pretty, you and your little dog, too!"

Rick came in around 11:00. Colleen could tell he had tipped a few himself, but he was cordial about her staying there. She said her goodnights, put on her borrowed PJs and got in bed with a book. She must have dozed off when a loud crash and a bark startled her awake. Colleen opened the door of the bedroom to investigate.

A dining room chair lay on its side next to a gouge in the wall. Julie was bent backward over the living room chair's back, her shirt gaped open, revealing the swell of her breasts. Colleen could see Rick's back muscles flex as he shook Julie by her shoulders. He was hissing something into her face.

Julie saw Colleen, and her eyes must have told Rick they had company. He relaxed his grip and backed away from Julie.

Julie straightened, "Sorry, the chair must have woken you. I'm so clumsy!"

Colleen was frozen, not sure what to say.

"We're just messing around." she took a few cautious steps toward Colleen, a nervous giggle escaped her. "Right Rick?"

"Sure, sorry, I kinda forgot you were here," he said and sat on the sofa without looking at either of them.

Colleen knew something was up, but what could she do? Certainly, she couldn't confront Rick in his state.

"Go back to bed. I am too . . . It's late," Julie said with Morse code in her eyes. *The storm is over.*

"If you're sure."

"I'm sure. Looks like Ricky may be falling asleep there on the sofa."

A noncommittal grumble from Rick. Clyde padded over from the corner to him. He patted the dog's head and laid down.

The girls walked back to their respective rooms, unsure of what to say to each other. Just before they parted, Colleen took Julie's hand and said, "I'm here, Okay? I'm keeping this door open."

Julie shot her a look filled with emotions she couldn't articulate, "I know." When she closed her door, Colleen heard the lock click.

Chapter 22

SUMMER 1979

Julie was dreaming . . . Beth reached out to her from somewhere bright and sparkling, like the snow on the day she died. Beth's hand was a beacon slicing through the dark space where Julie crouched. She stretched her arms up to touch the light, the hand. But she was being pulled back . . . darkness was winning.

Light spilled across the bed as Rick opened the curtains. "Up and at 'em, Sunshine!"

Julie pulled the blanket over her head, "Five more minutes."

Rick slammed the dresser drawer.

"Ok, ok, I'm moving." Julie swung her legs off the bed, wincing as she stood. Last night, she had tried again to address Rick's constant anger. It only got her a shove followed by a cold shoulder.

They were closing on the sale of the house today, hopefully that would give Rick some closure. Grandma was keeping half the proceeds for her own expenses. The rest would be split between the sisters. Beth's half would go to Rick and Julie, and Dawn in trust. The amount wasn't a lot, but Rick was glad to have some money to sock away.

They invited Dawn to get crabs with them that night at Glenmore Gardens. Rick was in rare good spirits. He ordered the largest crabs. When the pitcher of beer came, he poured Dawn some while the waitress wasn't looking. "Hell, you're 17, which is almost 18 far as I'm concerned."

The three tried to outdo each other with stupid jokes. Dawn laughed until beer came out her nose. That made Julie call, *pee-speed!* and run to the bathroom. Rick was feeling good—he had money in his pocket and his girls were happy.

After dinner, they took Dawn home. She and Leslie had plans—now that she had her license and Beth's old wagon, they had broadened their horizons.

"Let's hit Spirits, darlin'. I'm not ready to call it a night," Rick said. He took her hand and squeezed it.

"Good idea, I think Craig's playing solo tonight."

A group of their friends was on the far side of the bar. As they made their way around, Cups mixed drinks, "Drink of the week, 'Alien.'"

"Like the movie?" Rick asked.

"Yep, Kahala over crushed ice, topped with two raspberries and syrup drizzled around the rim."

He set two on the bar.

"It's staring at me!" Julie laughed, "and drooling too!" She sat down next to Val, Kevin, and Randy who had his arm around a hot little blond.

Randy said, "Helen, these two are my best friends in the world. Julie, Rick, this . . . is Helen." He squeezed her and beamed, "She's working at Padonia with me this summer."

Rick saw Julie and Val share one of their girl Morse code looks. Randy tended to fall hard and fast for pretty girls and just as suddenly, fall out of love a couple months later.

As Julie began a conversation with lovely Helen, Cups gestured to Rick to meet him in the back room. "Scored some stellar blow, man, thought you may need a pick-me-up after all you've been through lately."

"Haven't done that shit for a long time. Used to get me in trouble!"

"Older and wiser, man, and better shit." Cups laid some lines of cocaine out on the counter and handed Rick a straw.

"What the hell, I deserve a treat!" He leaned over and snorted up the snowy white powder. The familiar taste hit the back of his throat, and a lightning bolt of adrenaline shot right up to the center of his brain. Rick almost grabbed the top of his head to keep the euphoria from hitting the ceiling, "Woah! I forgot how much I like this shit!"

Cups took the straw and snorted up his line, half in each nostril, and jerked his head violently as the magic hit its mark.

"Got some to sell me? Half gram, maybe? I got money in my pocket and a girl I gotta keep happy!"

Rick made his purchase and went to find Julie.

"Hey, darlin', I got a present for you, follow me." Cups left the door unlocked for them. He pulled Julie inside the storage room and laid out a couple of lines.

"Oh! I don't know . . . me and drugs don't mix well."

"Come on, this is special stuff, baby, we're celebrating this money in my pocket. Just for tonight." He handed her the straw.

Julie put it to her nose and sniffed. Within seconds, he could see she was dancing inside. No muss, no fuss! Instant happy!

Rick watched the worried look she had worn the last few months evaporate; a smile spread across the face he loved. He kissed her with a passion he hadn't felt in months. *I'm back.*

They rejoined their friends in the bar, most of whom also had the coke high tickling their brains. Julie babbled intensely with Val and while Randy mooned at Helen.

Rick, Ty, and Kevin were deep in conversation about the sale of the Orioles as they watched them play Kansas City on the TV over the bar.

"I tell you, they keep playing like this, no way Williams will move to DC," Rick said.

"Got that right. Look at Palmer," Ty said, watching the Orioles' pitcher strike another man out. "Boy got an arm on him."

"They don't call it Orioles' Magic for nothing," Kevin said. "Look, Singleton's up next. Give us a home run, Kenny!"

A disturbance on the other side of the bar distracted them. Some guy was being loud and obnoxious.

"What's wrong with that guy?" Kevin said with a wry grin.

"Yeah, you never seen us actin like that," Ty said, and they all laughed.

The guy was pointing at them, "That's him. That's the guy from Halloween!"

His sloppy buddy tried to talk him down, "Not worth it . . . He's *mean*, man!"

"Hey SHITHEAD!" he was looking at Rick, "remember me?"

Rick looked up, took a sip of his drink, and replied, "Nope." He slid his eyes back to the game and muttered to his pals, "Asshole friends of Joanie, Bill or Barney or some shit name."

Kevin's face contorted into worry. Ty stood up, making sure the guy remembered just how big he was, "I got your back if you need to tussle," he said to Rick.

"Not worth it. Nothin's gonna spoil my good mood tonight."

Barney or Billy, or whoever he was, started around the bar. Cups headed him off, "You're out of here, buddy."

Ty sauntered over in his slow easy style and stood behind Cups. The waitress, Kathy was at the hostess stand, "Got my hand on the phone, pal. I need to call the cops?"

Julie and the rest were watching, on high alert. Craig was just coming back from a break and stood at attention.

The guy's eyes were shooting daggers at Rick, "I haven't forgotten you, Asshole!" Rick just sat there and watched the game.

His friend tugged on his arm, "Come on, man! I can't be here for cops."

Billy took a step.

Cups pushed him backward, and the friend tried again, "I got that court thing, man, don't screw it up for me."

Seeing he had to go through Cups and that big wall called Ty and seeing no arousal from Rick, he backed toward the door, "I'm still not done with you, big man! When you least expect me . . ." he punched a fist into his palm, "Bam!" and they were out the door.

Julie put her arm around Rick's neck and kissed his cheek, "Proud of you, Baby."

Rick just smiled.

Craig started his next set with "Bad, Bad Leroy Brown" replacing the names Rick and Ty in the song. Relieved of tension, the crowd laughed and sang along.

Julie got up and whispered in Craig's ear. He strummed a few bars and she sang with him, "I'd Like to Teach the World to Sing . . ."

By the end, the entire bar was singing. Then she sang "Where Away" and looked at Rick with those bedroom eyes. He called for the check. He wanted to take her home where he wouldn't have to share her.

They stumbled in the door, eager to undress, but first, Clyde needed to go out. "Let's do a line and take a walk," Rick suggested. "The bed can wait if I can hold your hand."

Glad to have time to talk, Julie found her hand mirror to lie out lines of sparkle, and they shared the lines, shared a grin, and then took Clyde out on his leash.

The night was sweet with summer. The smell of honeysuckle hung in the humid air. Fireflies lit their way around the block as Clyde sniffed and left wet messages for his doggy friends.

"Clyde's adjusted well, even puts up with the leash now."

"He's just happy he ain't getting kicked no more!"

"Floyd kicked him?" Julie asked, horrified.

"Hey, the asshole hit his kids, you think he wouldn't kick the dog when he got in the way?"

"Guess Clyde learned to stay out of the way, huh?"

"I guess . . . I don't want to talk about Floyd, I keep thinking of that Star Wars thing with Luke and Vader."

"Nooooo, that's impossible!" Julie imitated the famous Luke line, "That one?"

Rick laughed a big gut laugh that warmed Julie's thrumming heart.

"Oh no, I got her started."

Julie did her Clint Eastwood for him, "Ask yourself, do I feel lucky. Well, do ya, punk?'"

"I feel lucky, go ahead, and shoot. If I have you, I'll die a happy man."

Julie realized she got them off on a tangent and lost the Floyd thread. She had hoped that would lead to the anger thread. "Woah, my thoughts are going a million miles an hour. But I wanted to talk about something else and . . ."

"And we are back," Rick said as they entered their parking lot. "Let's get naked!"

He ran up the terrace with Clyde, barking happily, running beside him. Julie thought, my tail is wagging too, and followed the drooling boys into the apartment.

II

The college kids that rented Walt's old place moved out at the end of May, and the second weekend in June was slated for painting. Rick came home Friday night with a gram in his pocket.

"Guess what can make painting a lot more fun!" he pulled out a little amber vial. "I know . . . before you say anything, we said last weekend was a special treat, but . . ." he wiggled his eyebrows.

"I think this will be the best paint job we've ever done!" She ran in and got her mirror, "No time like the present!"

Rick tried to procure "sparkle" as Julie called it, a few more times that summer. Monday mornings were rougher than usual, but worth it. Didn't they deserve a little bit of fun?

He had fleeting thoughts of going down a dead-end road. He'd done that before and almost didn't survive. That was different, he thought, I'm older, wiser, and not hanging with those degenerates from up home. He'd just seen a news article. One of them was bludgeoned to death in the federal pen. It sent a shudder through him, thinking he'd dodged a major bullet. Yeah, everything was good now. He could handle this. One more weekend, he told himself, and I'll keep the rest of the money in the bank.

Julie dragged herself through the weekdays, exhausted and wary of Rick's temper. The hours before work were when she did laundry, cleaning, and grocery shopping. She snuck back to bed some mornings, knowing if he found out, he'd be pissed. She found out the hard way when they were out of coffee. She told him she'd been too tired to get to the store, so he threw the old coffee grinds against the kitchen wall.

The weekends they had coke, he was a different person, funny and sweet and sexy, the Rick she fell in love with. It was the magic wand she'd prayed for, or more accurately the fairy dust. They talked about future plans, buying a house, and having kids. Julie desperately wanted to have children. She watched Rick with her nephews and niece, the way he tenderly held Abigail every time they were with the Friedmans. He was great with kids. He hovered over Dawn like a protective dad. Rick would be a good father.

They had some money saved, maybe it was time, he said. Julie loved talking with Rick about houses, baby names and a fairy-tale future.

Then, the weekend was over and reality set back in.

The second weekend in July, Aunt Dorothy called to say their condo in Ocean City was free. Their renters backed out at the last minute, did Julie and Rick want to go downey ocean? They took Monday and Tuesday off for a mini-vacation.

On Sunday night, Julie made some ramped-up Bug Juice to go with the coke Rick scored from Cups. They took their treats out on the balcony that faced the ocean. Julie, still in her bikini, felt like this was heaven. The salty night air kissed her skin, lingered on her tongue and in her nose. The waves roared out a euphoric song. Her husband was sexy in his cutoffs, tanned and muscular. When someone talked about joining a gym, he liked to say *his* gym was The Gym of Hard Work.

The conversation rambled on, as it always did when cocaine was involved.

Rick told her about his past drug use; not coke much, not much of that around back then, more like quaaludes, black beauties, Dilaudid. The guys he ran with were a hard-core bunch, and he was getting sucked into some heavy shit. They planned a drug store robbery, and in his high brain, it sounded exciting. He was in until they told him he would be armed.

"That scared the shit out of me! Armed robbery. That made it real! I had to get myself out of this without pissing them off, they were a vindictive bunch."

"You didn't go through with it, did you?"

"Funny story there . . . So, back story . . . When I was a kid and Floyd was on the warpath, I used to hide in the oak tree out front. There was a V in the branches and I rigged some 2 by 4s in there for a seat. It kind of became my thinking spot, ya know?"

"You used to draw up there, didn't you?"

"How did you know that?"

"Finish this story, then we'll do that story." She told him, she put some more sparkle on the mirror.

He snorted, "The pause that refreshes!" and continued. "I had to figure out something, I was so *pissed* at myself for getting in this jam . . . so here I am, 18 years old, all six foot one of me climbing a tree. Oh, and of course I was high as a kite!"

"A kite in a tree, funny!"

"Yeah, funny till I fell out and broke my arm!"

"Oh, no! Poor baby." she bent and kissed his arm. "From now on, be the tree, not the kite."

"The tree, not the kite . . . I'll try to remember that."

He smiled at her and a feeling of pleasure flowed through her, her heart pumping it to the farthest reaches of her fingers and toes.

"Anyway, I wouldn't be no good to them in a cast, so I was out. Saved by the tree." He shook his head, remembering, "They went ahead with the robbery. Almost a year, later they got caught. Dummies still had the bottles from the pharmacy. That sobered me up fast! I started walking the straight and narrow."

"God works in mysterious ways, huh?"

"That tree saved my ass a million times, one way or another. Lightning struck it not long after that. Big limbs came down, hit the house. Put a hole in the roof and broke a window. Me and Floyd went out with a chain saw and cut the poor sucker down. Its wood kept us warm the whole next winter."

"I want to show you something." Julie went into her suitcase. She had the folder with her, hoping to talk about it this weekend. "Funny how pieces fall together," she mused as she handed the open folder to Rick.

"Where'd you find this?"

"In Beth's dresser when we were cleaning out. She told me about it that last day, when we were there for Valentine's. She was so proud of you! I should have shown you right off, but I was scared you'd be embarrassed. Then I thought, maybe I'd frame something and surprise you."

"Mom saved all this?" Rick's eyes clouded as he looked through his drawings, "I remember doing these, I was obsessed for a while. Course I hid it when Pop was around."

"You have amazing talent. You should start drawing again. It would be an outlet for you, you know like it was then?"

"Like I have time."

"You have time right now." She handed him a pencil and turned over one of the essays on the folder, "Draw me."

Rick looked at the pencil, hesitated.

"Come on, it will feel good, I promise. Get some of that emotion out on paper."

He began to sketch, slow at first, looking at her, then the paper.

While he worked, she broached the subject of his anger.

He told her, "You gotta understand, anger is what kept me alive, my anger kept Mom and Dawn safe from Floyd. Hell, it even drove me up that tree and knocked me out of it. Now sometimes it's like it has a mind of its own."

He kept talking, told her he was sorry he got out of line sometimes when she pissed him off. He knew he shouldn't get out of control, felt like he didn't have control over anything. He failed his mother; he was failing her . . . all the while he kept drawing.

Tears were now on Julie's face.

"I just want you to be happy. I get mad at myself when you aren't happy. I get mad because I'm not good enough." He lifted her chin to him and kissed her wet cheeks, "I'm sorry that I shove you sometimes, but I never hit you, I would never hit you." He handed her the drawing. There she was on the page, created by his hand, a beautiful girl with a tear on her cheek. He kissed her mouth then, and she was swept into the moment, the passion, the raw emotion they shared.

Later, she remembered what he said and thought back on the times he hurt her. He pushed, threw things, held her in death grips but . . . He had never used his fist. Except for their honeymoon, he had never even slapped her openhanded. He *did* have some control. Was that a good thing, that he could cap his violent acts? Did that mean he wasn't completely blinded by his rage? Did that mean he knew very well what he was doing?

III

A young couple moved into the apartment above them at the end of June. The husband was a new professor at Goucher College.

Julie took a peach cake up as a welcome. The wife invited her in. She was six months pregnant with their first. Jealousy stabbed Julie, as she looked at the woman's bulging belly. The force of it took her by surprise. She gave out some names of stores and restaurants, traded phone numbers, and got out of there.

Julie tripped down the steps and into her door, where she stood holding the knob. A great burst came from her chest—she didn't realize she'd been holding her breath—uncontrollable sobs wracked her, body and soul. A baby? How could she even entertain the idea? Her marriage was surviving because of cocaine! Exhausted, she curled up on the floor with Clyde and slept.

They were on a slippery, snow-covered slope and agreed it had to end. Rick wanted to start their family, and he'd be damned to let that happen while they were coked up. That was enough for him to quit.

He started looking at the real estate page and asked Julie to stop taking the pill.

"Let's get through the summer. We've had so much thrown at us this year, I need a couple months to regroup." She told him.

He felt responsible for the crap Julie put up with because of his family. He could give her a couple months. But it wasn't easy. Once he got an idea in his head, it was like a little dog with its jaws on a pants leg. He could shake like crazy, but it wouldn't come loose.

Julie was not so thrilled to give up the sparkle. It let her escape her troubles. She loved the surge of energy and creativity that flowed from its high, but mostly she loved what it did for Rick. Those few weekends, he lost his jagged edges, loosened the armor he wore, and let himself breathe. She could talk to him without fear of repercussions. But, knowing their histories, if they didn't call a halt to the sleigh ride, neither one of them would survive the slide.

Chapter 23

FALL 1979

Summer ended and so did their sleigh ride—Rick was adamant about the "no sparkle" rule.

The days grew shorter and colder and then daylight savings chopped another hour of sunlight, sending Julie into a downheartedness she couldn't shake. Days flowed one into the next with no joy. A melancholy had settled into her bones and cast shadows on her world.

Julie worked by herself on Fridays until 8:00. She did her regular closing chores: wiped down the counters, reconciled the register, vacuumed the floor. The vacuum was a huge and loud old beast, and she was almost done wrestling the monster around the store when she thought she heard the phone. Once the verru-ume! was silenced, there was no ringing sound. "Oh well, must have been mistaken."

She gathered the trash and took it to the dumpster, put the bank bag away, and did a final check on the back door. By now it was 7:59, finally! She locked the door and stood back from the store window to check the display she'd done that day. To get a full picture, she walked slowly, left to right, then crossed the street and looked again. *Looks pretty good. Now I can get home and chill out!*

Rick was sitting on the sofa, watching TV.

"Hi, baby, whatcha drinking?" Julie asked as she kicked her shoes off.

He held up a bottle of Blue-Ribbon beer.

"Think I'll make a vodka something, I'm beat!" she went into the kitchen. The wall phone's receiver was lying on the counter, its curly cord stretched across the width of the room. Julie picked it up and listened. It was ringing somewhere but not being answered, the monotonous sound repeated in her ear. "What's up with the phone?" she hollered to Rick.

"You tell me." He said in a deadpan voice.

"Huh? Should I hang it up?"

"You ain't gonna answer, so hang up."

What is he talking about? Julie hung the receiver back on the hook and wandered out of the kitchen.

He glowered up at her bewildered face and stood, "I was calling *YOU*! *YOU* didn't answer!" a step closer.

She took a step back; this was going to be bad. Clyde barked once, then sensing danger himself, cowered in the corner.

"I thought I heard the phone when I was vacuuming, but . . ."

"Save it," his hand went up, stop sign style. She flinched. "Tell me where you were. I called three times!"

"I was at work! I vacuumed and took . . . took the trash out!"

He was on her with signature speed, and she fell against the chair, knocking it over with a crash. Clyde barked again from his corner.

"WHERE WERE YOU?" he lifted her and threw her like a rag doll at the wall.

"Stop it!" she screamed at him. "I was at . . ." his hand shot out and slapped her. Julie's eyes grew wide at his transgression, and he slapped her again . . .

"Don't you look at me that way!" . . . and again, "This is *your* fault!" his breathing was heavy, ragged, "Tell me what the *FUCK you were doing!*"

Rick's hands wrapped around her throat and threw her to the floor. Then he tightened his grip until Julie was struggling for breath—terrified! If his fury drove him past his self-imposed limits, did he *have* no limits? That thought shot her with the adrenaline she needed. Julie pushed against his chest with all her strength. Now she was fighting for her life.

His hands loosened just enough for her to scream, "You're gonna KILL ME!"

"DAMN RIGHT I AM!"

One hand stayed on her throat, the other pulled back in a fist. It loomed over her, hesitating, then slammed down. In the same instant, she shoved again and the punch lost some momentum. It grazed the side of her head, just above the ear, and slammed into the floor. Pain shot up Rick's arm. He let go of her and she scrambled to her feet and moved, not caring where, just away from him, but he was quicker than she was.

He grabbed her by the hair and pulled her against him. His massive hand closed over her mouth. She whimpered; he growled in her ear, "You fuckin' around on me?"

Rick's other arm wrapped around her, lifting her feet off the floor. He carried her to the bedroom, threw her on the bed. Sweat beaded on his forehead, his ice-blue eyes blazed as he straddled her, pinning her arms against her body with his knees. Hands came down and lifted her head as he hovered over her. Her face only inches from his, Julie dared not even breathe. The sound he made was primal and he drank in the fear in her eyes, steeped in it. He was not the man she loved but an animal devouring its prey. Then, as he held her there with hands strong enough to crush her skull, there was a loud pounding at the door.

Chapter 24

He blinked, let out a rasp of air. His grip loosened.

Rick straightened, listening. The knock came again. Clyde started barking.

"Baltimore County Police, open up."

"Fuck!" Rick pulled himself off the bed and glared down at her, catching his breath before he went to the door.

Julie lay still and listened.

The sound of the door opening, "Yes, officers, can I help you?'

"We had a call about a disturbance. Is there anyone here with you?"

"Uh, yeah, my wife. She's in the bedroom."

A woman's voice, "We need to speak with her, please."

"Well, uh, let me see if she's . . ."

The woman again, louder, "We need to see her now, sir."

Julie rose from the bed, ran her fingers through her hair, pulled it over the side he punched, and moved gingerly to the door, "Here I am."

The cats came out of hiding and wound around her legs.

Two officers, a man and a woman, stood in the open doorway. Rick held the door with one hand and Clyde's collar with the other. Clyde was standing at attention, tail wagging.

When he saw Julie, the man said. "May I step in, sir?"

Rick moved back into the kitchen, taking Clyde with him. The officer came in and stood by the door while Julie moved to the patio. She was shielded by the door but knew Rick was listening.

The female officer spoke in hushed tones, "Ma'am, I'm Officer Jackson, I need to ask you if you are ok."

Julie hesitated, pulled on her hair, "I'm ok."

"Miss?"

"Mrs . . . Madsen, Julie Madsen."

"Mrs. Madsen, there was a call about a domestic disturbance. Has anything been going on here you want us to know about?"

"No, um, the chair went over, and um, I'm ok. Really."

"Listen, we can take you elsewhere if you don't feel safe."

"Well . . . I was actually . . . um . . ." *What should I do? Come on, dummy, think!* "I'm safe . . ."

"You're sure?"

"I'm sure, but . . ." Julie glanced over her shoulder. *This is your way out, Take it!* She spoke louder, so Rick could hear, "I was just going to the store . . . dog food . . . I'm ok though."

"Here's my card."

Julie took the card from her.

Officer Jackson held onto her hand for a moment and searched Julie's eyes, "Please call me if you need anything,"

Julie nodded and glanced over her shoulder.

"How about if we wait until you get to your car?"

"Yes, please wait. I need to get my purse."

"Officer Clark?" Officer Jackson spoke loud and clear, "We are ok here. I told the young lady we need to wait until she is in her car."

The officers walked to the patrol car and Julie slipped her shoes on, grabbed her jacket and purse. Rick stood in the kitchen's doorway watching her, fear and shame radiating from him, he didn't move.

"I have to go," she said.

"Don't leave me," Rick reached his arm out, saw her flinch, and lowered it again. "Please. Don't leave."

"I have to go . . . I'll call you."

"Julie . . ." she turned and ran to the car. She couldn't look at him. Officer Jackson waved as she pulled away.

Rick fell to his knees and a great sob escaped him. Clyde licked his face as he slumped against the wall. He stayed there, Clyde's head in his lap, for a long time.

Julie drove away from Towson, not wanting to see anyone she knew. The full moon leered down at her as she made her way around the beltway. After several exits flew by, she chose one blindly and pulled into a 7-Eleven. There was a payphone out front, covered with wads of gum and graffiti. She dug in her purse for 15 cents and called Colleen at Pete's apartment. No luck, no answer. Where could she go? No way could she go to her parents. She had gone to great lengths to hide all this from them, couldn't bear for them to know what she had been allowing to happen. Russ . . . she needed her brother. Another fifteen cents in the slot and Russ answered his phone.

"It's Julie. I need . . ." she started sobbing.

"What's wrong?"

"We had a bad fight. I don't know where to go!"

"Where are you now? You have your car?"

"Yes, I'm at a payphone. Somewhere off the beltway."

"You're okay to drive? Come here."

"There?"

"Yes, Julie, get in the car and come to me. Remember how to get here?"

"695 to 495 to . . . Yes, I can! I'll see you soon."

"Be careful and, Julie, breathe."

"Breathe, yes, I can do that now."

A few hours later, she pulled up to Russ and Linda's historic farmhouse. Russ met her at the door and pulled her into his warmth. Linda was right behind him. "Come in, honey."

Julie started crying again, couldn't help it. Russ sat with his arm around her and waited for the tears to subside. Finally, she composed herself enough to talk. She didn't tell of the police or his physical abuse, couldn't find those words. Julie told of his unfounded accusations, his insecurities.

"Hey, Buttercup, I told you long ago, you can't fix him. Rick has to do that for himself. The only thing you can do is support his efforts," Russ said.

"I thought we had gotten through it. I thought he was better, but he's never been so . . ." she pulled her hair around her neck, ". . . violent."

Russ shot a worried look to Linda, "Did he hurt you?"

Julie put her hand over her mouth.

"Julie, tell me. You know you can tell me anything."

She couldn't say it. That would make it real, and there would be no going back. So she said, "No, he pushed me. That's all, and I fell into the chair. He didn't mean it."

Another look passed between Russ and Linda.

"You've been through a lot this year, certainly more than your share," said Linda.

"That's for sure," Russ smiled at his sister. "You are only 19, Buttercup, your shoulders aren't that big yet!"

"Age doesn't have anything to do with it."

"True, but it's amazing the perspective you have when you look back on life," Linda said. "The best thing you can do is give yourself time; really think about what you want to happen with this relationship. You can stay here as long as you want, so take all the time you need. In the meantime, a good night's sleep will help."

Julie didn't think she could sleep with her mind in such turmoil, but Linda gave her a Benadryl and she was out like a light.

She stayed for three days. On Saturday, she called Colleen to tell her where she was and gave a watered-down version of what happened. Colleen told her to stay there a while, make Rick suffer. That sounded good in theory but didn't help her own suffering.

By Monday, Julie was ready to talk to Rick. When he answered the phone, an instinctual stab of fear went through her. *Pull it together, he can't reach through the phone!* Once he began to talk, it was clear that anger was the last thing on his mind. The sound of relief in his voice was palpable.

"You don't know how worried I've been. I was afraid you wouldn't even speak to me again."

"Well, I *have* to speak to you, Rick. I mean, of course, we have to talk about all this."

"I'm so sorry, I don't know what . . ." his voice faltered. "I'll do anything to make it right, anything you say. Just, please, come home."

There was an ache in her chest, hot and ragged. She longed for him with every fiber of her being, yet was terrified to walk back through that door. She remembered Beth's words about why she stayed with Floyd, and now she understood. But she wasn't Beth; she couldn't go on this way, something had to give.

"The way things are, Rick, I can't come home. I love you, but I can't live like this."

"I get that, and we can fix this . . . I can fix this. Like you said in Ocean City, I need to figure out why . . . what drives me to lose control."

"This isn't something you can figure out on your own. You need to get some help, we both do. This is too big, too complicated."

"I'll go to a shrink, or whatever you want. Just come home, I can't live without you."

Julie drove home that night. When she opened the door, Clyde barked a welcome, and the cats wandered in from the bedroom, stretching and mewing. Rick jumped up from the sofa and threw his arms around her, "You're home."

Julie laid her head on his chest where his heart was beating as wildly as hers.

"I'm Home," she echoed, but she wasn't convinced she could stay.

Chapter 25

DECEMBER 1979

Rick picked up hours in the retail store at Harbor Lumber to help sock away money for a house. A couple football bets paid off, too, so a down payment was within sight.

On Wednesday afternoon, a thin guy in a turtleneck approached the register with various doorknobs and hinges. "I could use some advice," he said. "I'm all thumbs when it comes to this kind of thing."

"Are you replacing existing hardware?" Rick asked.

"Well, I hope to find someone to do it for me. I've just moved into the house and I'm overwhelmed."

"If you don't mind me working nights and weekends, I'd be happy to take a look. I've been doing renovation as a side job for years."

Rick met him that night at the house in Homeland, an old-money part of Baltimore City. The guy was a musician with the Baltimore Symphony, an artsy type with no common sense, was Rick's assessment. He had inherited the house from his grandmother and moved in with his wife and four young children.

The house was enormous, right off Charles Street. Three stories with six bedrooms—each with a fireplace, and a dingy unfinished basement. Repairs and upkeep had been neglected for years. There looked to be 35 broken windowpanes that needed glazing. Locks, door hinges, and other hardware needed replacing; and most of the interior needed a paint job. More needed doing than one person could tackle in a reasonable amount of time. Rick hoped Julie would help him. She was a whiz with a roller, and he functioned better when she was around. When she wasn't close by, he worried about her.

When he told her what the guy was paying, she'd go for it. Rick had visions of pouring a drink, telling her about the job, and taking her to bed; maybe taking her on the sofa or floor, he didn't care where so long as his hands were on that silky skin . . . Just thinking about that made him hard . . . he needed to lose himself inside her. When he was fucking her, losing control was ok.

They started work on the house on Friday after work. Rick taught Julie how to burn the old putty to remove the broken glass from the window frame and then how to cut the new glass and apply new putty. Julie was a quick study and Rick was able to have her finish the glass while he spackled holes.

As the job progressed, he was amazed at the way these people lived. The wife was a lazy, unkempt woman with a large belly who walked around in bright colored caftans all day. There were mouse droppings everywhere on the second and third floors—not surprising considering the number of peanut-butter covered crusts, cookie crumbs, and dirty dishes they found. Here are people raised with culture and money, and lots of it. The guy had gone to a fancy private school and was the head Cellist or something for the BSO for God's sake! The wife didn't work, just laid around, reading, as far as Rick could see. Yet, they let their kids run around half-naked and in filth. *Pop beat the shit out of me, but at least Momma kept us clean, clothed and well fed. Way these kids are raised pisses me off to no end.*

Julie seemed to think the same because she made funny snide comments as she worked like, "Whole lota poopin' goin' on!" or "Look! Hansel and Gretel's bread crumb trail!" A couple of times he heard her down the hall singing, "Food, Glorious Food!"

The kids in the house appeared like pint-sized ghosts to stare at them as they worked. One day he heard a kid's eerie little voice floating up the vent, singing "Food, Glorious Food!"

"She's contagious," he said to himself and shook his head.

Julie suggested Randy help Monday and Tuesday evening. That was ok with him; Rick couldn't wait to get out of this house. He wished she'd picked another helper, maybe Kevin or Craig, because Randy did too much fooling around. Rick overheard the goof messing around with Julie while they were painting, and when they were washing brushes, he heard her giggling. Rick couldn't help himself, his back went up, like a dog when another dog pees in his territory. He saw Randy look at her all innocent and shot a warning glare—*I know what you're thinking, son, but you touch her, you're dead.*

"Keep it under control," Rick said to himself, but his new mantra was getting hard to follow. Good thing they'd wrap this up tonight.

Wednesday night, they returned to get their gear and do a walk-through with the owner. The guy handed Rick a check and shook his hand, "You all did superb work here. I'll keep your number for future renovations and recommend you to my neighbors." He walked Rick and Julie to the door, "It's hard to find a man who takes pride in his labor these days."

Rick wanted to show him a little pride with his fist, but that recommending part made him keep it cool. Plus, Julie was holding on to his arm like she knew what he was thinking.

When they got to the car, she said, "Thought you were gonna give him a Rocky demo there for a minute!" Her laughter rang out, his own private symphony. The sound of it soothed the burning in him.

"Yeah, I oughta beat some sense into that asshole. Mr. Superb and his tuba-shaped wife. All that money and you let your kids live like that. I don't get it."

"Money can't buy good parenting skills and a beating isn't going to change them either." They drove a while in silence, "But . . . now we have money. Lemme see!" He handed her the check, "Wow! That's a lot of dough!"

"Yep, let's go celebrate and figure out how to spend it."

II

They stopped in Spirits for a drink and dinner, and Julie was happy she didn't have to cook. Cups was sitting at the bar, "My pals! Pull up a stool," he said. "Kathy, give them one on me."

"How's your day goin, Cups?" Rick sat and pulled a stool out for Julie. Kathy set drinks and menus on the bar and lingered, smiling at Rick.

"Wednesdays, man, I live for them," Cups said.

"Got a drink of the week?" Rick asked.

"Yeah, 'Let it Snow' white Russian with a little something on the side. My night off is party night for me."

"We're celebrating the end of an obnoxious but well-paying job," Julie said as she perused the menu she knew by heart. "What are you getting, Rick?"

"Gonna hit the head, darlin'," he said, and she watched him follow Cups to the restrooms.

Uh oh, I know what that means. Guess we're snorting dinner.

Sure enough, Rick came back grinning ear to ear and slid a vial into her hand. *We aren't doing that anymore. It's a work night . . . but look at his smile . . . haven't seen that since summer . . . but the hangover . . . but the high!* Julie imagined a cartoon devil and angel on her shoulders, battling it out. The devil won, and she ordered another drink instead of a burger.

Since her return in November, she had been walking on eggshells, jittery in anticipation of the next bomb to explode. Rick seemed to be feeling the same way, on edge and over-solicitous. When they made love, he was frenetic, desperate. He had become so possessive, barely let her out of sight.

He saw a psychologist twice but was vague when he relayed what they talked about. Perhaps a night of sparkle would help him open up. *I need some good vibes, too.*

An hour later, Randy bopped in and came up behind them. With an arm on each of their shoulders, he said, "Hey, I really dug painting with you guys."

"It was fun having you on the crew," Julie said with a quick peck to his cheek. She caught a whiff of that clean Randy scent—Right Guard and Irish

Spring. Working with him on the house had reminded her of how strong their connection was. At one time, back in ninth grade, she considered pushing their relationship farther, but then he moved and that was that. *We could have been good together, though.* She smiled at the thought, "You going to Richmond for Christmas?"

"Yeah, but I'll be back by New Year's Eve," Randy patted Rick's back. "Can't miss the New Year's party, right Rick?"

Rick turned languidly, "Whatever you say . . . Kathy, get the boy a drink on me." He drew himself up and puffed out his chest, "Got some money for you soon as I get the check cashed."

Kathy brought Randy a drink. "Another round?" she asked Rick.

"Nah, got an early morning," he downed his drink and threw some cash on the bar, "Come on, darlin', bedtime." Rick stood and pushed Randy aside with his elbow.

Julie looked at her half-full glass, then at Rick. An alarm bell rang in her head. She shrugged at Randy, "Well, talk to you later."

"Yeah, later, *boy*," came from Rick. "Cups, Kathy . . . Adios," he pushed Julie toward the door.

She looked over her shoulder at Randy: his eyes wide, his palms turned upward in front of him like *What the hell did I do?*

The night didn't go as she hoped. When they got home, Rick said, "I been thinking about this all day," he threw his jacket off and dove at her, smashed his mouth against hers.

"Slow down, babe, let me get my coat off."

She grappled with her coat and was knocked off balance against the back of the living room chair.

"Can't slow down," he moaned. The coat came off and he pushed up the shirt beneath. His mouth moved to her breasts, teeth grazing against her skin.

"Ow, that hurts."

His eyes raised and sent a message as his hands worked at her pants, yanked them off, then unzipped his jeans, "See what you do to me?"

Somehow, they careened off the chair and he rammed his way in. His slammed into her violently like he was nailing her to the floor.

Her spine was crushed into the rug—his belt buckle gouged her thigh. "Rick . . ." she gasped.

His mouth was on hers again.

He didn't stop—either didn't hear or thought her passion was calling his name—she wasn't sure, but she pounded on his chest, "Stop!" it came out like a moan.

Rick drowned it out with primal sounds. At last, with a final thrust, his body shuddered with climax and collapsed.

Julie pushed him off. There was blood smeared up her thigh, her back stung from rug burn.

She wobbled her way to the kitchen and he lay panting, zoned out.

Water for her throat and paper towels for her leg, she assessed the damage. The skin was ripped and raw. The bomb she'd been expecting came with a new twist.

Julie opened the trash can to throw the towels away, "What the?"

There, among empty bottles and orange peels was her bonsai, roots reaching up to her like fingers. Gently, Julie lifted the delicate plant out and picked the trash from its tiny boughs. The tree's ceramic container was beneath, broken in two.

Julie put her tree in a bowl and grabbed a serving spoon from the drawer. Now she was crying. She stormed into the living room and pulled on her pants. Rick was still on the floor. She kicked his leg, "What the hell happened to my tree?" she yelled.

Rick's eyes opened and stared at her.

"Answer me!"

Rick stared a minute longer while she stood shaking with rage.

"Sorry about that. Cat knocked it off," a smirk appeared on his face.

Julie spun back to the kitchen and grabbed the bowl and spoon. Then she stomped outside and began digging up dirt from the lawn, tears pouring down her face.

Rick stood at the door, nothing on but his t-shirt, and watched until Julie turned and stared back, her face smudged with dirt and snot.

He laughed at her, "Don't you be bringin' that dirt into my bed." He was wearing a victory smile.

"Don't worry, I won't!" She screamed.

Julie went back to digging and he went to bed.

The next morning at 6:00 am, Rick woke to music instead of his alarm. Janis Joplin was begging him to take another piece of her heart at full volume on the stereo. Julie and the bonsai were gone.

Colleen met her at Pete's apartment that evening, and they spent the night there. They drank two bottles of wine and talked about what she should do. When her head hit the pillow that night, she had made her decision; she was leaving him.

The next morning, at the door to Boutique Picasso, sat a ceramic pot with a bag of potting soil in it; an envelope addressed 'Julie' was taped to it.

Julie,

I'm writing this because these things are on my mind now, and I don't want to wait- I might not be able to say it face to face-

Julie, my biggest thrill in life (no lie!) is pleasing you. It is one of the few things I live for. And when you're not pleased, I hate myself—feel bad—defeated, unworthy.

I don't know but I feel something and it makes me hate myself—when I yell and holler and hit you (which I don't do often- just when I do it's bad). I don't hate you, often I'm not even mad at you. I hate myself and can't stand to live with myself. When I met you, I was a nothing—maybe I still am—maybe I always will be but just having you makes me feel a lot better about being nothing.

I think my biggest problem is that when I know you have been with brighter men than me, better-looking men, wealthier, happier men than me, it frustrates me to the point where I hate myself like I just explained.

I guess a person can try too hard- I want to be everything to you- when I can't- I won't accept it and then I start the hate myself thing.

I'll go to a counselor with you or by myself if you like.

I made an appointment with someone for next week and I'll agree to whatever she says.

I have been in control since you came back! I haven't done anything out of control.

I know sex got out of hand Wednesday, but it wasn't vio-lence- it was passion. You make me get carried away sometimes. I love you so much.

The most important thing is you. Do what you want and I'll respect your decision. If you decide to leave though, please remember one thing (I know you're tired of hearing it but it's true) No one ever loved you more or tried any harder for you.

Your Husband (I hope)

Rick

PS: Sorry about your magic tree. The cat really did it. But I shouldn't have thrown it away.

PSS: Please come home for Christmas, you are my spirit.

Julie read the note over and over. When she thought about it, he had been in control—he'd been off kilter, and needy, especially in the bedroom department, but there were no outbursts, no tantrums, no violence. Just the opposite, he had been anxious about her wellbeing and attentive. She thought about their good times, about life without him. And about the strength it would take to leave.

She could give him one more chance . . .

Part Three

Chapter 26

MAY 1981

COLLEEN

Colleen was thrilled about graduating. She didn't care about the pomp and circumstance but was glad to be done with studying and eager to get on with planning her wedding. Her mother had invited the aunts, uncles, cousins, and so forth to dinner after the ceremony. It was a typical O'Malley family celebration: ham, potato salad, green beans, lots of desserts.

The best part was Julie was home and would be here. She moved to Charlottesville in January 1980 after a terrible incident with Rick—finally left him, thank God. She didn't even come home for Christmas. Her parents went down there instead. Colleen had seen her a few times. She'd gone to Charlottesville and Julie met her in DC a couple times, and they'd talked on the phone for hours—long distance bills to the max! Now Julie was finally back in Baltimore to stay.

Before the festivities started, Cathleen O'Malley pulled her daughter into the bathroom and closed the door. It was the only place in the house one could get any peace.

Cathleen hugged Colleen and then leaned back against the sink, "I needed to tell you this while I have the chance." She pulled off some toilet paper from the roll and wiped at her eyes, "I want you to know how proud Dad and I are. Me, never goin to college; your Da dropping out once we knew about you comin' along . . ."

195

"I know Mom and thanks for scrimping so I could do this."

"Now, no thanks necessary, and you got that scholarship. It's just I had dreams and—Now I'm not complaining—I wouldn't give you and the hooligans up for the world but . . ."

"But what mom?"

"Don't do what I did, Dearie," her voice raised a decibel. "You love Pete, that's grand. But you are young and have so much time. Don't be havin' eight babes in the blink of an eye!"

"Don't worry about that, mom . . . I don't plan . . ."

"Alls I'm saying is live whatever dream you have in that smart head of yours. Don't get rooted and tied. Lord, I haven't had a thought to myself in twenty-some years!"

Colleen looked at her mother, eyes wide.

"Now I'm not complaining . . ."

"Yes, Mom, you are."

"But not about you! Never about a single one a ya."

She glanced past Colleen at the bathtub, "Don't get so pulled thin that you don't even have a shower without washing the tub ring while you're in there."

"I guess I get your drift there. Don't worry, K? No babies yet and not eight *ever*. Promise."

Cathleen squeezed Colleen's hands, "That's my lassie." they were interrupted by a commotion outside the door.

"I gotta peeee! Let me in. I gotta pee weally bad!"

"Sweet Jaysus," Cathleen unlocked the door and Tracy barreled in with her panties around her knees.

"Thanks for the bathroom time, Mom," Colleen said. Then the doorbell rang, and the party began.

By 9:00, the uncles were singing "Danny Boy" for the fourth time, the aunts were gossiping in the backyard, and the young ones were running through the house like banshees. Colleen grabbed Pete and Julie's hands and pulled them toward the shrubs on the side of the yard.

"Time for the *real* party," she said over the ruckus. "Let's make a break for it!" and she nonchalantly backed around the hedge. Pete and Julie backed around after her and the three of them ran, breathless with laughter, to the cars on the street.

"Drive with Julie, I'll follow you guys," Pete told them, hushed as if someone would hear him.

Colleen and Julie piled into her Aspen, and as the car started, the radio blared out a strain of the Human League singing "Don't You Want Me." With a squeal, Colleen dove for the dial as they pulled from the curb.

"Oh, God! This brings back memories of sneaking out when we were in junior high!" Julie laughed, "Remember the night we tried to sneak out my basement window?"

Colleen said, " . . . and your dad called down from the window above us. 'Girls . . . ' was all he said in that stern voice. We stammered something about getting some air and retreated into the house."

"I can't believe he didn't ground me forever after that. Now here I am living back home. Mom said not to worry about a curfew tonight, guess I've outgrown them," Julie said as she turned onto the beltway entrance. "So, you think anybody besides your mother will even notice we're gone?"

"Nah, they're all sloshed. Plus, I told my mom we'd be leaving."

"Some stealth secret agent you are . . . You told the enemy our plan!"

They pulled into the parking lot at Christopher's Night Club. Cups tended bar there now, so Colleen knew they'd get a few free drinks. It was a regular hang out place for her, Pete, and their college friends.

Colleen was eager to get Randy and Julie in the same room. She perceived some tension between them since Julie moved to her brother's, something neither would talk about. She hoped that if they were face to face, they could resolve whatever it was.

Pete, being heavy-footed on the gas pedal, beat them to the place and was already ordering their drinks. Beside him, Randy stood with a few other graduates. Kevin was also there, leaning on the bar, his arm slung around Valerie's shoulders. They had just gotten engaged.

Val pulled Julie in for a hug, "Hey, stranger! We miss you around here."

Kevin said, "Glad you could join the *partae*! When did you get back to town?"

"Just this week, and I think I'm back to stay," she glanced over Kev's shoulder at Randy.

"Randy, look what the wind blew in," said Pete and winked at Colleen. Randy turned toward Julie. His shoulders tensed back and a nervous grin broke across his face.

Colleen nudged Julie with her elbow and whispered, "Talk to the man!"

Julie seemed unsure of how to proceed and then, to Colleen's delight, lurched forward and enfolded Randy with affection.

"Miss you, Crazy Randy," she said. The tension faded from Randy and his arms wrapped around her.

Colleen gave Pete a decisive nod. *I knew it! All it took was a nudge for them to be back on track. I am the grand unifier!*

"Congrats on making it through!" Cups lined drinks up in front of the graduates and friends. "Drink of the week . . . the 'Yellow Ribbon' . . . OJ, vodka, Cointreau with a lemon rind twist," he said and they all clinked.

"To the hostages, thank God they're home!" Colleen said. A cheer went through the crowd.

"Better a bottle in front of me than a frontal lobotomy," said Randy, grinning at Julie. "Now it's off to grad school for me. I got into the Computer Science program at Hopkins."

"Johns Hopkins? Wow! You always impress me."

"The night school so I can work. I applied to Westinghouse and Grumman Aerospace. They both contract with the Navy."

"Your dad will be so proud."

"Yeah, that's part of it, for sure. I figure I can serve without the uniform."

"You would look good in a uniform, though!" Julie smiled up at him.

Colleen grabbed their arms, "Come on, let's dance!"

They followed her and Pete to the crowded floor and danced to the boisterous, thumping music. Val and Kevin joined them, and they bounced off one another like bumper cars. The friends grooved to "Super Freak" and shouted along to "Rock This Town." When "Jessie's Girl" started, Randy hollered he was thirsty, so they all reconvened back at the bar for more drinks.

Colleen said to Pete on the way back from the dance floor, "Funny how that song bothers him."

"The kid wears his heart on his damn sleeve. He should make a move already!"

After Val and Kevin quit arguing about what kind, they ordered a round of shooters. Colleen slammed one back and joined in a loud discussion with some of the other grads.

Around midnight, Colleen heard Randy say, "Oh shit. Look who's here."

She looked, "Oh, shit!"

Julie saw Rick, too. He was scanning the crowd.

"Of all the vodka joints in all the world he had to walk into ours."

"You better get outta here," Colleen said. "I'll throw him off. Meet us at Souris' Saloon in an hour."

"Come with me," Randy took hold of Julie's hand and led her out the back exit.

RANDY

A thrill passed through Randy as they weaved through the crowd. Perhaps he could redeem himself, become the hero he should have been long ago.

The scene he witnessed played over and over in Randy's memory in sharp Technicolor. It was a Monday in January. He'd needed to borrow a wrench from Rick. He rounded the corner, and as he stepped onto the patio, there came a sudden jarring crash from within. The inner door was open, and what he saw through the storm door rooted him to the ground.

The coffee table was standing up-ended. Its contents—beer bottles, popcorn, spilled ashtrays, broken glass—strewn across the floor, a Picasso painting of football playoff remnants. Rick's hand was clamped to her arm.

He could see the man's fingers press into her flesh; her bruises bloomed before his eyes.

Instead of his friendly baritone, Rick's words came in a low staccato growl, "Clean. It. Up."

Randy's heart pounded in his ears as he watched, powerless to move. Rick propelled her into the wreckage. Julie fell to her knees, then shifted her gaze upward toward her punisher, the intensity of her pain etched on her face. Rick's foot, clad in steel-toed work boots, shot out and connected with Julie's ribs. And then . . . he began to turn around . . .

Randy trembled as the blood surged back into his frozen limbs. In flight mode, he spun and ran.

He couldn't puzzle out why he ran, nor could he forgive himself. He should have charged in to save Julie. He should have been her hero. But no, *he ran*!

He told himself he was sparing her the embarrassment of someone knowing. Wasn't it wrong to have barged into their home, uninvited? If Rick had turned and found him there—gawking at their intimacy, witnessing his brutality—Randy would surely be dead.

Should he call the police? He called their apartment instead, and Rick answered. He hung up, started back over there, saw Julie driving away. His body shook with relief.

Randy tried to wish the whole business away. Maybe it was not what it seemed, maybe his imagination had conjured up a movie scene from a minor transgression. This was surely a freak occurrence. He knew of Rick's volatile nature, but against Julie? The perfect couple he once idolized could not be these broken people!

He ran. And he told no one. He stayed away from any chance encounter with them, working it through in his mind, deciding what he should do. Until a few days later . . .

Julie was getting into her car outside the bank. He stopped short. Something caused her to turn, and the sunlight touched her face. Her cheek was swollen, mottled purple and gray, there were cuts on her chin, under her eye, a bandage on her hand. Her eyes found him, registered his reluctance to move, and she also hesitated. Then she got in the car and drove away. At that moment, he knew. She had seen him in the doorway.

Images tumbled forth—a splinted finger, a limp in her walk, bruises and band-aids explained away by clumsiness. Hindsight, they say, is twenty-twenty. Standing there, in the bank lot, it was all so blindingly, tragically clear. Julie had suffered Rick's abuse a long, long time.

Randy led Julie through Christopher's parking lot to her car. Her hands were shaking so badly, she dropped her keys. He retrieved them and opened the door for her, then got in the passenger side.

"Let's just sit a minute." He said.

"It's the first time I've seen him since I left Baltimore." Her hand floated up in a helpless gesture, "I mean I've talked to him plenty. He calls nonstop but . . . It's so stupid. Seeing him . . . it gets me tied in knots."

"It's not stupid. You have reason to get knots."

"Damn it! Welcome to celebrations with the Madsen family!" Julie was dripping with perspiration, "It's so hot! Let's open the windows and get some air in here."

"Super Freak will do that to you."

"Well, I was hoping they would play some Elton John so I could golden shower you," she emitted a quiet sound of amusement.

Randy joined her with a small chortle; their eyes met, and the sound grew louder. Before long they were howling, tears running down their cheeks.

"Oh, God! I've missed you and everybody! I had Russ and Linda down there, but that's not the same as my buddies. Mostly I was with the kids, being the nanny."

"I need to apologize. I didn't know what to say to you. I should have barged in there that day," Randy leaned toward her. "I came back, and you were already in your car. I was just so shocked!" he sat back again, against the door. "Then I heard you were gone for good."

After seeing her at the bank, he'd finally mustered up the courage to talk to her and to confront Rick. He was all set to do just that when Val told him Julie had moved to Charlottesville. So, he kept quiet.

"I decided to go that day, the day you saw us, but wanted to get organized first, not fly out without money and clothes," the corners of her mouth turned up, "and my bonsai . . . So, I was doing that, behind his back . . . sneaking stuff out to Colleen. Then he pulled a whopper,"

She took a deep breath. "Took me to this house he found for us. He was so excited . . . showed me the swing for our kids. I would have loved living in that house if, well you know. It tore me apart the way he could be so wonderful about some things and then so horrible. I told him I was leaving . . . should have kept my mouth shut." Julie gazed out the windshield and touched the scar on her chin. "Threw me through the plate-glass window."

Randy's mouth fell open.

She turned to him, tears in her eyes, "Randy, I was never mad at you. I was ashamed . . . you seeing us like that. And, Rick . . . you held him in such high regard. I'm sure you felt like you were kicked in the teeth."

"But you *were* kicked! I should have . . ."

"If I have learned one thing it's to stop the 'what ifs' and 'should haves.' It gets you nowhere. You know how I feel about you . . ." She put her hand on his shoulder.

Kiss her, dummy! Her mouth is right there, waiting. She wants you.

" . . . just like a brother to me."

Shit! Fucking shit, damn it! He knew it, she would never want him any other way.

II

Rick heard about the graduation, and he figured they'd be out celebrating. Maybe if he could just casually run into her, she would talk to him. Maybe he could convince her to come home.

He glanced around the place he was renting. Not much of a home. When the lease ran out, he had moved out of Towson Ridge; couldn't bear to be there without her.

Back then, he put a deposit on a house that was perfect for them! Three bedrooms, two baths with a nice kitchen and a little yard with a garden. The picture of their children playing on the tire swing in that yard was so clear!

He surprised her as a late Christmas present. Julie was pissed, said a grand gesture wouldn't help anything . . . said she was leaving. Just thinking about it gets him mad again . . .

Rick tried not to think about what happened next. He'd never had a clear picture of it. All he knew for sure . . . that red cloud came over him and he lost control. He saw flashes of himself as if he were watching a stranger. Like he was some sick voyeur—watching an act of violence and getting off on it. But it did not excite him; it made him sick. Physically ill.

He saw his father . . . but it was really himself . . .

He saw Julie shatter into a thousand sparkling stars . . . shards of her flying into the air. Her blood on his hands . . .

He stumbled into the bathroom and heaved what little he ate for dinner . . . rinsed his mouth. The reflection in the mirror barely looked like Rick anymore, those haunted eyes looked like his mother's . . . beaten, defeated eyes.

What he needed was behind the reflection. Rick jerked the medicine cabinet open . . .

Cooked up some chemical amnesia with a spoon and lighter he kept there, and pushed it into his vein . . .

Better

. . . threw some water on his face and swiped the electric razor across the stubble on his jaw.

. . . took a swig of bourbon, liquid courage . . .

Headed out to hunt her down . . .

After Colleen told him that Julie left, Rick came out of the club and searched the lot. He saw the car parked close to the exit, the windows open. He moved in from an angle—the blind spot in the mirror. He saw her sitting in the driver's seat and his breath caught . . .

"Hey, Shortcake."

Julie turned. She recoiled at seeing him so close, leaning on the windowsill. "You startled me!" a hand went up to her perfect heart.

"Sorry, I just want to . . . Can we talk a little?"

"We've been over and over it. There's no more to say."

"Please . . ." he reached in and touched her perfect hair.

"Don't!" she batted his hand away.

"Start the car, Julie! Drive!" a voice from the passenger seat.

It's Randy! I should have known. Rick's hand was still in the car and it grabbed the headrest, held on tight as the engine roared to life.

A kid in a beat up Gremlin was pulling into Christopher's parking lot when a silver Aspen went tearing onto Padonia Road. Two legs and part of a torso were protruding from the driver's side windows. They were kicking at the air as if to gain purchase of something solid. It was an extraordinary sight! The car slammed on its brakes and the body lurched forward, then scrabbled and disappeared into the vehicle. He zipped into a parking spot shaking his head, "Gotta stop smoking that weed, man, makes you see shit!"

RANDY

Rick dove into the back seat and somehow got himself upright. "Please, Julie. Give me five minutes." Tears were threatening, he didn't seem to care.

Julie shook so much she barely kept her foot on the brake. She steered the car into the lot on their right. "What? What can you possibly say that will make a difference?"

"I've been seeing that counselor. I'm figuring it all out. Floyd, guilt about Mom. I've been drawing. We can get through this."

Gripping the seatback, Rick pulled himself forward, "When I said you made me better, I didn't mean 'feel better' I meant you make me a better person. I can do this if you're beside me."

Julie looked at Rick, clinging there pathetically. Randy could tell she felt sad for him.

Randy stared out the window and listened. He sent up a silent prayer that she wouldn't swallow this. He understood how much she loved Rick, or at least *used* to. Now he could see why she hadn't left a long time ago. *He's good at this, I almost swallowed it.*

"You are high as a kite stuck in a tree, aren't you? I've heard all this before."

"But I can't do it without you!"

"It's too late. I'm going through with the divorce. Randy, let Rick out please."

Randy got out, pulled the seat forward, and stood guard. Rick was agitated. This could all go south quickly.

"*PLEASE!* I'll die without you."

"Put me out of your misery, Rick. I can't do this anymore. Get out!"

Randy offered his hand. Rick slapped at it and hauled himself out of the car. He sneered at Randy, low so Julie wouldn't hear, "You and me ain't done."

Randy sneered back but knew better than to say a word. He hoped his meaning got across, anyway. *I'll be waiting.*

Chapter 27

SUMMER 1981
JUNE

Julie landed a bartending job at Sh'nanigans, a busy restaurant in Cockeysville. The bar was even busier, with live entertainment several nights a week. The first night she worked, Craig and Eddie were playing. Julie hadn't seen them since she moved to Charlottesville, and it was nice to see familiar faces. Craig was in search of a new housemate. Eddie had moved in with his girlfriend and his house on Willow Haven Court was feeling empty. Julie took him up on the offer without thinking twice.

The house was a a two-story, three-bedroom, two-bath—with a cool club basement and a large kitchen. There was also a nice deck and a backyard with a large sassafras tree that provided shade for summer barbeques.

Colleen came to see the house and to finalize her wedding guest list with Julie. They sat on the deck with wine and lists. Julie looked around at her peaceful surroundings, "I love being able to have outdoor parties, and best part of rooming with Craig, besides the music, of course, is we both work nights. Let's drink to sleeping in!" They clinked and drank.

"Now, let's drink to getting this damn guest list done." Colleen opened her organizer, "Let's see . . . now, what about Walt?"

"It's no problem for me if he comes. Only problem is Walt stays with Rick when he's here. That may be . . . well, Rick *ain't* invited so . . . weird for him."

"And it *ain't* weird because of your dalliance?"

"Dalliance?" Julie brushed the air with her hand to dismiss the idea. "It wasn't fancy; we made out a little! One time, never again amen."

"You sure Walt looks at it that way?"

"Yes. Look, I was miserable, hurt, and every other adjective you can throw in. He made me . . . feel better, you know? Reminded me I was worth . . . something. Walt knew I needed that . . . *as a friend.*"

"You *still* need reminding. You need *something*, I worry about you."

"I'm okay, really," she raised her glass, "now that I'm here. To fresh starts."

"Speaking of fresh starts, what's going on with the divorce?"

"I met with a lawyer. There's still some red tape about the inheritance. I said I didn't want anything, but you know how lawyers are. Should be final in the fall."

"Thank God for that!"

"But . . . I have a favor to ask." Julie fidgeted with her ring.

"What? You know I'd do anything for you. Except maybe drink Peach Boone's Farm again."

They giggled at that. When they were 14, the friends got drunk as monkeys on Peach Boon's Farm Wine and Colleen threw up in the bushes outside her front door. She was sick for two days. They called her Peachy for a while after that.

"Nothing to do with peaches. But I need a witness, you know, to the abuse. For the divorce. The only witnesses I have are you and Randy and I certainly can't ask him."

"Just tell me where and when. I've been hoping for this day for a long time."

Julie hugged her, "Through thick and thin, you've been here. And you've never judged, though you had every right to."

Colleen, hugging back said, "Hey, no one should judge what goes on in a marriage. There are so many layers, so much emotion that only you know. I knew you'd find your way through."

Julie sat back and they both grabbed napkins and wiped their eyes, friendship spilling over.

"Now, back to the list so I can find my way to the altar!" Colleen said. She took a sip and got back to business, "Val and Kevin, check. Ruth and Guest? Think she'll bring . . ."

"Maybe . . . Not sure how public she is making her girlfriend. Oh! How about Randy? Will he bring the girl of the month?"

"Jenifer's been around a couple of months, they've been dating since April. This one may last."

"Huh, you like her?" Julie felt an irritating tickle in her chest and pushed it away.

"She's ok. Not you, of course."

"Oh, cut it out! Randy is like a brother!"

"He is nuts for you, always has been since seventh grade!"

"You keep saying that . . . cool it! On to the next name."

"All I'm saying is you are single now so . . ."

"I am not interested in dating Randy. It would be too weird! I don't want to date anybody for a while."

"Good idea. You have this tendency to jump too fast, you know."

"I know." Julie said, then changed the subject. "Heard Rick sold Baby."

"Yeah, he's driving Floyd's Bronco. Cups said he's been hitting the powder pretty heavy. Don't know if that's why he sold her. For money."

"Poor guy. That car cost a fortune to keep running . . . Oh well, no longer my problem." Julie poured more wine into her empty glass, "and I'll drink to that!"

Julie was usually scheduled to tend bar along with Chris or Mike—the other regulars. Mike was a beefy guy in his 30s, dark hair, dark eyes, and sometimes dark mood. You never knew what you were going to get—jovial Mike or cynical Mike.

Chris was Julie's age, quick and wiry. He had a tendency to break into song the way she did, and it became a game of theirs to use lyrics in conversation. Some patrons loved it, others found it obnoxious. Julie and Chris didn't mind the ribbing, they just kept on singing.

Even though the job was exhausting, Julie loved bartending. The fast pace and party atmosphere helped push away the thoughts that gnawed at her when her mind was idle.

It was a busy Friday night at Sh'nanigans. Craig and Eddie were playing as they did every Wednesday and Friday. The bartenders were swamped with a bachelorette party and a birthday group on top of the regular crowd. Colleen and Pete showed up around 9:00 with Randy and Jenifer. It was the first time Julie met Randy's latest. She was cute—long dark hair, perky figure, demure smile. She wore a pink and green Ralph Lauren sweater with a matching headband.

When there was a break in the action, Colleen corralled her in the bathroom.

"What do you think of Jenifer?"

"I haven't had time to pee let alone assess a Randyette. Besides, what should it matter what I think?"

"Don't get defensive, I was just curious!"

"I'm not. I'll give you a full report once I have time to talk to the girl, okay? Now let me pee!"

Colleen laughed.

Julie went back to the bar, and Randy flagged her down to order another round.

Randy bellowed over the crowd noise, "Hey, I heard about your new digs!"

"Yep, me and my bonsai have a new home." Julie saw Colleen listening in, "So, Jenifer, good to finally meet you."

"You, too. Randy's told me you guys go way back," Jenifer laid a hand on Randy's arm, "And that you and Craig are living together. You make a cute couple!"

Julie wanted to set the record straight about she and Craig, "Oh, we aren't . . ."

"To old and new friends," Randy said and raised his glass.

"But . . ." Julie said, but Randy had already turned away. I'll have to sort this out later, she thought.

Mike scooted around Julie to get to the rail bottles and slipped something in her pocket. "Some energy for you," he said out the side of his mouth.

Julie reached into her pocket—a vial. Her heartbeat increased just thinking about it, the loud conversations around her became that Charlie Brown's teacher sound, "Wah, wah, wah." *Don't be such a wuss, you can handle a few bumps!* The next chance she got, into the bathroom she went. *No muss, no fuss, instant happy!*

Last call was 1:30. Colleen, Pete, Randy, and Jenifer headed home. Lisa, the night manager, locked the doors. The bartenders poured drinks for everyone and started cleaning up, which was much faster with the help of Mike's vial. Julie and Chris sang "Working in the Coal Mine" as they washed glasses. Eddie hit the Pac-Man machine, and Craig hung around, hoping to make time with Lisa. They had gone out a couple of times, but she was keeping it casual. Over breakfast that day, Craig told Julie he wanted to pursue a real relationship with Lisa.

Once the chores were done, they all traded off playing Pac-Man and Space Invaders and wound down from a frantic Friday pace.

By 3:30, Lisa was ready to call it a night, turning down Craig's offer to come home with him, so Julie and Craig went home alone. They were still buzzing, so they made drinks and Craig pulled out his guitar. They sang and talked until dawn and then stumbled to their separate rooms for sleep.

The scenario became somewhat routine the rest of the summer; sometimes Lisa or the other guys joined them. Sometimes, when the sun peeked in, Lisa stumbled off with Craig.

Julie always slept alone.

JULY

Julie was spiraling down a dark hole. She couldn't stand to lie awake alone, dark thoughts and memories wrapped around and wouldn't let go. Alcohol and Benadryl helped, but she was jarred awake by nightmares that lingered in the back of her mind all day.

Work was her happiest place, but she was exhausted. Mike gave her bumps to keep her going sometimes, then she started buying her own—just to get her through, and then she couldn't sleep. A vicious cycle; a snake biting its own tail.

Julie was embarrassed by her abusive marriage, her inability to get over it, her drug use as a crutch; afraid to face the darkness living inside her. It was all her dirty little secret. To the world, she was determined to be just fine, forging ahead, same old carefree, optimistic Julie.

RANDY

July 29th was a typical hot, humid night. The buzz around town was about the royal wedding. Randy didn't care much about that; he was celebrating his Top-Secret clearance.

The position at Grumman Aerospace in the Federal Contracting division was dependent on that clearance, and now he was clear to start his dream job. Randy was drawn to it because of Grumman's ties with the Navy—that meant ties to his father, whom he admired greatly and where his strong sense of patriotism began. Dad was so proud when Randy called him.

Next, he told Kevin, "My little brother will be working with the Department of Defense, scary thought!" Kevin smacked him on the back, "That's great, bro! Let me buy you dinner to celebrate. How about Sh'nanigans?"

"I told Jenifer I'd take her out tonight if I heard."

"Hey, I'll even buy her dinner, we can pick her up on the way!"

The three of them ate in the restaurant and afterward moved to the bar where Kevin announced Randy's good news.

Craig joined the group at the bar after his set, "Congrats, buddy," Craig said, "guess a joint and a snort are out of the question!" Randy and Kevin laughed. Jenifer looked nervous.

Julie said, "I am so happy for you! My friend is a top-secret genius!"

Randy glowed in her admiration, especially the genius part. Even though he got A's in all his classes, they teased him for being slow on the uptake. As a kid, he could never explain how his brain worked. It took him a long time to understand it himself. He was not a dummy; his mind just took its time absorbing and analyzing *all* the data. Computer Science was what he had always craved; principles of mathematics, engineering, and logic to solve problems. Now he would be working on systems for fighter jets, maybe even NASA.

Chris sang a few bars of "Secret Agent Man" and asked, "What's the defense department working on these days?"

"I'd tell you, but then I'd have to kill you," Randy replied straight-faced. Jenifer laughed at that one.

After his beer was gone, Randy said they'd better head out. He had a big day ahead. Julie came from behind the bar for a proper hug.

"So happy for you," she said, and her eyes got watery. Randy smiled down at her, thinking maybe he was over the Julie crush, and finally feeling like a grown-up.

"Thanks, Jewel," he said. Then he took Jenifer's hand and headed home to prepare for his bright new future.

II

When Craig and Julie got home, the house was like an oven, so they threw the windows open to let in the sweet summer breeze. Julie was wound up and exhausted at the same time, like most nights. She kicked her shoes off, made a drink, and grabbed a beer for Craig. A bluesy riff of music danced its way through the humid air and into her ear. She smiled; Craig was playing his new keyboard. He started with a few disjointed runs and began to sing in his rich tenor . . .

"Da da lada weary . . ."

Julie stood in the doorway and listened.

"Try a little tenderness . . ."

Something welled up in her and spilled over. *What the hell? What is going on here?*

Suddenly, all the misery, shame, and heartache she'd been pushing down for so long poured from her.

Craig looked up, and his face fell, the music stopped. He came to her, took the drinks from her hands—she'd forgotten she was holding them—and held her. Julie clung to him and cried, surrendered to the release. Finally, her sobs subsided, she was wrung out.

"I'm ok now. I don't know what . . ." she backed away, took a Kleenex from the box. "I can't talk about it . . . can't even think about it."

"You don't have to tell me anything. I'm just here for whatever you need."

Julie didn't know what she needed, but the pain that invaded her every cell was somehow not quite so unbearable now. She turned back to her friend with the kind eyes and big heart and leaned into his arms again. Then, feeling safe there, tilted her face up and put her lips to his.

"I need to feel something good."

"I can do that," he said.

This time, they stumbled into the same bed.

When the sun rose, it brought with it another hot, humid day. Julie was dreaming of swimming in a tropical lagoon. The seaweed below kept reaching up like tentacles and tickling her. She swam toward the surface and woke to find the sheet wrapped around her legs and a sheen of summer sweat on her skin.

Craig wandered in from the bathroom with a towel around his waist. "Morning," he dropped the towel and pulled on some shorts, "tea?"

"Iced tea . . ."

"Lemon, lot of ice. Coming up," he knew the way she liked it.

Julie burrowed back into her pillow and dozed until she heard the ice tinkling in its glass. She sat up and felt no modesty when the sheet slipped from her naked body. Craig sat his tea on the side table and bounced back into bed, "So, we good?"

She knew what he meant—*any regrets?* "We good. We get each other, don't we?"

"That we do. And anytime you want to be gotten between the sheets again . . ."

She bonked him with a pillow.

"Is that how you wanna play?" he scooped up an ice cube and held it on her belly.

"Aah! Torture!" she laughed and pillow-whacked him again. "Colleen would say we had a dalliance."

"Dalliance," he tried the word out, tumbled it around. "*Dalliance*, I like that, good word for a song."

Julie smiled at him, then lay back on the bed with a sigh.

"I lost it last night . . . that song brought up some stuff."

"Want to tell me? Getting it out in the open helps sometimes."

"Rick," just saying his name hurt, "he used to shove me around. I thought I had it behind me but . . ."

"That's a lot to leave behind," he scooped her up.

"Yeah. No magic expunction here."

"I've suspected something was going on. His anger is pretty intense," Craig thought about the times he'd witnessed Rick in full-out fury. "How long? I mean when did he start taking it out on you?"

"Honeymoon," she said, barely above a whisper. She was glad her face was buried against his chest so he couldn't see it color with shame.

He kissed the top of her head.

"No one knows that. Not even Colleen . . . well, she may . . . she saw my black eye, but I never told her about the honeymoon."

She laid there in his arms, feeling safe for the first time in years, "At first, I guess I didn't want people to judge him. His life was really tough. Then,

I was so embarrassed about letting it happen over and over . . ." she grabbed onto him a little tighter. "I was damn good at hiding it, huh?"

"I remember you used to jump right in there, throw water on Rick's fire," he said as he stroked her hair. "The last time I was around one of his tirades you cowered like Clyde in the corner. That made me think something was up."

"I tried to make it work. I guess he tried, says he did. He saw a counselor before I left him, wanted to go alone first before we did a couples thing."

"And?"

"Came home and told me my actions drove him to hit me, that's what the guy told him."

"What? That's crazy!"

"I know, I'm not sure what the therapist said, but Rick had it all con-voluted. Oh, he knew it was *wrong* to hit me or whatever . . . but, I didn't make a couples appointment with that guy!" she sat back, turned her face to the window.

"Sad thing is, I did blame myself. A lot of times . . . Like, why didn't I clean up or why did I yell back."

"Nothing you could do warrants a beating, you know that, right?"

"Intellectually, yes. It's different when you're in it."

A light breeze rustled the curtain, cooling her sweaty skin.

"I told myself over and over I could heal him. If I could just break through, just love him enough, we'd have a happy ever after."

"So, what finally convinced you to leave?"

Julie thought of flying through that plate-glass window; her life shattering around her in sharp, reflective pieces.

"The bad outweighed the good," she quoted Beth, "When the scales tip big for the bad, then you gotta go."

AUGUST

The apartment looked just the same. Sofa with Julie's throw pillows, dog and cat bowls in the kitchen (even though Hank had reclaimed the cats).

The towels hanging in the bathroom were different. They resembled the ones from that hotel in Nashville. It was dark in the hallway; the bedroom door was closed. Julie was drawn by some warped need to see inside, so she put her hand on the knob and it was warm. She turned it and the door swung open.

"Hi darlin," Rick is sitting on the bed. "Glad you got home safe."

He pats the pillow.

How did I let this happen?

He stands up, holds his arms out, "Light my way, darlin."

Why did I come back? Gotta get out of here! Panic races through her, the room swirls in a cloud of vertigo.

"You listening to me?" he stands just a breath away now, leaning in to kiss her. "You fuckin' around on me?" His mouth is on hers, his arms wrap around, constricting her lungs. *I can't breathe! Can't move! You're Gonna KILL ME!*

She sprung up in bed and gulped air. Her ears were ringing, hands clutching the sheets, her nightshirt drenched with sweat. *Just another nightmare . . .*

On shaking legs, Julie crossed the hall and slid into Craig's bed.

He woke at her touch, "I'm here," he said as he pulled her in against his chest. "A bad one, huh?"

She nodded.

"Shh, breathe," he said.

Julie matched her breathing with his slow, steady beat and tried to think of nothing else. The bed was warm, a fat moon hung outside the window, casting silver light through the sassafras tree. Daddy always called them mitten trees because of the shape of the leaves . . . warm mittens . . . then it was morning.

CRAIG

That night in July—the first time—he was noodling around with the keyboard, and when he looked up, what he saw shook him. She was just standing there, tears pouring down her face as if a mask had been pulled from her. He had never witnessed such raw anguish come upon someone so suddenly, so completely. He stood and went to her, wrapped his arms around her and they stood, swaying to some internal metronome until Julie's sobs subsided.

When she kissed him and said, "I need to feel something good," he knew what she needed . . .

Tenderness and he could easily give that. That's what he felt for her.

When they made love that first time, his heart swelled with pure, unconditional love. He realized he needed it, too, had been depriving himself of feeling something good, of connection.

Social interactions had always been difficult for him, large gatherings were exhausting; he never knew how to act or what to say. Music provided a buffer and gave him a way to communicate without having to analyze what other people were thinking. But with Julie, he didn't experience any of that. With Julie, he was always comfortable.

Their physical connection, though it was mind-blowing, was not what it was about.

They got each other, were like kindred spirits, and the only strings they placed on their relationship were heartstrings.

The rest of the summer and into fall, he and Julie shared a bed a couple times a week. Sometimes their bodies wound together with unfettered physical and emotional release, other times they just laid next to each other, talking, sorting things out, and feeling that bond until they drifted off.

Craig knew Julie was thankful that she didn't have to face her fears alone. Some nights she crawled into his bed shaking and sweat-drenched, very real monsters still showing in her eyes. He held her until she could sleep again, and he slept better, too, when he was able to give tenderness to her.

That was something innate in him, the need to give to another, and sorely lacking because of his social deficiencies. He laughed at himself—did the need to give of oneself constitute a selfless or selfish act?

Thinking about it, maybe Julie was the same, they were alike in many ways. Maybe that's why she stayed so long with Rick.

One way they were different was that Julie was an extrovert in the extreme and went out of her way to talk to people, acquaintances and strangers alike. He was astonished when they were in the grocery and she'd strike up conversations out of the blue with complete strangers, and she talked to any kid or baby within shouting distance. That weird and wonderful trait was why she was such a good bartender. She told him she got it from her gregarious father.

In their difference, they were good for one another—the social animal she was helped him peek out of his shell. He had lived in the house for years and never met his neighbors. Within a month, Julie had met and introduced him to the whole damn block, even talked him into having a neighborhood barbeque. She knew of his social difficulties and became his training wheels. When he started to tip, she would jump in with that funny run-on way of talking and no one noticed his struggles.

Craig, in return, kept her on a more even keel. Julie tended to get carried away with emotions and leap before she thought things through. He grounded her, gave her a sounding board. Now that she was sleeping, her snake stopped biting its tail and she began to inch forward.

Craig gave up pursuing Lisa. She was not right for him, too self-involved. He still had hopes of a romantic relationship with someone, but in the meantime, this was a lovely dalliance. As far as he was concerned, one had nothing to do with the other. If romance came along, his friendship with Julie would resume its platonic status, as it would if she met someone. They didn't have to discuss these rules; they just got each other. For now, living together was what they needed—easy, uncomplicated, and never lonely.

As a bonus, his mind was free to write some of the best music of his career.

Dalliance

We are Space and time suspended.
In this dalliance we share,
Open arms are a safe haven
Where we can lay our feelings bare

Outside storms are raging, ragged
Ensconced together, we abide
The wicked world no longer rules us
Hearts aligned, we turn the tide

Limbs entwine; our souls symmetric
Salve to strengthen wounded wings
No rules, regrets, or repercussions
We are dancing without strings

We write our story open ended
Friends and lovers blended
Fly on wings our bond has mended
In this dalliance we share
I believe I'll tarry there
In this dalliance we share
All my life I will remember
This splendid dalliance we share

Who knows where time will take us
The roads we walk must be our own
A thousand miles may come between us
But your notes will echo in my song.
And I know, I know
Time and distance can't erase you from the room inside my mind
I'll open the door and just like that,
You will be there
to resume this splendid dalliance we share

Chapter 28

OCTOBER 1981

Julie picked up Colleen, and they spent the day attending to wedding details. They stuffed gift bags, bought the cake-topper and Bride Barbies for flower girl gifts, and hit Hutzler's lingerie department for honeymoon attire.

Julie stayed for dinner at the O'Malley's and enjoyed the chaos and a home-cooked meal. When she returned home, Craig was watching Taxi on TV and laughing his ass off.

"You gotta hear this! Jim is taking his driver's license test. He's asking what a yellow light means! They've been at this about 10 minutes, he just gets slower and slower!" tears were leaking out of Craig's eyes, he was laughing so hard.

Julie joined him on the couch. Once the scene switched to commercial, Craig composed himself, "You two have a fun day?"

"We did! It's coming down to the wire, and she is so excited! I remember how great that felt."

"Shame it can't last, huh?"

"Shame . . ."

"Two calls for you. First, Will called about coming up next weekend."

"Yay! I can't wait until they move closer! Did he say anything about the houses they are looking at?"

"Yeah, in the Annapolis area. Said he wants a boat . . . Does Marriott pay that well?"

"I guess if you work at corporate headquarters. What was the other call?"

"Rick."

Julie's shoulders went up and her hands became tense fists.

"Now, wait a minute," Craig said, "He had a reason. His grandmother died yesterday."

"Oh," Julie's heart thumped. "Oh, that's sad. She was pretty old but still . . ."

"He seemed pretty shook up about it. Also, he said Clyde moved on to greener pastures."

"Huh? Clyde died?" Julie was struck with an immense wave of loss. "Poor Clyde, he was such a . . ." she couldn't continue.

Craig swept her up and held her, she let herself have a minute and pulled away, "Enough of the boohooing. I'll call Aunt Meg to give my condolences."

She kissed his cheek and stood, "And now I'm going to go to bed. My bed."

"Sweet dreams."

"I'll crawl in if I need you."

He waggled his eyebrows at her, and she laughed as she climbed the stairs.

Julie called Meg the next morning. Meg said the week before she died, Grandma wandered through the house putting those Post-it things on her belongings, with names of who should get what. Grandma put Julie's name on something.

When they cleaned out Beth's house, Julie had come to know Meg and Grandma Ackerman. Each trivet and trinket had a story behind it. Julie relished every tale, and Grandma enjoyed the audience. Her remembrances and anecdotes made a fairy tale of their chore. Now she wondered which trinket earned her name.

The next week, she stopped by Meg's house.

"Come in, honey." Meg said when she answered the door.

"I can't stay. Just wanted you to know how dear she was to me. I was so sorry to hear the news."

"And you were dear to her," Meg said. "I hope you'll keep in touch."

"Thanks, I will."

Dawn came down the stairs and stopped abruptly when she saw Julie.

"How are you, Dawn?"

"I am jest peachy, no thanks to you."

"I miss you, ya know."

Dawn raised her palm, a stop sign, "I cannot talk to you now. I have to keep on one loss at a time." She spun on her heel and flounced away.

Julie had tried to contact Dawn after she left Rick, but Dawn wanted nothing to do with her. She felt terrible, but hoped it was for the best. She didn't want Dawn to hear negative stories about her brother. He was a knight in shining armor in Dawn's eyes, as well he should be. That's the way Julie thought of her own brothers.

"She'll come around. Just give her time," Meg said as she handed Julie a bag.

The gift from Grandma was an antique silver frame holding a photograph of Grandma, Beth, Dawn, and Julie at her wedding. She touched the glass at each beautiful happy face, mourning the loss of all four of them.

NOVEMBER 26, 1981

Thanksgiving dawn was frigid. Icicles hung from the trees and the eves of the house. Julie wrapped her quilt around her and went downstairs to put the turkey in the oven. She could hear Oprah talking about traditions on the TV, but the kitchen was dark. She flipped the switch on the wall and her heart did a flip—Beth is sitting at the table of the house in Hereford. *Why am I always in this house?*

"Won't be long now!" says Beth, and Julie can smell the turkey, the air is infused with its scent of home and family . . . Comfort.

"Holidays with the Madsens, darlin'" Rick is behind her, his whiskey breath hot on her neck. She struggles to get away before he imprisons her, but the quilt wraps around her legs and she falls to her knees.

Julie reaches for Beth, "Help me!"

"I'm sorry, honey, you made your own bed."

Rick is over her, wearing predator's eyes, the electric carving knife buzzing in his grip.

She woke, drenched in sweat, rubbed her eyes, and surveyed her surroundings, sure she was in Rick's old room. Her familiar surroundings came back into focus, her childhood room. "Thank God it's morning," she said and went down to help Mom with the turkey.

WILL

Will, Diane, Tyler, and two-year-old Heather drove up from their new house in Annapolis and were first to arrive. Russ and the wild bunch were driving up from Charlottesville. Julie stayed overnight so Mom would have early help and not be 'in a dither.'

Mom had just thrown the potatoes in the pot when the rest of the family descended in a flurry of kisses and warmth. Aunt Dorothy and Uncle Jack bustled in ladened down with pies of all kinds.

Will kept stealing glances at Julie. Even though her smile was radiant, she seemed off-kilter and had dark circles under her eyes.

Julie grabbed up the kids for hugs so much that Luke finally said, "Aunt Julie, you sure are mushy! Let a kid breathe a minute, will you!"

Everybody laughed.

After dinner was cleaned up, Will waggled the bottle of Bailey's at her, and Julie met him in the kitchen.

"Some traditions should never rest," Julie said.

"You ok? You seem a little weirder than usual."

"Gee, thanks, something only a brother would say," Julie held her cup up for a glug of sweetness. "I'm ok, just had a crazy dream about Beth last night . . . well, and Rick, too."

"Tell me."

They sat at the kitchen table with their cups, and Julie tried to verbalize her dream. When she got to the Rick part, she probably didn't realize how it sounded until the words were hanging there in the open.

"Last year when we talked about this, that he shoved you once or twice, I was crazy pissed. But you downplayed it, didn't you?" Will could feel his face color as his own words sunk in, "I should have known. Damn it, Julie, you can't sweep this stuff under the rug!" He stood up, then sat down again, "I should have trusted my first instinct about him."

"Will, it's ok. In September, when his Grandma died, I called him. You know, to give my condolences. He told me he was glad I hadn't come to the funeral . . . said it was too hard to be around me."

"That sounds suspicious to me," Will said. "Unstable. Who knows what he could do? I heard about the graduation stunt from Kevin when he installed our dock electricity. Pretty funny, Rick's legs hanging out of your car."

"Ha! Electricians named Kevin should mind their own business."

"Not pretty funny, pretty crazy, Julie. Really crazy."

"Well, I am getting on with life and letting him be crazy all by himself. The divorce should be final in a couple weeks." She raised her cup, took a sip, "Besides, my best friend is getting married in two days. I'm focused on that."

"Glad you have something positive to focus on, and glad to hear you sounding happy, but I worry about you. If you need me—for anything—you'd better call."

"You aren't a million miles away anymore, I'll call you." She took a sip, "Hey! There's an after-party at Freddie's. You should come! You haven't seen the crew since . . . Gosh, two years?"

"Diane's got a whole weekend planned for us, but thanks for the invite." He stood nonchalantly then lunged for her, "Noogies!"

Julie squealed with delight as he knuckled her head, the brother equivalent of true affection.

II

All day, as she reveled in her family's love, Julie could hear Beth's little tinkle of laugh in her mind. She kept looking over her shoulder, expecting her to appear. Julie hoped wherever Beth really was today, she was at peace.

But on the way home, Will's words sunk in. *Unstable, really crazy.* She shuddered when she thought about what Rick was capable of.

When she went into the house, she was glad Craig was home. "I need a sleep buddy tonight," she said. "You ok with nightmare duty?"

"My pleasure," he said, and they climbed the stairs together.

Chapter 29

NOVEMBER 27 & 28, 1981

Julie woke to a soft and misty morning. Birds tweeted and twitched. Squirrels dashed, a frantic dance in search of winter fuel. Tonight was the rehearsal dinner! She slipped from under Craig's arm, careful not to wake him, tiptoed down the stairs, poured some tea, and dialed the phone. Little Tracy answered.

"May I speak to Mrs. McDonald?"

"Is this Julie?"

"Why, no, it is Snow White. I'm looking for a princess, are you one?"

Giggles . . . "It's for you, Collie, even if you *are not* a princess."

"Give it here, dingbat . . . hello, if you're looking for a princess, sorry! Only toads live here." More giggling in the background.

"Only 29 hours until you are a Mrs. Toad!"

"I can't believe it!"

"I'll be over to get you in an hour, make sure the girls are ready to roll."

"Are you kidding? They've been ready since dawn!"

Evie and Harry paid for manicures for the girls in the wedding party: Colleen, Julie, Clara, Caitlin, Molly, and little Tracy. Evie and Cathleen joined them for lunch afterward.

The day progressed in a flurry of activity. The rehearsal dinner was at Glenmore Gardens. Pete's parents kept a Maryland theme for the out-of-town relatives: crab cakes and oysters, Smith Island cake, champagne, and Natty Boh beer.

Colleen slept in her parent's house for the last time and Julie slept without nightmares . . . then it was Saturday morning.

A crisp breeze herded little cloud sheep across a brilliant blue sky. Bob Turk, the weatherman, predicted higher than normal temperatures and a zero percent chance of rain. Perfect.

"Only four hours, Mrs. Toad!"

"Get over here! I need my maid of honor to zip my dress!"

"On my way!"

Craig drove Julie to Colleen's house. "You look beautiful in that dress," he told her and kissed her cheek. "Go do the girl thing and I'll see you at the church."

All the girls were being transported to the church in a limo, much to the glee of the sister brigade.

The wedding was lovely; Colleen, beautiful; Pete nervous but handsome in his tux. Walt did not attend, but Ruth was accompanied by her girlfriend, and Randy brought Jenifer.

After the reception, they moved the festivities to the Friedman house.

Now it was Colleen and Pete's turn in the limo, and they had the driver ride around for a half-hour before dropping them at Freddie's. When they finally arrived, Pete told Julie, "Col wanted to take me for a test drive. Make sure being in front of the priest didn't wither me."

Colleen said, "He still works fine."

There was a reception at Spirits, so Gravy and Ty had to work, but they made it to the after-party. When they entered, they held up four bottles of champagne for the bride and groom.

Ty announced, "Three for now, and one for the honeymoon. The party may begin!" Cheers went through the crowd.

Gravy hit the kitchen in search of Cups where he was concocting a wedding cocktail and pulled him aside, "Rick was at the bar looking for you. He was fidgety, if you catch my drift."

"Shit, man. I told him I wasn't selling anymore, especially to him. He owes big time to his new supplier, not to mention his bookie right over there," he pointed to Freddie. "I don't want to get involved with that."

Gravy knew about the new supplier. One of Rick's old pals, Red Wilder, had been released from prison, and he was bad news big time. "Bigmouth Kathy told him you were at a wedding and he probably knows whose."

Gifts were piling up by the door. Julie pointed them out to Colleen, "Hey, how bout I take these home so you can keep your mind on honeymoon things?"

"Good thinking, thanks. We can have an opening party when we get back."

Craig opened her trunk and she began loading. Though the porch light was bright, Julie navigated the steps carefully, holding the hem of her long bridesmaid dress as she descended with a big bowed box. She didn't notice the old Bronco sitting across the street.

"Hey, Shortcake."

Julie spun around, the gift fell from her grasp.

"Hope that wasn't breakable," he smiled at her and touched her cheek, "beautiful as ever."

She froze, her feet rooted to the ground. *Am I dreaming?*

"Must be fate, running into you like this," his eyes swam with longing. He took a few steps and put his big hand on the car's roof, "She runnin ok?"

Now he was between her and the house.

She had a sudden flashback of the 1980 New Year's party here . . .

He was irate about something before they even got in the car. First, he fumed, then when she refused to turn the car around and go home, he smacked her and told her she was going to be sorry when the car stopped. Once they were parked on the street, she threw the door open and tried to run for the house. As always, he was faster. He grabbed her by the hair and pulled her back to the car. She screamed, but the party music was too loud for anyone to hear. Julie could see her friends through the window, oblivious to what was happening right outside. Just like a Horror movie.

Julie made herself speak, "No. You shouldn't be here."

"Is that any way to talk to your soulmate?" Softer, "Remember you told me that? I'm your soulmate?" He took a step closer, still smiling that pathetic smile, she took two steps back. They went on that way until she backed into the car in front of hers. He reached out again, "Come on, don't be like this . . ."

"Julie?" it was Craig. He couldn't see them from the back door.

Julie started to yell out, but Rick, quick as ever, slammed his hand over her mouth.

"That your new lover-boy?" he pushed his body against her, his bourbon-laced breath sour and hot against her cheek, "Nobody will love you like I do."

"Julie!" Craig was in view, "Hey, Rick . . ."

Rick lowered the hand from her mouth but kept hold of her arm and turned toward Craig.

"It's the music man! What's new? Oh yeah! I hear you are FUCKING MY WIFE!"

"You got it wrong, man, we're only roommates. Hey, Colleen's looking . . ."

"I don't care WHO is looking for her, I am having a conversation WITH MY WIFE!"

A couple other guests wandered out at the sound of shouting. Pete and Cups out the front door, Randy and Kevin out the back. Craig inched forward, and Randy moved toward the open trunk. He knew Julie's Ball Buster was still kept there. She called it her security bat. He pulled it out and clenched it, muscles taut, ready to swing.

Pete, in front, wore a menacing look. "I'm not gonna let you ruin this day, Rick," he hollered.

Craig was getting closer now, "Come on, man. You don't want anybody to get hurt."

"Please, Rick, let go of me," Julie said.

Rick scanned the crowd. He loosened his grasp a little, at least enough that Julie could feel the blood flowing back into her hand, and she let out a rush of air and relaxed her stance in relief.

Everything stopped for a second, as if the crisis would be averted. Until a voice from the porch called out, "That's it! I'm calling the cops!"

"Don't you do it!" Rick yelled back. He yanked Julie to his side, his left hand went behind him and reappeared with a gun, his .38. The world whooshed and sharpened, and Julie cried out.

Rick aimed the gun at Craig, "Back up, fucker."

"It's cool, man," Craig put his palms out in a sign of peace.

"I didn't come here for trouble. You are the trouble," he waved the gun in an arc, from Pete to the brothers that had moved closer, "my so-called friends." The barrel of the gun stopped at Randy, "You first."

Randy took a step forward.

Rick sent daggers with his glare, "Pow!"

Randy took another step, vibrating with adrenaline, bat high, until his brother's sudden grip on his arm stopped him. He tried to shake Kevin off, but common sense prevailed—gun trumps bat.

Cups spoke, "Rick, got what you came for, bro. Right here." He pulled a baggie out of his pocket, "Let's go, my treat."

"Tell her! I came to see you. This . . . this just happened," he gestured toward Julie with the gun, and Colleen gasped. The barrel was pointed right at Julie's head.

Julie could see Colleen now. She had come down next to Pete. *I've ruined her wedding.* She had to fix this.

"Rick, I love you," she turned to him and rested her free hand on him. "will always. . ." she kissed his cheek. "The cops . . . you gotta put the gun away."

Rick was knocked off guard by her profession of love, and the gun lowered, grip loosened. She held him, "Soulmates are forever," she whispered. She gave him what he needed.

"Let's go see Cups and get you out of here."

He looked at her, confused, like he wasn't sure where he was, but she took his hand and he walked with her. Julie beckoned Cups to follow to the Bronco. She opened the passenger door, and Rick wrapped his arms around her. She hugged him back, "You better go, that gun will get you locked up for a long time . . . Don't be the kite, be the tree."

"Julie, I . . ."

"I know." She pushed him into the car, "I'll call you tomorrow, promise."

She said to Cups over the car roof, "Get him away from here, anywhere." Cups nodded and got in the driver's side.

She leaned in and ran her fingers through his curls. Rick smiled . . . somewhere in there was a glimmer of *her* Rick, the goodness in him. She kissed him for the last time . . .

III

Rick heard from Walt about the wedding. He was sorry his buddy wasn't coming up, he could use a friend. Most of his friends were kind of fading away. He supposed that always happened with divorce, hard to stay close to both sides. Even old Clyde left him. He, Dawn, and Uncle Marty buried him in the woods up home where he loved to run. Rick hoped his own demise would be as peaceful.

Clyde had been a true friend, even when Rick was at his worst. That got him thinking about Red Wilder. He would never consider Wilder a friend; fucker should have stayed in jail. Instead, he came around and started Rick down a bad path again. Ol' Red had gotten into the cocaine trade along with his pill trade and wanted Rick to sell for him, fronted him product. Probably he knew Rick would consume more than he sold. Now Red had him over a barrel. Rick owed him for the goods he was fronted, plus his debt from long ago. He'd taken to carrying the .38 with him, in case any bad shit went down.

I'm not like him, I'm done with all that! Gotta pay him back and be done with him for good.

That reminded him of the money he owed Freddie. He had to stop betting with his heart. *Fuckin' Colts cost me money this year, better stick with betting the horses.* "Ha! Colts–horses," he laughed at his unintentional play on words.

At least he was back to being a mechanic, got a job at Ed's garage in Hereford. He missed Baby, but he could still get under the hood of some nice cars. He liked the way an engine worked, all its parts together in harmony, with nothing on its agenda but moving forward.

Today he was feeling mighty low, knowing all his buddies were at a wedding he wasn't invited to. He wondered if Cups had been invited, no love lost between Cups and Colleen after Rick showed up at Christophers. She blamed Cups, is what Rick heard. He was back working at Spirits, couldn't handle the nightclub crowd. Maybe Rick should drop in and see what's buzzing. *This is the last weekend, then I get my shit together.*

He made himself presentable, tucked the .38 under his jacket, and headed to Spirits. The other bartender was working, Kathy. *She's cute; maybe time to wet my whistle.* Rick sat at the bar and ordered a bourbon-rocks. There seemed to be a wedding going on in the back room. That couldn't be . . . just then the bride came rustling out toward the ladies' room, a very large woman surrounded by organza ruffles. *Definitely not Colleen!*

Rick smiled his most charming at Kathy, "Where's Cups tonight? He's usually here on Saturdays."

She smiled back, "He took off tonight for a wedding, I think. Let me refill that." She poured more whiskey into his half-full glass, with a dreamy look, not taking her eyes off him. *I believe she's flirting with me!*

"Heard about that wedding. One here, too, huh? Love is in the air."

She blushed, "Hope so . . . Yeah, Cups called off, but Gravy and Ty were already scheduled."

"Shame for them," Rick sucked down his second drink. "Refill me, darlin', I'm thirsty," he winked at her. *May as well warm her up, come back for some TLC later.* "Think the wedding party will continue here?"

"I wish, I could use the tips! But I think I heard Gravy say something about Freddie's."

The kitchen door opened and Gravy bustled out, "Ty and me are heading out . . . Oh, Rick, Buddy!"

"How's your day goin'?"

"Can't complain."

"Just stopped in to have a word with Cups," he shook the ice around in his glass. "Know where I can find him?"

"Nah, man, but if I run into him, I'll tell him you're looking."

"You do that, cause I'm lookin."

While Rick gave the boys a head start to Freddie's, he finished the drink. *I'll see Cups and make a deal with Freddie, all or nothing against the Colts.* Rick stood and threw some money on the bar, "You work till close?"

Kathy nodded and gave him a grin that told him all he needed to know.

"I'll be back, then," another wink.

First things first, he stopped at the payphone and dialed Fred's private number. It rang three times and went to the machine, "Yo, it's Rick. Gimme the Jets Sunday . . . You heard me right. I'm taking the Jets over the Colts for $300. By the way, I'm coming over there . . . lookin for Cups. Tell him to meet me outside."

Rick pulled up to Freddie's and parked just across the street. He had just gotten out of the car when motion in the driveway caught his eye. The Aspen's trunk popped open and somebody went back into the house. And then, there she was, the porch light kissed her perfect shape as she moved, just like the night of their first date, the night he fell in love with her. He watched, mesmerized, wishing for pen and paper so he could draw her. *See that? She makes me better.*

After the Christopher's fiasco, he promised himself he'd stay away from her, but . . . *What are the odds that I pull up just as she's coming out?* He couldn't help but think this was meant to be, they were meant to be together. He approached her, "Hey Shortcake."

He must have surprised the hell out of her, because she dropped the box she was holding. He smiled and joked, "Hope it wasn't breakable."

God, she was beautiful, all flushed, hair flying out. He couldn't help himself, he had to touch her, but she flinched at his hand. He tried to tell her he hadn't planned to see her. It was fate, but she didn't seem to get it. *Stop being all heavy, jerk! Just be nice! Talk cars, she likes that . . .*

Julie didn't like that either, "No, you can't be here."

Why was she pissed at him? He was being nice! "Don't you remember? I'm your soulmate."

She kept backing away from him.

"Come on, don't be like this . . ." *I'm not gonna hurt you, I love you.*

Then Music Man spoke up. *Why does somebody have to ruin it every fucking time!*

Julie started to call out . . .

NO! I need more time with you! All on its own, his hand slammed over her mouth.

Rick knew she was living with him. He'd sat outside and watched their house a few nights, and he saw the way Craig touched her. Didn't Music Man know the code? You don't mess with a friend's woman. Just thinking about it lit him up, started a fire he couldn't control. He pushed his body against her to drive home the truth of his words, "No one will love you like I do!"

The jerk kept talking!

"FUCKING MY WIFE?" *She is my wife . . .* "I'm trying to have a conversation WITH MY WIFE!"

He's trying to play you . . .

Now there was a fucking crowd around them, what the hell? He just wanted to talk to his wife.

"Please, Rick, let go of me." But she wasn't his wife anymore, he failed her. All these people knew he failed her. He should go . . .

"Calling the cops!" Val's big mouth.

That can't happen. "Don't you do it!" He panicked, pulled the gun. He tried to explain. This was their fault! He didn't come here for trouble, they were causing the trouble!

Then he saw Randy—his little brother. That's how he thought of him ... until he found him in her car that night: FUCKING AROUND WITH HIS WIFE!

"You first," *you broke the code. Pow! You're dead, muthafucker!*

Cups spoke, "Rick, got what you came for, bro—right here." He pulled a baggie out of his pocket, "Let's go, my treat."

"Tell her," *I don't care about the drugs, I don't want to hurt anybody. I just want her to understand!* Then the gun was pointing at Julie. *How did that happen? Never! He loved her!*

"Rick, I love you," she touched him, "I will always . . ." she kissed him. *She's playing me, don't fall for this!* "The cops . . . you gotta put the gun away."

He looked in her eyes, they never lied, felt her arms go around him. "Soulmates are forever," she whispered. *She means it, she remembers.* All the fury and fight dissolved. He would follow her anywhere.

They walked to the car, and he held her, smelled her hair, lemony and sweet. Julie held him like she used to when he was her everything. He knew he had to go, let her go.

"You better go, that gun will get you locked up for a long time . . . Don't be the kite, be the tree."

Our words. Only ours . . . I'll be the tree.

"Julie, I . . ." *sorry, love you, Can't live without you. Have to let you go . . .*

"I know." She pushed him into the car, "I'll call you tomorrow, promise." He knew she always kept her promises.

She leaned in and ran her fingers through his hair like she used to.

He smiled, the first real smile in a long time. *She loves me, Heaven!*

She kissed him. That kiss would be what he held on to as he died . . .

Chapter 30

Julie watched the Bronco drive away and turned back to the crowd across the street. There was Randy. She pictured that gun pointed at him and suddenly saw him anew. The thought of losing him . . .

Everything was slow-motion, rippling, underwater. Randy let the bat fall and was coming toward her. She crossed the road, reaching out . . .

Jenifer ran from the front porch, nearly tackled Randy from behind. He stumbled and turned; took her in his arms as she blubbered and kissed his adorable face.

That's where he belongs, I'm bad news.

All at once, she was surrounded by Colleen, Craig, and Val. They swept her into the house, talking over each other, crying, laughing—sounds of relief.

Marilyn threw her arms around Julie, "Oh, honey, honey, thank God!"

Through the window she saw Randy and Jenifer locked in a lovers embrace. Julie turned away.

Freddie hollered, "Open that fucking bubbly, Ty. My heart is beating out my chest. The hell with what he owes me."

Marilyn got busy getting drinks for everyone, and the party atmosphere resumed. Julie sat down heavily on a kitchen chair and accepted a glass of champagne from Ty.

"Here you go, sugar. Doctor Ty's got just what you need."

Julie smiled up at him and took a big swallow, then let out a burp.

Ty laughed, "See that? All the bad stuff just burped its way out!"

Sometime later, the phone rang. Marilyn answered, "Hello? Hey, Hon . . . Gravy, phone call!"

It was Cups, looking for taxi service back. Gravy swung by Julie on the way out, "Everything is copasetic. The wayward boy is sitting on a barstool at the Pioneer House."

He signaled Ty, "You coming along?"

"Hell, no! He's in redneck territory. You ever noticed I'm *black*?"

"Aha, I assumed that was from being over a stove all day! Hey, guys! My best friend is black! How cool is that?"

"Get out a here, mo-fo," Ty waved his big black hand toward the door as Gravy grinned and exited.

Ty eyed Julie with a sarcastic grin, "That mo-fo called me his best friend! Sheeit, ain't I lucky!" He mimed a serious mug and shook his head, "Doesn't know I'm black . . . my black ass, he doesn't!"

Julie laughed so hard, she had to go pee-speed to the bathroom. *God, thank you for my friends!* After her bladder was empty, she threw some water on her face, sprayed some 'Love's Fresh Lemon' on her neck. Better. On the way downstairs, she peeked into Abigail's room. There she was, an angel in designer flannel, sleeping through the chaos. Glad the uproar hadn't woken her, Julie envied her innocence. She tiptoed back down the stairs.

Colleen was just coming to find her, "There you are! You okay?"

"Are *you* okay, is the question. I ruined your wedding."

"Julie, nothing could ruin this day. It's been perfect, at least right up until this bump."

"Weee! Welcome to my roller coaster." Julie said. "Seriously, this was a big fuckin' bump!"

Colleen laughed. Julie rarely used the "F" word, so when she did, it was appropriately shocking.

"Come on, there's a party going on." Hand in hand, they joined the others.

When they entered the living room, it surprised the girls to see Will sitting on the sofa with Craig.

"You came!" Julie said.

"Yeah, I miss this crowd," Will stood and gave her a squeeze, then Colleen. "You look stunning!" he told the bride.

Pete appeared behind them, "Kev and Val are leaving. I need to steal you away from Julie."

"Go on, Julie and I need a minute, anyway," Will took Julie's hand and led her to the back porch. "We need to have a chat."

A chilly November breeze fluffed through Julie's hair, and she shivered. Will threw his jacket around her shoulders, "Craig filled me in on the hoopla."

"Oh, boy."

"Julie, this has gotten out of control."

"What can I do about it?"

"That's what I asked myself, and I had a brilliant idea!"

"I'm listening."

"How about if you move to Annapolis? You can stay with us until you get a job. Plenty of bars down there and good money."

"I don't know."

He tried again, "Wait, listen—you'll be far away from Rick but still close enough for your friends to find you!"

Julie could see Will was thrilled with the idea. *Will—Mr. Fixer.*

"Just give it some thought."

Julie looked out over the yard. Leaves covered the ground. The trees were almost bare. She hated this time of year, when everything died and winter stretched out before her.

"I'll think about it . . . tomorrow. Right now, I'm full to the brim."

"I can live with that."

"I'm so glad you're here." Julie fell against her brother, her comfort since birth, "What would I do without my brothers, my shining armor brothers."

BEYOND THE BROKEN WINDOW

JENIFER

The cuckoo clock in the dining room sang out eleven, and Jenifer was ready to leave. She had enough of this group for one night. They were nice, but she felt like an outsider with all their private jokes and rituals. When she joined in, it seemed awkward, forced. And the drama tonight! Jenifer was conservative, introverted, not made to handle all that. Seeing a pistol pointed at the man she loved just about put her under.

It was exhausting!

"Randy, you about ready to call it a night?"

"I believe I am, and you, my sweet, may drive!" he handed the keys to her. "Let's go say our goodbyes and fly."

He held her hand and flapped the other arm like a wing as they went to find Colleen and Pete.

He was cute when he'd had a few, mushy and silly. She stole a sideways glance at his handsome profile—his big brown eyes and strong, chiseled jaw.

The man of her dreams: handsome, brilliant, successful. But . . . Randy kept a part of himself locked away, and she couldn't find the key. Tonight, after the drama, the door seemed to crack open and he stayed glued to her side.

Out of nowhere, he said with a big grin, "I love you, Jen. You make me happy to be alive."

Their relationship started slow back in April, but since his graduation, Randy was around all the time. On the night he got his clearance, he said he loved her, but that damn door stayed closed until tonight.

Something was different. Perhaps a brush with a madman did it.

They headed to the car and Julie and Will were on the porch. Jenifer tensed at the sight of Julie, another obstacle she had yet to overcome.

Randy insisted they were just friends, but . . . her intuition said otherwise. Julie was so different from Jenifer; bubbly, emotive, always touching people. Jenifer was uncomfortable when Julie touched her unexpectedly, and even more so when she touched Randy. The way she talked was irritating, how she'd go off on a tangent and her words would get jumbled. Her emotions ran all over too, and there they were, always right on her sleeve. The worst was she was naturally pretty, she didn't wear makeup. *How do I compete with that?*

Thank God Randy didn't linger with more goodbyes. They walked past Julie's car to his Datsun and she got in the driver's side. Randy dropped his sport coat, bent, picked it up, and after some fumbling, finally opened the door, threw the coat in the back, and got in.

When they got to her place he said, "I ought to keep some stuff here so I don't have to cart a bag around."

"Good idea." She tried to sound casual, but her insides were jumping for joy.

"That whole thing with Rick . . . I was shaking in my boots."

"He is one scary guy!"

"Oh, no, I'm not scared of him, but I am scared to lose my clearance. Rick seems to have a vendetta for me. He knows things about me, recreational drugs, and the like. One wrong word and my career could be in the shitter." he sat down, pulled her down next to him, "I should find out about that promotion Monday. I will not let Rick or anything screw that up for me."

He kissed her, "I'll be transferred, you know."

"I know, but not too far, right?"

"New York. Long Island."

Her heart sank.

"What about grad school?" she asked, grasping at straws.

"I'll take the exam for this semester, then transfer. St John's has a campus near Grumman."

I knew he was too good to be true. Jenifer turned her face away to hide her disappointment.

"Come with me," he said softly. His finger traced the side of her face and tucked her hair behind her ear.

She turned back.

"Come live with me!"

Her jaw dropped; a little drool dripped from the corner of her mouth.

"Would you come with me? I know you just landed your job, but we could figure it out!"

Jenifer didn't care about any job, her answer was yes.

Randy smiled and took her to bed to consummate the deal.

RANDY
NOVEMBER 29, 1981

When Randy woke Sunday morning, he found Jenifer wrapped around him. He couldn't move without waking her, so he laid there; muscles cramping, bladder crying out for relief, brain replaying every word he uttered the night before. Trepidation set in. *What was I thinking? What did I get myself into?* He had visions of a fox chewing off its own leg to get out of a trap. That made his stomach roil. The hell with chivalry, he rolled her off and ran for the bathroom.

Once he evacuated the contents of his stomach and bladder, he could think past the panic. *Jenifer is great! Calm and steady. No surprises… and she worships you! Just right to share your fresh start in a new city.*

He was eager to get away from the constant turmoil of everyone around him; Cups and his drug life, Val and Kevin's constant bickering, being treated like everyone's little brother, Rick's self-destruction, and . . .

Julie. *Don't think about Julie, it only gets you in trouble!*

Rick's insanity last night was the final straw. The man was sick. *Can't believe he pointed that gun at me, at Julie! All she ever did was love you! Ungrateful son-of-a-bitch!*

When he thought about all Rick had put her through . . .

Jenifer's voice floated in through the door, "Got everything you need in there?"

"Yeah, stomach's a little upset. Too much to drink last night."

"Take your time, I'll make you some coffee and toast."

"Thanks, you're a doll!" he tried to sound chipper. It was hard to do with the murderous thoughts that were coursing through his brain.

"Pull it together, Asshole," he said to the man in the mirror. He spit out the sour taste in his mouth, brushed his teeth, and put on a smile, but he couldn't shake the feeling that there were loose ends to tie before his fresh start.

Chapter 31

NOVEMBER 30, 1981

When the phone sang out at 3:35 Monday morning and jarred her awake, she knew—tragedy was calling.

"Julie, it's Dawn. You have to come."

"What? Come where?" she answered, bewildered. *Am I dreaming?*

"The hospital, GBMC. It's Rick."

"Wha . . . ?"

"He's . . . in a coma. They found . . . Just come! Come!"

Julie shook her head to clear her thoughts. Why would Dawn call *her*? Dawn had shown nothing but scorn since the separation. "I still don't understand . . ."

"You're his agent—those stupid papers he signed after Mom died. They say if . . . if . . ." Dawn stammered. "There's nobody else to call!" She burst into tears.

"I'll come. Of course, I'll come," she assured Dawn as her mind raced. "I'm leaving now."

Craig poked his head out his door, still half asleep, "What's going on?"

"It's Dawn. Something's happened to Rick. He's in the hospital."

"Julie, stay out of it."

"I can't! She needs me," Julie felt her eyes tear up. "He's in a coma."

243

"Oh God, what happened? Let me . . ."

Julie touched his arm, "No, you stay here for now. You are fuel to the fire at the moment."

The corner of his mouth went up, "Yeah, guess I am." He gave her a quick hug, "Keep me posted. I'll be here."

"Thanks. What would I do without you?" She kissed his cheek and headed down the stairs.

The temperature had plummeted with nightfall and the trees and power lines were crusted with silver. Julie slipped on a patch of ice and almost went down as she hurried to scrape the film of frost from the windshield. Even the sky appeared icy, with a waning moon and sharp little stars. Her frigid fingers gripped the wheel as she made her way down Charles Street and turned into GBMC. Once parked, Julie sat a minute to say a silent prayer.

"Please, no more," was all she could muster. She headed to the hospital doors and whatever waited within.

A disheveled, tear-streaked Dawn met her as she entered the intensive care unit and she fell against Julie. Her skinny body hitched and shook with sobs. Julie wrapped her arms around her and murmured calming sounds into her newly cropped hair.

"Shh . . . I'm here. Shh, I've got you."

Julie understood Dawn's grief. Her protector, the man she thought could lasso the sun, lay unconscious.

"Hey, I need some caffeine. How about you?" Julie asked. Dawn nodded as she swiped her face with her shirtsleeve. "How bout I go talk to the doctor and you find us some coffee or something?"

"Thanks for coming . . . Aunt Jo and them are away and I really can't handle this stuff so good."

"I'm here. Now go get us some fuel." Julie dug some bills out of her purse and handed them to Dawn. She wandered away, glad for a chore that would give a few moments of respite.

Julie turned to the task ahead. Doctor Craig met her at the door to Rick's room. She took Julie's hands in hers. The irony of the situation was not wasted on the doctor as she spoke, "Julie, I'm so sorry to tell you Rick has suffered a blow to his head. We are monitoring him closely, but his skull is fractured, and there is damage from bone fragments and swelling in his brain."

"But he's alive?"

"Alive, but in a vegetative state. We've put a drain in to ease the swelling and he is on a ventilator to help him breathe. But I must warn you there is little chance of him recovering."

"Dawn said you've got papers or something."

"Yes. He named you health care agent. I remember how you all suffered with his mother. Rick was smart to draw this up, as it's a rather new procedure," she handed Julie a copy of the document Rick carried in his wallet. "There is not much we can do at this point but wait."

She stood by the side of the bed, among the monitors, their beeps a metronome keeping time with her thoughts.

Here lay the man who tore her life apart, whom she had loved and hated and feared. The force of those emotions was unparalleled.

Now, as she stared down at him, lying quiet and still, she experienced a sense of deep sadness. Regardless of what or who put him here, he had let his anguish and anger strangle him and was reduced to this.

She literally had his life in her hands.

Julie contemplated document she held. Rick had insisted she sign it after Beth's funeral. He was adamant he did not want to go through what she had. He said he couldn't bear to have his family watch him waste away before their eyes. Now Rick was lying here.

Was that karma or somebody's twisted sense of humor? And who could that person be.

Chapter 32

JOE MINELLI

Joe Minelli was a grizzled veteran of the United States Marine Corps and the Baltimore County Police Department. He had a year left until retirement and didn't mind what they said about his new partner.

Detective Rowina Lopez was low man on the totem pole in the Baltimore County precinct. It wasn't because she was the newest or youngest detective in homicide. It was because she was a she. This was a case nobody wanted. It wasn't a homicide yet, but odds were it soon would be. The victim, a nobody with a couple juvenile charges and a DWI, was vegetative and hanging low on the vine. Joe knew Detective Rowina Lopez didn't mind the snubs or the low-profile cases, she was on the job to get the bad guys so he treated her like any other young upstart. Teaching the fine finesse of interrogation was his forte, and Lopez needed some finesse. She was all fire and brimstone. At least she was nice to look at and, being as he had no one at home to look at anymore, that made his day.

The detectives were called to a rutted drive off a narrow road in Hereford. The sky was just hinting of cold morning light when they arrived. A crime lab van was on the scene with a tech busy dusting for prints. Joe hauled his large frame out of the car and approached the patrolman standing beside a rusty old Bronco, its front bumper nudged against the trunk of a thick oak tree, "What we got here, officer?"

"Victim was in the Bronco. Door was ajar. He was found by another tenant. The house has a double entrance, two separate apartments." He showed Minelli the Polaroids of the victim before the ambulance took him away. The guy was slumped across the steering wheel, mighty bloody, with a gash on the back of his head behind the left ear.

Joe pulled on a pair of plastic gloves and examined the Bronco and the surrounding area, "No blood on the ground. Splatter pattern on the outside of the vehicle," He stuck his head inside and saw the steering wheel, seat, and windshield all had blood on them, "Think this guy drove himself here?"

"That's what it looks like to me. He got bashed over the head somewhere else and made it this far until he hit that tree."

"So, the perp thought we'd fall for the ruse."

"The ruse?"

"Tried to make it look like an accident."

"I guess so."

Joe riffled through the photos, "You took some good shots here." He pointed at one, "See how the angle is here? This was done with some major force. Broken hand too, I see. Interesting."

Lopez spoke with the officer inside the house and reported what was found to Joe, "drug paraphernalia, ammo for a .38, a lot of drawings of a woman. Got his address book and some letters, you can sort through all that. Where's the list of what was on his person?" The officer handed it to Detective Lopez.

While she read it, Joe had a further look in the Bronco. Other than cigarette butts in the ashtray, there was a glass pipe, "Make sure they dust the pipe for prints."

His guess would be the residue in it was rock cocaine, expensive high and all the rage these days.

He opened the glove box. Nothing of note there. He shone his penlight under the seat and saw a glint of metal, "Look what we have here." With a pen from his pocket through the trigger, he pulled out the .38 and sniffed the barrel, "Been fired, let's get this to ballistics. Did somebody bag the hands?"

"Not sure, they took him pretty quick."

"Call the hospital. See what we can get on those hands."

Joe examined the tree that the vehicle's bumper had nudged and worked his way to the top of the drive, following tire tracks. About 50 yards from the top, he found what he was looking for. The Bronco's tracks swerved to the right of the entrance, before continuing down the drive. Behind them were another set of tracks. It looked like a car pulled right up to the Bronco and stopped, then backed out. The dirt was scuffed like somebody was doing the electric slide all over the place.

Erased the foot prints, smart. Fortunately for Detective Minelli, the perp couldn't get rid of the blood that had seeped into the earth and froze with the drop in temperature overnight. He just found the primary crime scene.

After gathering information at the scene, they arrived at GBMC to question the family. Joe let Detective Lopez take the lead.

II

Julie stood vigil next to the bed, her mind whirring. Who would do this? Maybe it was random. Maybe he was robbed. That guy, Red Wilder, came to mind. He had been trouble before.

She was so lost in her thoughts; she didn't notice Walt enter the room. He touched her, and she jumped. A small squeak escaped her.

"Sorry, I really startled you!" he hugged her. "Dawn called me."

"Walt, I'm so glad to see you."

Walt approached the bedside. "Ah, man . . ." his eyes grew watery as he took Rick's hand. "What the hell happened, buddy?" He turned to Julie, "Has anybody else been in, you know, to see him?"

"Just me and Dawn. I sent her to change her clothes and feed her dog. Promised her I'd stay until she got back. Tried to call Randy and kept getting the machine," Julie sunk into the chair and blew air out the side of her mouth. She fidgeted with the ring Will gave her years before, "Will said he couldn't come up . . . stuck at work. My parents said they'd come. I told them not to, they'd make me nuts hanging around here."

"I talked to Rick yesterday. Man, he was a wreck . . . couldn't make much sense of the story, except he saw you and things went bad."

There was a tap at the door.

"I'm sorry to bother you, Mrs. Madsen, I'm detective Rowina Lopez of Baltimore County Police, and this is Detective Joe Minelli."

"Oh, yes. Come in."

Walt stepped up, and held out his hand, "Walt Jackson. I'm a friend of Rick's. Just came up from Charlottesville."

Joe Shook his hand and Detective Lopez continued, "I know this is a difficult time for you, but we hoped you could answer some questions. Help us sort this out. The hospital has provided us with a room down the hall."

"So, you think . . . I mean, what do you think happened?" asked Julie, feeling flustered.

"Looking at the medical reports and the scene, we have reason to believe there was foul play. Any information you have will be helpful."

"What can I tell you? I saw Rick Saturday, my friend's wedding. Before that, it's been months since I even talked to him."

"We just want to go over a timeline with you, and possible suspects."

"Everybody loved Rick. He had his problems but . . ."

"How about you, Mr. Jackson? What can you tell us?"

"I talked to Rick on Sunday. But I don't expect I can give you anything of use."

"Did Mr. Madsen tell you his plans for the day?"

"No, he was feeling kind of low, I think. He seemed pretty down on himself. Worried about getting involved with a guy from his running days, Wilder's the name. Rick owed him money from years ago."

"Yeah, I thought about him, too," Julie said. "And what if it was some random robbery?"

"We think that's unlikely. There was a credit card and twenty dollars in his wallet," Detective Lopez said. "Please, can we sit down and talk with you? We won't keep you long."

"Sure, I'll tell you anything you want, I just . . ." she glanced at Rick. After all he did to her, she should be dancing at the sight of him lying there, but she felt lost.

Such a feeling of helplessness came over her, she was always the one to spring into action when tragedy struck, but she could do nothing except wait. At least talking with the detectives would be something positive. She looked at Walt, "I told Dawn I'd stay with him."

"I'll stay. You go ahead."

Julie said, "Thanks." She squeezed Walt's hand and followed the detectives.

ROWINA LOPEZ

Joe handed Julie a cup of coffee. "Cream and sugar," he pointed to the countertop. As Julie fixed her coffee, he continued, "Now that you've had time to speculate, any names pop into your mind?"

"Only the one, Red Wilder. Rick was friends with him back in high school. He got out of prison last spring, I believe."

Joe wrote in his little log book. Detective Lopez took over the questions, "Mr. Madsen and he got reacquainted?"

"I am only going by what I heard. I've only seen Rick a couple times since our separation."

"You are separated then, for how long?" Rowina glanced at Joe.

"We separated January 1980. The divorce will be final next month. I was living in Charlottesville for over a year, then came home this past summer."

"I see, living in Charlottesville with Mr. Brooks?"

The question visibly flustered her, "No! Why would you think . . . no, I lived with my brother and his family. They needed a nanny."

Lopez thought she hit a nerve. Joe gave her his 'go easy' warning glance.

"Just a coincidence then, that Mr. Brooks lived there, too. Did you see Mr. Brooks while in Charlottesville?"

"A couple times, but he was Rick's friend, so it was awkward . . . but that has nothing to do with Rick's . . . whatever you are calling it."

"Felony assault, for now. That may be upgraded as the circumstances change."

"What?" Julie was confused. Rowina watched the meaning dawn on her,

"Oh, if he dies."

Joe stood up with a grunt and grimaced at Rowina, "Mrs. Madsen, let's not get ahead of ourselves, we simply need to know who to look at for this."

"Wilder. Look at him," Rowina detected vengeance in her voice.

"Oh! And there was this guy at our party . . . well, and at Spirits last year, threatened revenge on Rick."

"Revenge for what?"

"Oh, it was nothing really, the guy spilled beer all over our apartment. Rick took exception to it and kicked him out . . . well, I guess not kick. Punched him."

"How long ago did you say?"

"Jeez," she considered a minute. "It's been a couple years since the party. Also, he showed up in Spirits maybe Summer 79? And I heard they got into another scuffle recently."

"You don't know the kid's name?"

"No, he was friends with Joanie Janowitz, she could tell you. I can find her number for you."

"That would be helpful. So was Mr. Madsen in the habit of punching people?" Joe asked, eyes cast down as he scribbled in his book.

"He had a temper sometimes, but . . . he never . . . never really hurt anybody *bad*."

Rowina watched Julie rub her arm—*Was that a bruise there?*—and pull her sleeve down over her hand. She got a vibe and made a mental note to follow up. This woman was not telling the whole story.

"You say you haven't been in contact with Mr. Madsen the last year or two?"

"Right, except on the phone. He used to call me all the time. Try to get me to come home."

"That sounds annoying. Would drive me nuts!" Rowina said. "Had an ex like that myself once."

She shot a look at Joe. *See—I can commiserate!* He gave her a half smile.

Julie continued, "I finally stopped answering. I mean, what didn't he get? It was over!"

Rowina nodded her head, scanned her notes, "There is evidence your ex-husband was a drug abuser. Do you know about that?"

"Yes, long time ago and I understand he was getting back into it."

"I have to ask you this so we understand the depth of your knowledge. Please don't be offended," said Detective Minelli, in a kindly tone. "Do you use drugs?"

Julie's face flushed, "Well, I have . . . but I don't. I mean, in the past, but not in a long time."

"With your husband? We just want to be sure of any connections he had. You know, dealers and the like. I assure you anything you tell us is strictly for this case. You won't get in trouble for it."

"Once or twice," she answered, talking slow, then sped up. "But I don't know where he got it. He just . . . he brought it home with him."

"Brought what?" Rowina asked.

"What?"

Her voice rose, "What kind of drug did he 'just bring home'?"

"Coke." She said it so softly they could barely hear her.

"Speak up, Julie," Rowina could tell the girl was embarrassed, but what else was going on?

"Cocaine! We did it a few times, ok? It made him . . . well, he coped better. With everything."

Rowina changed the subject, to throw her off balance, loosen her tongue.

"Mrs. Madsen you said you saw Mr. Madsen at a wedding on the 28th. Was he arguing with anyone then?"

The detectives watched the blood drain from her face. She took a minute to answer, "Uh, it was a misunderstanding."

"Go on," Rowina said. Julie said nothing. "Miss, are you ok?"

"Oh, uh, sure. I just, well . . . I've been up since three and . . ."

"Please," Joe said in his fatherly voice, "tell us about the wedding."

"Well, it was an after-party. Rick came up to me outside. He surprised me since he hadn't been invited. I . . . I guess I kind of overreacted," she sucked her bottom lip in and bit at it. "There was some yelling. My room-mate, Craig, came out and Rick yelled at him, thought we were a couple. Anyway," she took a sip of coffee, stalling. "Some others came out to see what was up . . . but I got Rick to cool down and he left. I kept my promise to call . . . he didn't answer."

Tears filled her eyes, probably part of the show.

"Here you go," Joe handed her a box of Kleenex, and let her wallow in her sorrow a little. Rowina knew Joe's big key to interrogation; time is your friend, let them stew. You'll be surprised what comes out when they retreat into their head.

"So, I want to be sure I have this straight. Mr. Madsen showed up at the party uninvited. He surprised you outside the house before he ever entered?"

Julie nodded.

Joe moved a chair next to her, sat, "So you yelled at him, he yelled at you, your friend heard the ruckus and came out. Madsen yelled at him because what?"

"He thought Craig and I were dating. But we're roommates . . . friends."

"Hmm," Joe leaned forward. "He was jealous in any event, even if you aren't intimate with the guy. Your husband is unhappy you are sharing your life with somebody else. That would upset me in his shoes."

"Yes, well . . . I get why. But Rick, he started waving the gun around . . ."

Rowina slapped her hands on the table and lunged toward Julie, "Woah, hold on. A gun?"

Joe gave her a look of exasperation.

Shit! Rein it in, Ro!

Julie blinked several times, figuring out what she said, "Yes Rick had a gun. He didn't aim it. I think he just . . . you know, like . . . a prop, to get everybody to back off."

"A prop. I imagine that worked. Got people to back away, huh?" Joe's hands gave a little pushing motion.

"Yeah, then I talked nice to him, told him he had to go because somebody said they were going to call the cops."

"Who said that?"

"Not sure, maybe Marilyn? It's her house . . . or maybe Val?"

Joe said, "So this gun. Seen it before?"

"It was Rick's. I had forgotten he even owned it. He showed it to me when we were cleaning out his mom's house. I think it kind of scared him, you know, to have it around. He stashed it away in the back of the closet. Never saw it again."

"What kind of gun? A Pistol?"

"A .38, he said. I don't know much about guns."

"Your husband was left-handed, yes?"

Julie nodded.

Rowina said, "So help me out here. Someone said they were calling the cops, and he just left?"

"I talked him into it, like I said. I talked nice, told him I loved him and I would call him."

"And he just did what you said after all that?" Rowina asked.

"Sometimes I could get through to him. Sometimes not so much." the tears started again.

Joe and Rowina shared a look across the table.

Joe patted Julie's shoulder, "We'll leave you alone for now, but one more thing. Can you give us a list of people at the party? Just in case someone remembers something helpful."

Rowina handed her a pad and pencil.

She wrote names and numbers. "Can I go back now? I've been gone too long."

JOE MINELLI

Later that day, the detectives spoke with Dawn Madsen. She was a skinny girl and appeared much younger than the age she professed to be . . . until Joe looked closer. Those eyes said she'd lived through more than her share. She willingly entered their little room to extol her brother's virtues.

"We are so sorry that you have to be here, Miss Madsen. What can you tell us about your brother's recent activity?" Rowina asked.

"Ricky was goin through a hard time. When Julie left us, he jest fell apart. Didn't do much but work and sit on a barstool," Dawn sucked in some air, "broken heart'll do that to a man."

"Were you aware he was using drugs?"

"Yeah, I knew. He needed some numbing is all. He was in . . ." she looked at the ceiling, "anguish, yeah, that's the word for it, but he was still the best man you ever met. Took care of me and my mom all those years." her words dissolved and she reached for a Kleenex and blew her nose. "He always came when I needed him. Guess now he won't."

Rowina handed her another tissue, "Do you know a man named Redmond Wilder?"

Dawn's back went ramrod straight and her face became a sneer, "He is evil. As my Pop used to say 'lower than a snake's belly in a wagon rut.'"

"I like that description," Joe said as he covered his grin with his hand. He saw Rowina smirk a little, too. "Why do you say he is evil?"

"All he done. He tried to get Ricky in trouble. Rick was too smart to go for it. Plus, he broke his arm."

Joe was having trouble following, "Redmond broke Rick's arm?"

"No, Rick fell outta the tree."

That cleared everything up, clear as mud. Joe tried again, "So the arm had nothing to do with Mr. Wilder."

"Right. But Reddie come around looking for Rick right before the trial. He was out on bail an . . . uh," she looked at her lap this time, "he was mean . . . said mean things about Rick. He's the one did this I'll bet," she drifted off again. "I was only a little girl, a couple days before my 11th birthday."

"Your birthday?"

"Never mind. He was pure evil, that's all."

"What about your family, Miss Madsen? Anyone have a beef with Rick?"

"Nah, everybody loves Ricky, like I said. He's the best one of the family on Pop's side. Guess you heard about Pop being in jail, sombitch. My Uncle Jessie don't come round no more, but he loved Ricky. Gave him money to paint Baby."

Rowina screwed her face into a question mark.

"My momma's sisters are jest happy Rick helped with me. I was a little wild time to time . . . not that the Little Women were saints. Now . . ." Dawn stared down at her hands, twirled the ring on her finger, "He gave me this ring for Christmas, couple years ago." Her expression clouded over, a veil of devastation.

Joe rubbed his eyes. They would get nothing but non-sequiturs from her today. Normally he'd let her babble on and hope some gem of information would pop out, but time was their enemy right now so they could circle back to this one. He walked her back to her brother's room.

On the way down in the elevator, he said to Rowina, "Poor kid. He was a good brother it seems. Meant the world to her. One thing I always take from the interview room . . . everybody gives a different view. People are multi-faceted, not all evil and not all good."

"Notice she said 'Julie left *us*,' not him?"

"Yeah, and sounded like Wilder put a scare in her, too. Poor kid."

The detectives' next stop would be the home of Fred and Marilyn Friedman.

"Battered wife, I'd lay odds on it," Rowina said as they made their way through Towson. She had seen her share of domestic abuse cases, and it pissed her off. *Why do these women put up with it? I'd be out of there so fast!*

"I got that vibe, too, sounded like she was used to having to talk him off the ledge," Joe scratched the back of his neck, where the hairs were standing up. "Wonder if the roommate is *really* only a roommate. I recognize I'm old-fashioned but . . ."

"That Coke thing, I'd lay odds that was more than twice, too. Classic, drug abuse to curb domestic abuse."

"That's a thing?" Joe asked.

"That's a thing. Wilder may be the obvious choice, but my money is on the wife." Rowina looked out the window, "The other guy that threatened him at the bar? That was an awfully long time ago."

"Revenge is a dish best served cold."

"Where do you come up with this shit?" she laughed.

"How bout hell hath no fury like a woman scorned."

"Yeah, that one may fit good."

Chapter 33

DECEMBER 2, 1981

Driving the back way to the Madsen home, Julie took a road called Poplar Hill, barely two lanes that traveled from the Loch Raven Dam up and over, then down, steep and winding to Paper Mill Road. On that narrow stretch was a pair of trees—a dogwood and a weeping redbud—that had grown together. Their branches entwined as they reached for the sky—a marriage of magnificent blooms, white and magenta, mingled in haphazard symmetry—their roots and trunks bound together; a lover's embrace for eternity. She looked up the phenomenon. The scientific name was inosculation.

She always slowed to gaze upon its beauty and wondered; if one died, would the other continue? Would the survivor still bloom into the sky even with lifeless branches clutching at it? Or would the branches of the dead tree slowly strangle the living one until it could no longer bloom itself?

When Dr. Craig told her Rick showed no cerebral perfusion and it was time to decide, she thought of those trees. Even in death, she knew he would be forever clutching at her life. She prayed she had the strength to grow beyond his grip.

Julie grappled with the task at hand feeling like she was playing God. A part of her damaged psyche reveled in revenge, and though she was ashamed, she couldn't help but feel a sense of justice.

A Dr. Josefson spoke to Julie and the aunts about organ donation, and the idea of others surviving made the task easier to accept. After much persuasion, she and the aunts convinced Dawn it was a way to let him live on.

Jo told her, "That alone will earn him a place in heaven."

"He will be with Beth and Gabriel," said Meg.

The ventilator was removed and the machines turned off. The room grew quiet.

Dawn, Jo, and Meg were at his side. Julie hung back and let them say goodbye.

Dawn sobbed and threw herself over him, "Don't go!" she moaned over and over. Finally, Jo and Meg pulled her away and nodded at the nurse to take him.

Dawn backed against the wall and began twisting the ring on her finger that Rick bought her for Christmas. Julie was glad Dawn had it, a talisman from her first love, her knight in shining armor.

As they wheeled him out, Julie asked them to pause. She thought of all she'd been through with this man, only three and a half years, but it seemed like a lifetime. The song by The Who, "Behind Blue Eyes" played in her head.

She traced his profile with her fingertip and thought he finally looked at peace, "No one knows what it's like . . ."

She hoped she could also find peace.

They whisked him away to harvest his organs. To the recipients and their families, he would be a hero.

MINELLI AND LOPEZ

It was now a homicide.

"What have we got here, Lopez? Let's go down the list," said Joe Minelli as Rowina wrote names on their wall board and the headings; motive, alibi, profile.

Joe looked again at the medical and pathology reports and read parts aloud, "Evidence of intravenous and nasal narcotic use. Skull fracture, force, left rear . . . blunt object. Consistent with baseball bat . . . broken bones, left hand. The guy was left-handed. Let's see . . . The tox screen reads like a pharmacy inventory: cocaine, Demerol, Dilaudid, nicotine, ibuprofen . . . blood alcohol content . . ." Joe looked at the ceiling calculating, "Madsen was in that vehicle a good six hours before they found him, and his BAC was still .14. This guy did some drinking."

Rowina wrote a name on the board, "Number One, Redmond Wilder. Released from Jessup Prison in May. Back in the business according to narcotics. They're keeping an eye on him. They think he was passing off to Madsen to distribute."

She scanned the notes she had from the Narcotics squad. "Wilder's not so stupid that he'd sell them himself. He's on parole."

"Far as we know, a lot of it went in Madsen's arm. Hence this report." Joe gestured to the paper he was holding.

"Madsen apparently owed him money from before he was put away as well."

"Motive, money. No moral compass," Joe said. Lopez put it on the board.

"The guy has a shaky alibi—girlfriend. Bartender at the Pioneer House told us he and the girl were there Sunday night and talked to Madsen."

Joe took a cruller out of the bag, propped his feet up on the desk, and took a bite.

"Monday morning," Joe said with donut in his mouth, "he saw his PO who said he was cool as a cucumber."

"The guy is a career criminal. He knows how to play parole."

"True. Let's talk to the bartender again. Maybe his memory will be jogged now this is homicide."

Rowina noted the bartender and continued, "Let's go on to number two, the Ex."

Rowina wrote as Joe talked, "Strong suspect. Suffering, sorrow, and sacrifice; she played it well in the interview. We know he was abusive. Randall Barrett mentioned it to you, and your friend Officer Jackson was sure of it, right? Remind me, when was the domestic Jackson was called in on?"

"November 79. Jackson said the girl was a mess—bruised and scared to death. Asked them to stay until she got out of there. Yet wouldn't press charges, and the stupid girl went back! Didn't leave him until January." Rowina shook her head.

"Anyway, that's the motive."

"A *strong* motive. Especially after he held a gun to her head 24 hours before he was attacked. This is my . . ." Rowina wrote a big #1 next to the name.

"Alibi is shaky. The friend she," she made quote signs with her fingers, "lives with. He had a look down the barrel of that .38, too. He could want revenge, or maybe did it for his roomie."

Done with the donut, Joe gnawed on his pencil, "Guy's a pacifist . . . hippie type. Doesn't fit."

"Would he fake an alibi for the femme fatale?"

"Probably." Joe gnawed some more. "How bout the Mazzotti guy? We got all kinds of witnesses saying he threatened Madsen—at least twice. That gal at the bar," Joe glanced at his notebook, "Kathy, said he'd been in recently asking about Madsen."

Rowina looked at the mug shot they'd pulled of William Anthony Mazzotti, "Long time to hold a grudge . . . I know, served cold or some shit."

"If he just happened upon Madsen and had opportunity, he'd take a swing, I'll bet."

"How bout Barrett?" she asked. "The kid who was threatened. He seems incapable of premeditation but, like you say, still waters and all that."

She wrote Randall Christopher Barrett on the board.

"The guy has top-secret clearance, clean as a whistle," Joe thought a moment, "and another pacifist from what everybody said. Still . . . still waters *do* run deep. Does he have an alibi?"

"On the phone Monday, he said he was with his brother Sunday. Of course, brothers lie for each other. Both were vague . . . Randall said he had to be in New York for his new job and couldn't come to the station. I've been calling him for a follow-up to no avail."

"Now you say it, the brother, Kevin, seemed vague," Joe looked back at his notes from the Barrett brothers. "Look here, their timelines didn't match, and suddenly Randall is out of town. Let's pull him in again soon as we can."

Rowina drew a circle around Randall Christopher Barrett.

"The bartender who drove him. Anything there?"

"Nothing we've found," Joe reviewed his notes from Eric Lucas Johansson aka Cups. "Told us Madsen had calmed down. Said he talked about owing Wilder money . . . how Wilder was pressuring him to pull a heist." Joe looked at Lopez. "Tell me if I'm wrong, but the guy seemed like he genuinely cared about Madsen."

"I can agree to that. He has a solid alibi too, right?"

"Him and the two cooks, Grady Demarco and Tyrone Jones, all worked Sunday. Would have been really hard to get out there and whack him, considering the timeline. Still, everybody seemed intentionally closed mouth about him."

"Pretty tight group."

"Let's go over the Friedman interview again," Joe was tapping the pencil against the desk now.

"They're the only ones that have seemed to break from the pack, told us about the bartender driving him. And exactly where the gun was pointed."

"Low-level bookie trying to cover his own ass," Joe said. "Pretty ironic him hearing that message from Madsen the day he died. Winning that bet whittled down Madsen's debt. Took Old Freddie off the suspect list."

"Nothing on the rest of the party people. We may be barking up the wrong tree, thinking the incident is related." Rowina Lopez still had a feeling about Julie, "Let's get the ex-wife in again. She's hiding something, I feel it in my bones."

Detectives Lopez and Minelli escorted Julie into a room with a table, a few old metal chairs, and the requisite mirrored wall. Detective Joe Minelli gestured to a chair beside the table, "Please, have a seat. Coffee? Water?" He moved to a small table against the far wall and poured a coffee for himself.

"No, nothing thanks."

Detective Lopez perched her perky bottom on the edge of the table across from Julie and looked down at her clipboard, "Mrs. Madsen, will you be keeping that name . . . Madsen?"

"I'll go back to Fairburn after the divorce."

"I see. It was not an amicable split, I understand."

"What's that got to do with anything?" asked Julie.

"It goes to his demeanor . . . and yours."

"Mine? Look, I haven't slept much since . . . well, I've practically lived at the hospital. Please, just tell me what you need to know."

"Why have you kept vigil for a man who abused you, Julie?"

"Who told you that?"

Lopez's glare bored into her, "It's true, isn't it?"

"Yes . . . but I loved him. I was afraid of him, but I loved him, still do."

" . . . Monday?"

"I'm sorry, what? I lost you."

"Something on your mind?"

"A lot, actually. What the hell do you think!" Julie was losing her patience. "I've got to go. I need to sleep." She rose abruptly from the chair and it toppled over.

Lopez dropped her clipboard on the table with a clatter, "We're not done here."

"Don't bully me!" Julie's voice was loud and raw.

Joe stepped in, with his father image, set the chair right. "Mrs. Madsen, Julie, please. I know you want to catch whoever did this, just . . . other than Wilder and Mazzotti—they have alibis—who should we be looking at? You knew him best."

"But I don't anymore. I left him two years ago!" she slumped back into the chair.

"You have talked to him. He called you all the time, you told us. Then we heard about several times he barged back into your life, yes? Threatened you?" Lopez was leaning on the table, looming over it like snoopy on his dog house. Julie barked out a laugh.

"I'm sorry, is something *funny*?"

"No, sorry, I . . ." a ragged sigh, "I don't know who did this. Maybe he owed somebody besides Wilder . . ." She put a hand over her eyes, "Headache . . ."

"You bring up an excellent point, Mrs. Madsen," said Detective Minelli. "Who else did your husband do dealings with? Did he owe money elsewhere?"

"I told you before, I never knew any of that. I don't know much about drugs."

"We know Mr. Wellington said you were home all day on Sunday. What did you do that day?"

"I had a late breakfast with Craig and my brother, Will, and then Will went back to Annapolis," she ran her fingers through her hair, recounting her day, "watched the football game, I took a shower. Craig and I well . . . we watched TV . . . and I went to bed early."

"What time?"

"Not sure. After 'Archie Bunker.' Wait, then that next show . . . 'One Day at a Time,' the one about the single mother."

Joe believed Julie, even though his partner had a hard-on for pinning this on her. *Do I say 'hard-on' for a woman detective?* He scratched his head and scanned his notes again, "We know he testified against his father at trial. Any family members take exception to that?"

"Floyd's family is just about all dead, or in jail. The Ackermans hated him."

"There is a brother. Jessie?"

Julie thought a minute, rubbed her neck, slumped into the chair, "He liked Rick. Didn't like Floyd so well, so no."

Joe consulted his notebook, "Rick's sister, Dawn, agrees with that."

"You talked to Dawn?"

Rowina said, "We spoke with her at the hospital."

Joe said, "What about the sister of Floyd. Bonnie? Seems there were letters from her."

Julie sat up straight, and her eyes got round, "Oh my God! You have the letters?"

"Yep."

"Well, I need to get them back! It's . . . you didn't say anything to Dawn did you?"

"No, we hadn't read them yet. Why? Dawn doesn't know about her?"

"No, she doesn't, and besides Bonnie is dead. I want to spare Dawn all that sordid family history."

"I can understand that. What those letters intimated . . ." Joe's meaty hand ran across his jaw as he thought about what he had read and what it would do to young Dawn, "I assure you I will keep their contents to myself."

Julie blew breath out the side of her mouth, "Thanks . . . I'd hoped they weren't somewhere she'd find them. Can I have them back?"

Joe legally shouldn't give them to Julie, but he didn't want them getting into the wrong hands, either.

"Of course, I'll see they go directly to you."

Detective Lopez broke in, "Now that we're done talking about what we aren't going to talk about, can we get back on track?" She glared at Joe from under her lashes, clearly irritated to be out of the loop.

"Of course, where were we?"

"Barrett," said Rowina, pointing to her clipboard.

"What about this Randy fellow? Rick threatened his life. Would he retaliate?" Joe asked in a low, even tone.

Julie looked up with wide puppy eyes, "Oh, no, no, absolutely not Randy! He idolized Rick. And he's the kindest person . . ." she started crying.

Joe watched her react to the name. *She's got a thing for the guy! After Madsen, 'still waters' must be appealing . . .*

He handed her a tissue and sat, waiting to see if anything pertinent would squeak out in her emotional state.

Lopez took a step forward, but Joe waved her back, warning not to get too close. Sorrow uncorked needed a chance to breathe. Sure enough, she began to babble.

"Randy and I have been friends since seventh grade. Well, he moved and came back. We just picked up like no . . . no time passed, you know . . . like you do with good friends." She sniffed, wiped her eyes, "He . . . he's got that nice girlfriend now . . ." and the tears came again.

She's wrung out. He felt sorry for the kid, all she'd been through. *If she did it,* Madsen deserved it, "Ok, you've had a rough week. Detective Lopez, maybe we should resume after she's had a couple hours sleep." *We need to find Barrett. See how deep those still waters go.*

"Sure, go home, Julie," Lopez said with a sigh. "But, Julie . . ."

"What?"

"Don't leave town."

Chapter 34

Julie was surprised when they called her in. She'd told all she knew, but they kept badgering her. In the hospital before he . . . officially died, they kept at her: 'just one more thing,' 'could you confirm,' blah, blah, and she couldn't clear the cobwebs from her mind. *Now, were they accusing her?*

Julie heard Beth talking in her head. "*I loved him, still do.*" *Do you, Beth? Still love Floyd after he killed you? Is that the only way you could let go? Is killing Rick the only way I could?*

She wanted suddenly and powerfully to get out of there, the walls were closing in.

She sprung from the chair like it was on fire. Hot tears rolled down her cheeks, rubbing salt in her wounds.

Craig was waiting just outside the interrogation area and stood when she pushed her way out the door.

"Get me out of here."

He hurried along beside her to the car, "What?" he unlocked the door and Julie bundled herself in and slammed it.

"Julie, what?" he asked when he was behind the wheel.

"Just get me home!" She dissolved.

Once they were in the door, Julie threw her coat off and started talking, "That bitch said, 'Don't leave town.' I feel like I'm on Columbo or something!"

"I told them you were with me. I can't believe they would think . . ." Craig said.

"She's got it in for me. Don't know why," Julie plopped onto the sofa. "But the list goes on. First, they asked about Randy. Again, why? I haven't been able to get in touch with him, have you?"

"Kevin said he got the promotion and split to NYC."

"Without saying goodbye?" her eyebrows knitted together. "Anyway, then I thought about Cups. Rick owed him money! He was the last of us to see him!"

"You don't think he would do this, do you?"

"Of course not, he loved Rick. Stayed close with him when everybody else drifted away. But they don't know the whole story."

Her mind whirred. She surveyed the room. It was a mess. Empty glasses on the table, crumbs on the floor, wedding flowers from Will's car wilting on the dining room table. That reminded her there were still gifts in her car.

"Come on, I think better when I'm busy."

"What?" Craig asked as she pulled him out the door.

"Let's get those gifts out of my car. Then we are gonna clean the house."

"My favorite activity," said Craig with a sarcastic grin.

Julie popped the trunk. They carried packages into the house and returned for more. When Craig lifted the last of them out, Julie stared into the trunk, empty except for an ice scraper.

"Huh, where is it?" she said.

"What?"

"The Ball Buster, where is it?"

She looked in the back seat and around the car.

"Last I saw, Randy was holding it."

Julie stopped searching and looked at Craig, "Randy?"

"Yeah, don't you remember? Saturday night."

She envisioned him, a hateful look across his features, wielding the bat.

She ran her fingers through her hair, trying to remember, "What did he do with it after that?"

"I don't know. Maybe he carried it into the house? Or just left it there by the car," Craig worried through the chain of events. "I don't remember. Wait, you think that's the weapon?"

"Ironic, if it is, huh? They said the wounds looked like a bat did it."

"Well, Randy didn't do it."

Julie shut the trunk and he followed her into the house.

"Let's think about this. The cops think it was someone from that night. They aren't saying why."

"So?"

"Could they have the bat? Do they know about it? Would they tell us?"

"No, they wouldn't tell us if we are suspects."

"Randy's fingerprints will be on it. Probably mine and yours, too."

"Let's be rational here. We don't know what happened to it. The odds are it's just a coincidence. Let's see if it's at Freddie's. I'll call over there."

Craig dialed the phone and held the receiver tilted so Julie could hear. Marilyn answered, "Hey, weird question, is Julie's bat sitting around over there?"

"What? Bat?"

"You know, the Ball Buster. From her trunk. It's not in the car."

"Oh! I get it now. No, I haven't seen it. Randy had it Saturday. He probably just flung it down. Why?"

"No big deal, really. You know how things bug you when you can't find them. It's a mystery, that's all."

"Oh," Marilyn laughed, "Rick used to say that. 'It's a fouckin' mystery!' remember?" she started crying. "Sorry, we just heard he's gone. I can't believe it."

"I know. It's tough," Craig looked at Julie. *What else was there to say?*

"Any funeral arrangements yet?"

"Not yet, let you know when the family tells us."

"I guess Julie is beside herself. After the way she was with him on Saturday. I kept hoping they would get back together."

"Just let us know if the bat turns up, ok?" Craig was done with this conversation, "See you." He hung up.

"No bat."

"Call Kevin."

"Julie—"

"Call Kevin! I need to know where it is!"

Craig dialed the phone, mumbling under his breath. Kevin answered.

"Hey there, weird question . . . You know what happened to the Ball Buster, after Randy had it?"

"Shit, man, he just dropped it, I think. What's going on?"

"Julie is concerned. It's missing and well Rick's uh, head."

"Christ! The cops don't know about it, do they? That Randy had it?"

"Not that we know of. It probably has nothing to do with it."

"It sounds bad, though. Fuck! I already lied for him when I said he was with me. Val was asleep so she went along with what I said.

He didn't come home until midnight . . . said he was driving and thinking. He asked Jen to move to New York with him."

"Heavy, man."

"Yeah . . ."

Julie had been listening in, and a shiver ran through her. This was all so surreal! Her head was spinning and her legs threatened to give out.

Craig took her by the shoulders, "Don't let this get to you on top of everything else. No one at the wedding did this. The bat has nothing to do with it."

"I'm calling Cups, give him a heads up." She turned away from Craig's imploring looks and punched in the number. After four rings, he answered.

"Thank God!"

"Julie? What's up?"

"I just got questioned by the police again. They asked about Rick owing money!"

"So?"

"Just I know he owed you."

"What are you trying to say here?"

"Oh! I don't think you did it!"

She saw Craig shake his head and roll his eyes.

"I hope not, you're the one who put me in that car!"

"I know that . . . I'm so sorry how things worked out, but . . . I just want you to know. I didn't say anything, about . . . you know."

"Well. Thanks for that, but I was working Sunday night so I'm off the hook."

"Thank God! Ok, sorry."

"Julie, chill! Get some sleep. You're talking like a madwoman."

"You're right. My brain is fried. I'm gonna take a nap."

She hung up the phone.

"Good idea, baby, you need sleep." Craig held her a minute and walked her to the sofa.

Julie kicked off her shoes, curled up, and drifted off to dreamland, a place filled with detectives wielding baseball bats.

CUPS

Cups didn't tell her the whole story about Sunday night. Thought it best she didn't know, considering her mental state.

When he and Gravy came home, the front door was unlocked. Nothing seemed to be missing: TV and stereo untouched, Gravy's jar of coins intact. The only things missing belonged to Cups. A baggie of Coke and $240 in cash was gone from his hiding place. Few people knew where he kept his stash. Besides the super, only one person they knew of ever had access to the key. Both pointed to Rick.

Cups recounted the drive on Saturday night to Gravy, "I asked him where to, he told me the Pioneer House. It was eerie how calm he was, considering . . . I guess that was the Julie effect."

"She had that effect on him, that or the opposite." Gravy said, "I've seen Julie talk him down but also witnessed Rick's rage turning on her, yelling in her face. Speaking of the opposite, what about the gun?"

"He tried to hand it to me soon as we got away from the curb. Told me to put it under the seat, but I didn't wanna touch the sucker. Told him to put it in the glove box."

"Did he partake of your bag on the way?"

"Yeah, he snorted some. Then you could see his brain pop into gear. You know the look."

"Yep. You think his little light bulb going on told him to rob you?"

"He started talking about how he owed Wilder and Fred. He wanted to get out from under that. Said Wilder wanted him to hit a drug store and he couldn't do that. Talked about disappointing Julie. The whole thing was hard to follow. Bottom line, he knew where he could find money or at least product—here."

"To pay off Wilder. Wonder if he ever got a chance to do that?"

"I don't know, but I ain't gonna ask Wilder. And I damn sure ain't gonna tell the cops!"

Gravy scratched his head, "If he did pay him off, does that let Wilder off the hook for the murder?"

MINELLI AND LOPEZ

The forensics report finally arrived. Joe guessed now that it was a homicide, it got legs.

Fingerprints in the Bronco matched the victim, the bartender who drove him from the wedding, and Wilder. Even better, the pipe in the ashtray had Wilder all over it.

Ballistics said the gun was operable and partially loaded. The hospital had erased any evidence of powder from the hands when they tended to his wounds.

The three sets of tire tracks were also analyzed. One was the vehicle of the victim, one the truck of the man who found Madsen, and the third were

185/70 SR14 tires. Minelli had an officer get a list of cars that wore those tires. In the meantime, he called for a warrant to search Wilder's residence.

Then he and Lopez took a drive to the Pioneer House to talk with Bartender Lou. The night shift was just coming on at 5:00. Joe pulled up a stool and ordered a beer. Rowina asked for a coke.

"How ya doing on the case, detective?" he asked as he tapped a draft and sat it in front of Joe.

"Now a homicide."

"Aw, that's too bad. I really liked Ricky. He was a good guy. I'll never forget the day I had to pull him off his father."

"Tell us about that, would you?" said Rowina as she wiped a smudge from the rim of her glass with a tissue.

"Floyd was sitting on that stool," he pointed, "the one that Rick always sits on when he comes in now . . . Aw, sorry he *sat* on . . . anyhow, he was in a snit over something his little girl did. Stole his cigarettes, I think it was. Had himself a couple bourbons and was mumbling to himself. When Rick come in the door, looking for him. Man, he had fire in his eyes, I tell ya," Lou gazed at the empty stool, remembering, "Ricky stalked over to Floyd and hauled him off that stool like he was a rag doll . . . Strong sombitch he was. Said something like, 'Don't ever hit my sister or I'll kill you.' Well, he almost kilt him right then! Took three of us to pull him off, and by then Floyd was pulp."

Lou rubbed at a spot on the bar with his rag, "I gained respect for the boy that day. Standing up for his little sister. Looking back, shame he didn't kill Floyd. His mother'd still be alive and maybe he would, too." Lou wiped at his eyes with the rag and cleared his throat.

"I'll tell you, Lou, you could be a big help in this case. Tell us exactly what went on in here Sunday night."

"I talked it over with George since you been in. He was sitting over there that night," he pointed to the other side of the bar, "put our notes together, so to speak. Anyhow, Rick was sitting on his stool. Having a drink when Wilder and his sleazy girl come in, like I told you before. They started talking, then . . . this is the part I forgot . . . but George remembered . . . Rick paid up, and he and Red went out the door. Left Sleazy here. She was pissed when Red told her to 'sit!' just like she was a dog, he did!" Lou laughed.

Joe did, too, "So did they come back?"

"Wilder did. Rick didn't." Lou got a look on his face like he just figured something out.

"How long was he gone, Wilder?" asked Lopez.

"Jeesh, let's see. The girl had two more beers waiting—she drinks fast, but 3 beers? Maybe half hour? Wait, she went to the payphone, too. Called somebody but got no answer. So, 45 minutes, it coulda been."

"Anybody leave around that time that could tell us whether they left the parking lot together?"

"Hmm, not that I remember. Weren't too many in here. George and a few others that stayed till close. One guy I never seen before. Had a drink and left. Paid cash. Only remember him because he left a good tip. Couldn't say he woulda seen anything. They probably woulda been gone by the time he left."

"Was he any of these guys?" Ramona showed him photos of their possible suspects. Lou looked them over carefully.

"No, none of those fellas were in here Sunday, nor any other night that I know of."

"You've been very helpful, sir. May have wrapped this case for us."

The detectives got up to leave and Joe threw a twenty on the bar, "Keep the change." To Rowina, he said, "Let's time how long it takes to get there and back, with time for a murder in between. If it's under 45 minutes, I bet we got our man."

After they confirmed it was indeed possible for Wilder to commit the crime, they picked up the search warrant and raided Wilder's house.

Nobody was home, so they busted the lock. The place was a dive. Dirty clothes and dishes everywhere. No drug items out on display, but after digging a bit, they came up with a couple syringes and pipes. Then they hit the jackpot. In the back of the closet was a box with bottles of pharmaceuticals, several kinds—with *PARKVILLE PHARMACY* on the label.

"Dummy didn't even change out the bottles," said Joe with a lopsided grin, "how he got caught the first time."

In the bottom drawer, under a pile of old tee-shirts, was a baggie of rock cocaine and an antique pocket watch engraved inside—*Henry Ackerman, 1924.*

"Rick's grandfather, I bet." Lopez slipped it into an evidence bag. "Must have grown legs and walked here."

"Wilder must have knocked Madsen over the head and taken what was owed him."

When they returned to the station, a list of vehicles was lying on Minelli's desk.

"We got the third car right here," he said and read down the list. "Chrysler Lebaron, Audi, Dodge Charger, Datsun 200 . . . What kind of car does Wilder drive?"

Lopez looked over the notes, "A 1972 Buick Skylark."

"Bingo!" A wide grin spread over Joe's face.

"On the list?" she asked.

He turned the paper to face her and pointed. She had a sudden urge to kiss the old fart! *Ah, what the hell . . .* She planted one on his stubbly cheek.

"We got robbery, felony drug charges, and a real good case for murder." Joe was practically doing a jig, "Honey, we got the bad guy!"

Chapter 35

1982

Redmond Wilder was convicted of the murder of Richard Henry Madsen in March 1982, just three days shy of Rick's 29th birthday. The trial lasted three days and the courtroom was packed with press and supporters of both the victim and the accused.

There was a woman that sat in the back row and always left before the end of the day's proceedings. She was striking; dark curls pulled up and cascading down the back of her head, high cheekbones, and a strong jaw that framed full pouty lips. She wore sunglasses when she entered, but Julie noticed when she removed them, her eyes were big and dark—dark as black ice. She was a Madsen.

Julie was in the courtroom holding Dawn's hand when the verdict was read. As they turned to leave the room, she saw the woman slip out ahead of the crowd. They walked out with the Aunts, cousins, and friends to a barrage of reporters on the courthouse steps. The trial was getting coverage because of the Wilder family's criminal infamy and the Madsen family tree.

From the top of the courthouse steps, Julie saw the woman cross the street. She hopped up on the side wall so she could see above the crowd. Before the woman disappeared around the corner, she turned and saw Julie watching her, smiled and raised her hand, a sort of wave. Julie waved back to the woman with Rick's smile. Bonnie Madsen was alive and well.

The night of the conviction, Julie had supper with her parents, Will and Diane.

"This chapter is finally over," Harry said as he raised his glass of wine. "Let's toast to moving forward!"

"I'll drink to that," Will said, and drank down half his glass. Diane gave him a worried look and sipped from her own.

"I'm thinking of going back to college," Julie said.

"Here, here! I'll even pay for it!" said Harry.

Evie sighed loudly, as if she'd been holding her breath for a very long time, "Oh, thank goodness. What a wonderful idea!"

"Let's see, with credit from your classes before," Diane's math brain was whirring, "you could do it in two semesters! Will can put in a good word at Marriott when you're ready, can't you Will?" Diane nudged Will's arm.

"What? Oh sure, anything you say, Di."

"Where are you tonight? I swear, you are always off in your head lately!"

"Just thinking about the trial. Can't imagine being in jail for 25 years."

"Well, I hope he rots there! Now let's eat!" said Evie, cheerfully.

That night Julie snuggled into her bed, thinking she could finally move forward. The next thing she knew Rick was at the door.

"Miss me, darlin'?"

"No, go away! You're dead!" she yells out, but it comes out a whisper.

"Ain't goin nowhere, darlin'. You are stuck with me forever." He laughs, then his eyes go wide . . . his head caves in, a bloody soufflé.

Randy is behind him in a coat of armor, holding a silver bat.

On April fool's day, Julie awoke to Craig calling her name,

"Julie, phone!

She staggered out of bed and took the receiver, "Hello?"

"You're going to be an aunt!"

"Huh? Wait, Colleen?"

"Yes!"

"Oh My God! Craig, get tea! I need to hear details!"

A confused Craig wandered back to the kitchen and poured iced tea, lots of ice, and lemon.

"When? Tell all!" Julie screamed. Colleen was pregnant. The baby was due in November, just in time to celebrate his parents' first anniversary.

Three of Craig's songs were picked up by a popular singer, Tamyra Shepherd. He flew out to LA in early April to meet with her and her people and sign a contract. He spent the next couple months working out arrangements with Tamyra and the band. Seems she took a liking to him and wanted him to sit in on the recording.

With Craig spending so much time in LA, Julie was lonely, so when one of the regulars at Sh'nanigans asked her out, she said yes. He was recently separated and had two young daughters. She enjoyed her time with him, especially when the girls were along. They went to the circus and the zoo; took day trips to Harpers Ferry and Hershey Park. It reinforced how much she wanted her own children, but David wasn't ready to commit. He wanted to date around, and she didn't blame him being newly single, but she wasn't into that kind of relationship. Although she would surely miss those girls, she broke it off.

Her friends were all moving on with their lives. Kevin and Val finally got married, *after* their twins were born, and were happily bickering about child raising. Gravy met the love of his life and was living in sin. Cups was still bartending but had been scared straight by the events of the wedding weekend. He was keeping his nose clean. Eddie scored his dream job, as an entertainer for a cruise line and sent postcards from exotic ports of call. Randy was still in New York with Jenifer and a rising star at Grumman. Julie felt she was just spinning her wheels.

In July, Craig got a call from Tamyra Shepherd's manager saying her lead guitarist was in an auto accident. Could Craig fill in on their national tour? If things worked out, it could be a permanent gig.

Craig was nervous about the whole social aspect, but Julie pushed him, "You have to do this, it's no different from playing anywhere, your guitar will still be right there in front of you, a stringed shield."

"It's when we are off stage I'm not so sure of. I'll have to face multitudes."

"Just act weird or stoned like every other rock star! They expect it, and you can call me anytime you need a pep talk."

"Maybe Randy will invent a phone you could carry with you, like in your pocket. Then I could call you from the road when I get jammed up, and you could ramble on for me," he laughed.

"Good job title for me—official rambler-oner!"

In the fall, she started taking classes again. This time was not a race to a Degree. Julie truly enjoyed going to class, and absorbed everything her professors had to offer. She had missed out on the college experience and was determined to get everything out of it she could.

She went out with a guy in her cooking class a couple times. He was 21 but seemed like such a kid. Her experiences made it hard to relate to most of the other fresh-faced students. She felt jaded.

Kevin introduced her to a guy from work. He was nice but wanted to party hard on the weekends. She was done with the party hard life. She broke it off.

Craig started calling her Ruby Tuesday because she was blowing in the wind, changing direction day to day.

1983

Julie hadn't seen much of Dawn. They chatted on the phone at Christmas, but it was awkward small talk. That's why Julie was surprised when she picked up the phone and heard Dawn's voice.

"I got news," she said. "I'm pregnant! Due in May."

"Wow! That is news! You sound happy."

"I am over the moon happy. The father ain't, sombitch, but that makes it better. Don't gotta be putting up with him butting in."

Julie laughed, "You don't need him, I'm sure you will be just fine."

"I been goin to church a lot, that helps me, and Meg retired and begged me to move in with her. She's gonna watch the baby while I finish barber school. It's a boy, by the way, gonna name him Richard Henry Madsen."

A guy at the gym asked her out and they dated a few months. Maybe, she thought, this is the one. It all seemed perfect until . . .

They were in the heat of passion and he spanked her butt, not hard—she was sure it was playful so she let it slide.

The next time they made love, he flipped her over and knelt behind her. She was losing herself in sensation when he pulled her head back by her hair and *SMACK!* His hand hit hard against her ass and *SMACK!* harder on her thigh. Julie was transported back to Rick. She twisted her body away and scrambled from the bed.

"What's wrong?" he was blocking the door. She couldn't breathe, her vision blurred, her heart was bursting.

He reached out to her.

"Get away," She whimpered and collapsed against the wall.

After she'd calmed down, she tried to explain, but he didn't understand.

"I wasn't being abusive, a smack on the butt? Come on, Julie! It was a love tap."

That was the end of that relationship.

She ached for the intimacy she shared with Craig, but his music life had taken off like a rocket and now he was not just Tamyra Shepherd's guitar man; he was her lover. Craig told her that Tam, as he called her, had invited him to her room one night on the road and they'd been sharing a room ever since. He tried to downplay how head-over-heels he was, but Julie had witnessed them on stage together at their concert in DC. She could tell he had found love. She was happy for him, but she missed him and although she would never tell him—when she heard Tamyra singing "Dalliance" on the radio, she switched the station.

With all the money rolling in, Craig needed an investment, so he bought the house on Willow Haven Court.

He came home for settlement and they went to the Prime Rib downtown for a celebratory dinner.

Craig raised his glass, "This is just what my anxiety-riddled ass has needed—an Anchor."

Julie said, "A what?"

"Look, living on tour is exciting. Playing my music for multitudes . . . and Tam is great…" he sat his glass down, and his shoulders relaxed. "Knowing I have a home somewhere, an anchor, relieves the anxiety like you wouldn't believe."

Julie smiled over her wineglass.

"I'm hoping you'll keep living there. You will won't you?" he asked, his eyes searching hers. Then with his show voice he said, "You can be the official caretaker, rent-free of course!"

"That's the best offer I've had in years!"

1984

Julie finally got her AA degree and got a job as Banquet Manager at Hunt Valley Golf Club. The job called for many hours but Craig was in LA or on the road most of the time and the house was lonely. She dated guys, one after the other, but the magic wasn't there with any of them.

After one of her breakups, she called Craig in tears, in need of his calming voice.

"Why does everything seem to slip through my fingers?" she cried.

He said, "You know you urged Rick to a counselor, and though that never worked out, you could see someone now."

"I don't know . . ."

"My dearest Ruby, I will listen and love you, but I'm no expert. You need some guidance. It's been years and you are more wounded than you know."

"And you are more wise than you know. Ok, I'll look into it."

There was a place on Charles Street, a women's counseling center. Julie made an appointment.

What she learned about her life over the next few months surprised her.

The therapist's name was Carolyn Hiraoko. She was easy to talk to and Julie filled her in on her background and marriage.

"I come from a very loving family. No abuse, no history of anything abnormal. Why did I marry a man who abused me? Why did I stay there?"

"Not all abuse comes from past abuse. It seems that Rick's did, and probably his father's before him. It was learned behavior and a defense mechanism: beat or be beat."

Carolyn leaned forward in her chair, "Let's look at your history. You told me your father and brothers were the most important people in your life growing up. Your father went on business trips often. Both brothers, with their wives who were like sisters to you, moved away. Your first boyfriend joined the Navy. The next one went away to college. Now think about your friends. Where are they?"

"Well, there's Colleen. We don't see each other as much. She's so busy with work and the kids. Randy moved away. Twice. I miss him more than I ever thought I would. He hasn't even returned my calls. All I get are generic notes in Christmas cards. Craig is always on the road. I'm happy for him but . . . Val and Kev moved to the Eastern Shore. Even Liz moved away." Julie sat a minute, then looked up wide-eyed, "Everybody leaves me!"

She pondered the revelation for a minute. She could add Beth and Dawn to that list, too. "I do have trouble letting go of people. It's from this?"

"Let's say your fear of abandonment is great."

Julie thought it made sense. She always clung to relationships, friends, as well as lovers.

Maybe that's partly why she couldn't let go of Rick.

Another session . . .

"Why did you choose Rick in the first place?"

"I don't know, I was dazzled by him, and have to admit, liked the bad boy vibe."

"But you didn't go looking for an abuser."

"Of course not."

"He didn't show you that side of him until you were already hip-deep, so to speak."

Julie said through an ironic grin, "I was neck deep."

"Now, what were his positive traits?"

"Well, he was smart and self-reliant. Never saw anyone work as hard as he did. He protected his mom and sister, would do anything for them. Was always helping out his friends, too."

"His friends looked up to him, did they?"

"Oh yes, at least before he lost his way. Course he was older than everybody, too."

"Your father was a strong personality. He protected you, took care of every aspect of your family, am I right?"

"Yes, he was larger than life, but in a good way."

"Of course, a good way. Perhaps you were seeing that strength and protection in Rick. He was self-reliant, watched out for his family, the patriarch of the friends' group," she paused a minute to let it sink in.

"When his flaws appeared, however horrible they were, you thought you could fix them."

"By giving him the kind of love, I had always known. Unconditional love." Julie felt a veil lift from her thoughts. "I couldn't fix him."

"He had deep psychological damage and no one could fix that for him. You need to stop blaming yourself for that." Carolyn said in her kind manner. "He left you terribly wounded, physically and emotionally. No one can fix that for you, not Colleen or Craig, not your father or brothers, and certainly not a new love. You must do it on your own. Until you do, you'll be carrying all that baggage with you."

Though they had diminished, memories crept in when least expected, and nightmares of Rick still haunted her. They probably would for the rest of her life. Her challenge was to come to terms with what she had lived through and hope she could grow as a person because of it.

Julie did a lot of soul-searching—examined her scars and her relationships. She needed connection. It was almost an addiction, she hated so much to be alone. Craig had been her safety net, and she loved him. She could imagine a life with him. But he had a new, exciting life, the one he deserved. It wasn't fair for her to cling to him.

Each time she felt the smallest spark with a man, she latched on, optimistic that this was the one. But something was always missing, something was always flawed. She broke up with them before they left her.

Fear of Abandonment. Now I know, so how do I tackle it?

Julie figured out it out. To be okay, she needed to learn how to be okay on her own.

Chapter 36

MAY 1985

C olleen, swung baby Lilly onto her hip and hollered out the back door to Pete and Peter, "Come in from the sprinkler. The guests will be here soon!"

They were having a cookout with the old gang.

Colleen smiled as she swatted Peter through the kitchen and handed Lilly off to Pete.

"Go on, Daddy will help you dress."

Walt, in town on business, sat at the kitchen table cutting vegetables while she made hamburgers.

"Catch me up on everything. I've been so out of touch with everybody."

"Well, I suppose you know Val and Kevin's twins are starting preschool in the fall. They haven't settled on where yet. He wants to move back to Baltimore, but she likes Cambridge."

"That sounds like them," he said. "I still get a chuckle that the babies were at their wedding. They gotta be what—three?"

"Yep. They were three in February."

"I guess you've heard about Craig. Left Tamyra Shepherd after the tour ended but stayed out there and does session work, whatever that is. Julie says it's his dream job. I haven't seen him in ages, but he comes home every so often. Bought that house that Julie lives in so he'd have a landing pad, I guess. The whole thing is strange. He's got his LA life but can't let go of Baltimore."

"Probably can't let go of Julie. I can understand that," Walt said. "Speaking of Julie . . . She settled down yet?"

"Oh, our Julie! Pete jokes he's going to buy her a revolving door," she said with a sparkle in her voice. "First it was the guy with the kids. Then, the restaurant owner. After that was, let's see . . . the sailor, the bookie, the teacher—not sure of the order."

"She's just playing the field, huh?"

"No, she truly loved a couple of them in some way but . . . it's always flawed. Rick damaged her in so many ways. Her men either can't understand where she's coming from or they're damaged themselves."

Walt gazed down at the carrots he was cutting and tried to clear the lump in his throat.

"So, who's the lucky man this week?" he attempted a laugh, but it fell short and only a "Ha" came out.

"Nobody right now. Last one was a golf pro, wanted her to travel the circuit. She wouldn't go for that. She has that great job at Marriott."

They heard the front door open and in walked the devil herself. Julie saw Walt, threw her packages on the counter, and jumped on him, "Walt! It's been too long!"

Walt was thrown off balance by her force and bumped against the counter. Then he lifted her from the floor and kissed her sweet cheek, "That's the best hello I've had in a long time!" He set her down and patted her head, took in her smile.

"What can I help with?" she spied the carrots Walt was attempting to cut. "Here, let me do that," she took the knife from him and had them sliced before he blinked.

"Learned some fancy stuff in that school, I see," said Walt. "Here, show me celery!"

Julie laughed and explained the fine art of slicing, "See, if you hold it like this . . ."

The doorbell rang, and they heard Pete say hello to the arrivals. Two seconds later a tornado of kids swept through and out the back door, all arms, legs, and laughter. Behind them came Val and Kevin, and Gravy, carrying his six-month-old son. Ruth and her girlfriend, Patti, strolled in next. They were excited to tell about the house they were renovating.

"These old row house neighborhoods are going to be the next big thing because of the Inner Harbor Renovation," Ruth said. "You ought to get in on the ground floor."

Julie thought that was a smart move if she could scrape up the down payment. It would be exciting to live in the city and work at the downtown Marriott. She'd have to look into that idea.

Everyone followed the kids out back for appetizers and drinks.

Julie begged to take the baby from Gravy and had him on her lap, cooing and burbling with him.

"Hey, it's the wayward son!" Pete said.

Julie looked up from the drooling angel. There was Randy, handsome as ever, shaking hands, patting little heads, and making his way to her.

Julie hadn't spoken to him for years. Cards were his only communication. He and Jenifer came back for Kev's wedding, but he barely spoke to her. Colleen said to give him his space; they needed to respect the fact that he had moved on without them. She respected that—but there was a hole in her life without him.

Colleen took the baby from her so she could stand to greet him. Before she got all the way to her feet, he had his arms around her.

He kissed her square on the lips, "I've missed this face!"

Pete handed him a beer, "How goes life in DC? You settled in?"

Randy took the beer but kept one arm around her, "Yes, I have a fantastic apartment. I can see the monument from the balcony," he turned to Julie. "I'm on contract at the Pentagon. Just moved to DC last week."

Colleen plopped the baby on Gravy's lap and scurried back over with a conspiring look on her face, "So good to see you, Randy. Wasn't sure if you could make it."

"Now that I'm only an hour away, I hope to be coming to Baltimore more often."

"You are always welcome to stay here if you can handle the chaos," Colleen smiled at Julie, a quick twitch of face that was their Morse code. "Pete, start the grill, people are hungry."

Pete got the Morse code, too, and followed his wife to the grill.

"DC, that's exciting!" Julie said to Randy. His arm was still at her waist, "I'd ask to hear all about it, but then you'd have to kill me."

Randy smiled, "Couldn't do that, could I?"

"Where's Jen? She didn't come with you?"

"We split a while ago. She stayed in Oyster Bay, I moved closer to the city."

Randy and Jenifer had been living in Oyster Bay, Long Island where Jenifer found a job at an insurance agency. Randy was a star at Grumman and loved doing his part for the Department of Defense but worked long hours. Many nights, he went right from work to his grad classes. When he returned home, exhausted but happy, Jenifer would be waiting with a list of complaints that put a pin in his happy bubble.

Jenifer hated how they lived. She hated insurance, all numbers and paperwork. She wanted to get married, but Randy wasn't ready. She hated that he was gone all the time and knew she was a nag, but she was miserable. When they were together, all she *could* do was complain. Then she began an affair with her boss and stopped talking to Randy altogether.

Julie reached up and wove her fingers through Randy's cropped hair, "I like it short. You look like a grown-up."

Julie noticed Colleen casting furtive glances their way. She waved her away and picked up her cup. "Come sit with me on the glider," she said to Randy, "I want to hear about life in The Big Apple and the nation's capital."

By the end of the evening, they had plans to tour the Smithsonian the following weekend.

RANDY AND JULIE

Julie met Randy at his condo in Crystal City on Saturday morning. She parked in the garage and took the elevator to the 10th floor. He opened the door at her first tap.

"You're here! Good, come on in."

"I wasn't so sure about the weather yesterday, but I think the rain has ended," she said. "It's a perfect day out there!"

He took her in and said, "Yes, perfect."

She looked out the sliding doors at the view, "Beautiful."

"Yes," standing behind her, he admired her admiring the view.

"What shall we do first? I haven't been to DC since our school trip. Ha! Just realized I was with you, CR!"

"It's RC, ya know," Randy felt a warmth spread through him right up to his grin and saw Julie was grinning, too. "It's so nice out, let's do the zoo."

"Great idea!" She raised her arm in front of her like a trunk and made a trumpet sound.

"Yes, they have elephants. And lions and tigers and bears."

"Oh, my," they said together.

On the way to the bathroom before their departure, she peeked in the room set up as a home office.

"Oh, my gosh! You have a computer? I mean, we have them at work but I don't know anybody that has one at home."

Randy leaned against the door frame, arms crossed across his chest, and watched her marvel over the electronic beast on his desk. *I'm not the little brother anymore.* He smiled, "Maybe later you can play around on it."

"Cool! I won't look at any of your secrets, promise. You won't have to kill me."

"Good, I haven't had to kill anyone in a long time. But it may be fun interrogating you," he came at her with fingers moving.

"Oh, no, you don't!" Julie skirted around him and ran giggling into the bathroom, "Ha!" she said and shut the door.

They spent the day among the animals, reminiscing and catching up. Their natural cadence fell into place like they'd never been apart. She was his same Julie, but something was different about her. He couldn't put his finger on it. *Perhaps we've just grown up.*

"It has indeed been a perfect day," Julie said. "Now feed me, I'm hungry!"

"You will never change," he laughed. "Come on, I made us a reservation."

They took the metro to The Capital Grille.

The maitre d' greeted Randy like an old friend, he'd been in here with Senator Goldwater just last week. He was called in to work out the technical aspects of the Goldwater-Nichols Act, the Government was relying on computers and guys like Randy for everything.

"Frank, this is Julie, my very best friend."

Julie smiled at that introduction. *Some things withstand the test of time.*

He took her hand, "Lovely to meet you. We have a special table for you tonight, just this way," they followed. Frank pulled out her chair and handed menus, "a drink for the lady?"

Randy said, "Wine? Still like Chardonnay?"

She nodded.

"A bottle of Trefethen Chard, Frank. And a couple crab cocktails, the lady is hungry!" he smiled at her.

Dinner was magnificent. They lingered over dessert and Irish coffee in honor of Colleen. "You know she's in a dither over me being here. I wasn't going to tell her, but you spilled the beans."

"Couldn't help it, she badgered me!" Their laughter mingled and Randy reached for her hand on the table, "You are staying tonight, yes? It's too far to drive. I have a guest room."

"I would love to stay, but not necessarily in the guest room." She waggled her brows at him and he ducked his head, wearing a tentative smile.

When they got back to the apartment, Julie pulled him onto the balcony to look at the monument in its nighttime glory.

"Thank you, this has been the best day I've had since I can remember," she said.

"For me, too, this is a great place to live, but I admit I've been lonely."

Julie wrapped her arms around his neck, stood on her toes to put her cheek against his. Then gave him the kiss he had dreamed of for 15 years.

When they parted, he looked in her eyes, took a deep breath before he could articulate, "Julie, I can't take this any farther unless . . ." He shook his head, "I want you to stay tonight, but I can't be what Craig was." In their conversation earlier in the day, Julie had touched on her friendship arrangement with Craig.

"Ok, I get it."

"No, I don't think you do," he turned away, thought a moment, and turned back. "I want to make love with you, Oh God, I want it so badly!" he slid a lock of hair behind her ear, "but not unless its Love, with a capital 'L.' I know it sounds like junior high, but that's the only way to differentiate . . . That's how I feel about you."

"You know I love you," her nose crinkled with her smile.

"Please, Jewel, until it's the real thing . . . I can't. Take your time, let's get to know one another again, then decide how you feel."

"I like the idea of getting to know you again. We've both been through some changes."

"Stay tonight, we can spend tomorrow together, just no sex," he laughed. "I can't believe I said that!"

Julie giggled, "Okay, I'll keep my hands to myself . . . except this!" She dug her fingers into his ribs, knowing where he was ticklish. A battle ensued until they were laughing so hard, they had to stop.

"Come on, let's pretend it's a 12-year-old sleepover."

"Without the sleeping bags, I hope."

"No sleeping bags. I have a nice king-size bed."

He gave her a nightshirt; he wore sweatpants. They slid into his bed, and Randy turned on Saturday Night Live. By the closing credits, Julie was asleep. Randy laid awake most of the night, watching the moonlight caress the shape of her—dip of her waist, rise of her hip—breathing in the scent of her. Every fiber of his being craved her . . . but he knew once they crossed that line he could never go back to being just her friend.

The next morning, they had a quick workout in the gym on the first floor. Then Randy showed her how his computer worked. A sound of whirs and beeps emanated from its speaker and the screen lit up with green letters. "That sound is the binary language talking through the ARPANET. See, it's a system of . . ."

"Sorry! You lost me at binary," she laughed.

"Here, I'll just show you." He sat at the keyboard, and his fingers started whizzing along. Julie was mesmerized by the whole process. They spent an hour or so experimenting with technology, then had lunch in Georgetown.

Julie told him more about her job as banquet director at the Hunt Valley Marriott, "I really like it, busy as all get out, but the staff is great and it's a happy place. I was lucky to swing this weekend off. I have a great assistant that can handle events once I get everything in place."

She ran her fingers through her hair, "Anyway, I am in an ok place. Well, not ecstatic, but ok. Finally stopped searching . . . and leaning on everybody."

"It's ok to lean on your friends, that's what they're for."

"I've abused the privilege, I think. I'm glad you weren't witness to my last few years. Kind of self-destructed."

"You don't seem destroyed."

"Not so bad anymore. I figured out how to be content with myself, I guess."

"Good place to be, but don't be so hard on yourself, all you've dealt with," Randy shuttered internally at the thought of Rick; what he put her through, and of his own last moments with him.

"Enough of that, I'm looking forward, not back."

"Good! So, want to do the Smithsonian next Monday?" he asked. "I can take the day off."

"Good idea, unless you wanna monkey around at the zoo again."

Randy made monkey sounds, Julie did her elephant, and the table next to them stared and shook their heads.

They laughed like 12-year-olds.

Julie was struck with a brilliant idea, "Hey, come to June week with me! Well, it's not June but . . . I don't know why they call it that, but . . . it's great! Wednesday and Thursday at Will's. I think Colleen is coming and . . ."

"Jewel, take a breath!"

She did.

"Ok, now, start with what it is."

"The Blue Angels over Annapolis; they're amazing!"

"That they are. They do the Naval Academy Commissioning! I get it now."

"Oh, duh, of course, you know about the Naval Academy, your dad and all."

"He took us to see them every chance we got when we were kids," Randy said. "I'd love to come to Will's. Bet he has front row seats in his backyard."

Chapter 37

Once Julie left, Randy sat on his balcony and pondered the changes in his life.

He knew he'd never been fair to Jen. He'd jumped into their relationship as a means of escape. As the years went by, he kept hoping his love would evolve, he would love her the way she deserved, but it just wasn't there. Part of him was relieved when he found out she was having an affair with her boss. He was hurt, but it gave him an out.

He dated a couple of women after the break-up, but purposely kept his distance. After Jenifer, he needed some time for soul searching. All his life, he had trouble fitting in. He chose swimming over team sports because of the body/mind connection as he powered through the water. His brain seemed to be wired different than most people. He felt like the weird little brother, the naïve goof, and he realized that was the way he had viewed himself.

Now he understood; he didn't have to prove himself to anybody, just had to like himself. The big revelation was that he did!

When the opportunity to move to DC presented itself, it was kismet. He was ready to go home. He missed Kevin; was sorry he didn't really know his nephew and niece. He would be closer to his parents. He missed all his friends and he could be Julie's friend, if that's how it had to be.

He thought about Julie. She still rocked him after all these years. A warmth enveloped him as he replayed their weekend.

Sitting there, gazing out as the lights of the city came on, he put his finger on what was different about Julie—she, too, was finally comfortable in her own skin.

All week, Julie's mind strayed to Randy; the way he truly listened to her with that cute half-grin on his face, those funny monkey sounds, his brilliant intellect. He always had all those wonderful traits, and she had taken him for granted.

Now he was so confident, so in command of his life. He had a new natural ease when talking to people that suited him quite well.

She recalled the way his fingers danced along the keyboard. Now she imagined those fingers dancing on her skin and heat rose through her.

Her Randy that she'd loved forever. Somehow, she was seeing him in a whole new light. *How could I have been so dense? I've wasted so much time looking for what I already had!*

She called on Friday morning.

"Are you doing anything Sunday night?"

"Not a thing."

"I want to take you out to dinner this time. I'll be there at six if traffic allows."

They dined at the JW Marriott. Julie arranged a booth tucked away in a quiet corner. Finally, her employee status paid off!

"You seem to know your way around a wine list. Why don't you order us something?" she said once they were seated.

"It's become a hobby of mine, learning about wine. It's wonderful how much better a good cabernet tastes after you've given it time in its bottle. The best things in life need time," he perused the wine list. "I've come a far way since our Boone's Farm days."

"Oh, gosh, remember the peach Boone's Farm that time? Colleen got so sick! To this day she doesn't like peaches."

"That was the time we were in the graveyard in Towson!"

After dinner, Julie suggested Irish coffee again.

"I'm glad you weren't busy tonight. Couldn't wait until tomorrow."

"To see me? That's sweet."

"To tell you, I haven't stopped thinking about you all week. To tell you I've been so stupid and blind," Julie slid closer on the banquette. "To tell you I love you, capital 'L,' and don't want to spend another minute without you."

Randy felt the world tilt. With a trembling hand, he reached for her and drew her in, "I'm going to kiss you now," and he did; a deep, passionate kiss, and he didn't care who saw. Then he said, "Check please!"

Julie laughed. When the waiter brought it over, she said, "We'll put it on the room, please."

Randy's forehead got that crease in it that signaled he was questioning.

Julie waggled a key and handed it to him, "Didn't think you'd want to wait for a cab. I reserved us a room here, okay?"

The crease smoothed, and his grin was ear to ear as he led her to the elevator.

They had a suite on the concierge level, with a view of the Capitol, but they didn't notice the view until later. There was a bottle of Moët & Chandon in an ice bucket. They let it chill a bit longer.

Randy put the 'Do Not Disturb' on the door and turned to her with that crease between his eyes.

Julie put a finger to his lips, "I've never been surer of anything in my life. This is right."

The tenderness of the kiss was exquisite. His arms surrounded her, found the zipper of her dress, pulled it down, felt the smooth skin beneath. She unbuttoned his shirt, slipped it from his shoulders to join the dress on the floor.

Randy took her hand and led her to the bed, lay her down, and took off his pants.

Then he kissed the scar on her chin, her neck, breasts, lost in the taste of her. Julie wrapped her hand around his erection. Just her touch almost caused him to come.

"No rush," he said. "We have all the time in the world."

Randy touched his lips to the bump of her mis-mended rib. He continued down her body and slipped her panties off, caressed the silky skin of her bottom, kissed the scar on her thigh, ran his tongue down her calf to her ankles, the arch of each foot. He wanted to experience every bit of her, commit her to memory instead of fantasy.

He worked his way back up her body, lingering between her legs at the button that undid her and made her shudder. Then, braced on his elbows so he could see her face, he eased into her. Her eyes closed and her mouth became an O as she sucked in air. Her heat enveloped him and she surrounded him with arms, legs, heart and soul.

Their rhythm was perfect harmony. Slow, sensual, building. The world outside, the past, forgotten, as if one could live forever in such a cocoon of sensation.

"I love you," he said and heat became flame. Every nerve felt the eruption they shared.

He rolled sideways, but stayed inside, savoring the aftermath of her muscle spasms. He didn't want to break the spell.

Julie's eyes were misty, so close he could feel the words brush his skin, "I love you," she said, . "Forever I love you" and ran her fingers through his hair, down his back.

"This is real," he said and his body responded again to show her the overwhelming elation words could not express.

Julie stayed with him Monday and Tuesday night, too. When Randy came in from work, she had dinner waiting, along with a bottle of Cabernet and soft music on the stereo.

"This looks wonderful!" he said. "Guess I don't have to order pizza like most nights. This wine's too good for pepperoni, anyway."

He uncorked the bottle and poured, "Let's have a toast."

Julie picked up her glass.

"To the first of many Tuesday night meals together," he said, and they touched glasses.

"Hope we can add Wednesday and Thursday soon," Julie said and sipped, "mmm, delicious. Let's drink to eight days a week!"

"If it's good enough for the Beatles!" Randy drank and then that crease showed between his eyebrows, "We don't have to go so fast. I don't want you to feel pressured."

"If eight days were possible, I'd ask for nine."

The corners of his mouth quirked up, "Nine it is. Now let me feed you."

After dinner, Randy turned up the music while they cleaned up and their old friend Elton John began to sing "I Guess that's why they call it the Blues."

They stared at each other, eyes bright.

"Elton just gave us a new song," Julie said.

"Amazing . . . come here." Randy pulled her into his chest, *this is real,* "Everything falls into place. Let's go roll like thunder."

On Wednesday, she went to work and stopped at home to pack. Then she was in the car, speeding down the highway, to be back with Randy again.

Thursday morning, they packed Randy's Porsche with overnight bags.

"Far cry from your old Datsun 200," Julie said.

"Ah, that was a great car! Took us on many adventures."

"I like the adventure we're on now."

Only Will and Diane knew they were arriving together. When they pulled up, the Fairburns and McDonalds were on the lawn.

"Holy shit, look who's with Randy!" Pete said.

"Pete, language, Evie is right over there," Colleen said under her breath. Then she looked, "Holy *SHIT!*"

Pete doubled over with laughter. Everybody's heads turned to Colleen's outburst, then followed her gaze.

"Isn't that nice? Julie drove with Randy," Evie said, clearly oblivious to the possibilities of what that could mean.

"Evie, dear, Randy lives in Washington now. Isn't it odd that they would drive together?" Harry said, raising his eyebrows.

"Oh, they were always together," she said and patted his arm like he was the ditzy one.

"You may be right about that, Mrs. Fairburn," said Kevin.

Julie and Randy approached, holding hands and overnight bags. Will took Julie's bag and kissed her cheek, "Glad you two made it . . . and gave everybody something to gawk at for an opening act."

"I'll bet," said Randy, and shook his hand.

"So, Kev and crew are not staying the night. Mom and Dad, of course, are staying in the house. Peter wants to bunk with our kids, so Colleen and Pete are housing it, too. That leaves the boat for you two."

"Love it!" Julie said.

Colleen's jaw dropped. She was speechless. Julie gave her the Morse code smirk for "having hot sex!" and watched her friend grin and bounce on the balls of her feet.

They planned to watch today's practice from the lawn. Tomorrow they'd take the boat out for the actual show. They had a buffet lunch, played horseshoes and volleyball, fished off the dock. When the first plane sounded, the moms put hands over little ears and they watched in awe as six blue angels practiced their choreographed and synchronized displays at incredible breakneck speeds.

Randy and Julie had slipped away to the boat to change into swimsuits. They couldn't resist a quick tumble while the sounds from the sky vibrated the earth.

Afterward, he said, "I've always wanted to do that when they were doing *that*." He pointed upward.

"I'm glad you saved me a first," Julie said, adjusting her bikini.

"I have a couple of firsts I saved for you."

"Ooh, is it naughty?" she rubbed her hand against his crotch. "We could get nekid again."

"Not naughty . . . nice."

Just then, three of the planes dipped a low fly-by right above them. Julie jumped in surprise, right into his arms.

"I paid them to do that," he said. Then, with a crooked grin, "Let's get back before your dad notices. Don't want to ruin my reputation."

They walked nonchalantly back to the group. With all the planes and kids, no one even noticed how long they were gone—except Colleen. She winked at Julie and slipped her arm around Pete's waist, thinking, ain't love grand?

Two weekends later, Colleen got a call from Washington DC. It was Julie, "Guess who is wearing a new diamond ring?"

"WHAT? You are kidding me!"

"No joke, he asked me last night and I asked him 'what took you so long?'" Her laughter danced through the telephone line.

"But it's only been what, two weeks?"

"It's not like we had to get to know one another! And we aren't waiting, we're thinking end of July."

"Tell me everything!"

Life with Rick had been like walking on a perilous ledge in a landslide. She never knew what would crash down or where to step, which root or rock would send her over the edge. Sex with him was desperate, aggressive; violence lurked behind the love.

Being with Randy was a languorous glide down a river, a discovery unfolding at each turn, awakening all her senses, she was immersed in feeling without fear of drowning. She could spread her wings without fear of being shot down.

They had known each other forever, their quirks and habits, likes and aversions. They could finish each other's sentences and read the other's emotion tells. Yet, they were learning each other anew. The adventure was extraordinary.

Craig flew in for the wedding three days ahead of time so he could go over the music Julie and Randy had asked him to play at the ceremony. Julie scrunched up next to Craig on the sofa and put her head on his shoulder. "My last two nights here," she said. "Guess you'll have to find a new caretaker for this place. I'm excited to live in DC, but this house has been a wonderful refuge."

He threw his arm around her, "Think I'll put it up for sale, I won't be coming back here so much, and I can always stay in a hotel."

"You kept the house for me, didn't you? Made it sound like I was doing you a favor but really . . ."

"No, really, Ruby, it was a good investment. This is prime real estate!" His words had that false jocularity to them she knew as his show voice. "I'll get a painting crew in here, update the kitchen . . ." He stopped and looked at her, "Don't you worry about it. Your job is to let yourself be happy. Randy and you are meant to be."

Julie kissed his cheek and stood up, "Funny how time pushes and pulls us into the right place. Me finally with Randy and you on the list for Song of the Year, with that cute Elle waiting for you back in LA." Craig had told Julie about his new girlfriend. She was a script writer for a drama on NBC, an introvert like him. He said they were the only two in all of LA and that's why they clicked. He'd shown Julie a picture of her, a natural beauty with perfect skin the color of caramel and a shy alluring smile.

"Yeah, funny how things work out. Guess I can't call you Ruby anymore," he kissed her hand. "Now get to bed, you have a big day tomorrow." As she climbed the stairs, she heard his guitar and stopped to listen. He was singing "Dalliance" and she knew it was his way of saying goodbye.

Before dawn, Julie woke to the sound of rain pounding on the roof. The night air had been sultry, so the window was open. Wind howled and whipped the curtains in a frenzy. She jumped up to shut the window, tripped over her half-packed suitcase, and fell to her knees.

She pulled herself up and just as her hands reached the sill, a branch from the Sassafras tree smacked against the top pane.

Glass shards filled the air like glitter and caught in her hair, tiny cuts sprung out on her forehead. *Thank God I closed my eyes in time!*

Julie stumbled to the bathroom to assess the damage, flipped on the light.

"You're bleeding, darlin'."

The world swirls around her; she grabs the edge of the sink to stay upright. It's Rick, holding a towel, reaching for her. The towel is blood splattered—was it her blood or his?

How did I get here? I've got to get out! Julie wracks her addled brain for an escape plan. *Think, stupid!* Leftover spaghetti sauce is running down the walls. Everything is red.

Keys clank into the sink. As she reaches, Rick sneers at her and clamps his hand around her wrist. "He'll never love you like I do."

Now she's in the car, her old Aspen—back seat—desperately trying to reach the brake as they careen down 695.

Rick says, "Better figure it out, darlin'."

"No! You can't be here! Where's Randy?"

They are in the Friedman's backyard. Lightning strikes the ice-covered trees surrounding them, shattering them like fine crystal. Thunder booms out.

Rick has the gun, raising it . . . aiming it . . .

"POW!"

Randy!

A sinkhole opens in the ground. As the earth crumbles, its gravity pulls her until she is tilted over its yawning mouth. Monstrous tree roots protrude from its sides, stretch toward her, seeking purchase. With all her strength, she pulls herself upright. She watches as Rick tumbles past her, sucked down the vortex.

She stands, toes at the edge. Randy stands across the chasm. *My love.* His radiant smile lights her from within. Randy reaches out to help her across. In his hand, he holds a shiny aluminum baseball bat.

She woke, sweaty and shivering, gaped at the window. To her relief, the summer sun streamed in. The curtains wafted lazily and not a sign of rain or broken glass anywhere, but the image of Randy and the bat stayed with her. *Could he have . . . ? No, he is not capable of such a thing! Besides, Red has been convicted! I won't even entertain that idea.*

Still . . . if Randy were capable, he would have done it to protect me.

Chapter 38

JUNE 1987

Julie felt like a Macy's parade float. She propped her feet up on the rail of Will's newest boat and said to Diane, "I don't remember you losing your ankles like this."

"Honey, I had my babies in the cold weather for a reason!"

Randy handed Julie her iced tea, "Personally, I adore your fat ankles."

"Very funny." She was interrupted by a minor earthquake behind her belly button and rubbed it, "Hello!"

"Rolling like thunder?" Randy asked, smiling.

"Uh-huh . . . you taught him that."

"Sounds like we have another athlete in the family," said Diane as she put her hand on Julie's belly to feel her new family member, "hey little fella, you gonna play baseball like your uncle or be a swimmer like your daddy?"

"Don't forget lacrosse, Russ won the championship with the Hopkins Blue Jays," Randy said and kissed Julie's forehead.

Tyler poked his head out of the cabin, "Hey Uncle Randy, you ready to fish?"

"Sure am! Come on," Tyler and Heather scrambled up, and the three of them joined Will on the dock.

"They'll be occupied awhile. I'm going to bring lunch down from the house," Diane stood and threw her cover-up over her slender bikini-clad body.

"Think I'll ever wear a bikini again?"

"Of course, you will! Besides, the way Randy looks at you, with that beam of love, you don't need a bikini."

Diane was right, Randy did beam! Julie had never been happier. They were about to celebrate their second wedding anniversary. Their baby was due in three weeks.

They took Ruth's suggestion and bought two row houses in the same block as hers. After they were renovated, they sold them for four times their purchase price and bought a house on the Magothy River, with a big backyard, a pier, and trees to climb. Randy had given her a Chocolate Lab puppy for Christmas last year. They named him Elton. Life was grand.

She watched her brother and husband having a ball with the kids on the dock, and a rush of pure joy filled her. Will was a devoted father, and she had no doubt Randy would be as well.

Diane brought lunch down, and they all gathered on the boat to eat.

The kids talked over one another to tell their fish stories as Diane made them plates.

Another kick from her belly nearly knocked Julie's plate from her hands.

"Wow, Aunt Julie, I saw that one!" Heather exclaimed.

"So, what do you think? Baseball or swimming for this guy?" Diane asked the kids.

"That's a swim kick!" Heather said.

"Nah, baseball like Dad," said Tyler.

"Hey, Aunt Julie swung a mean bat, too!" Randy said. "She used to keep one in her trunk called the Ball Buster!"

Julie looked at Randy, surprised at the mention of the bat.

"Wait, wasn't that what was on that bat in your trunk, Will? The one you found?" Diane asked.

Julie looked at Will, who was suddenly sweating profusely. "Will?"

Diane didn't seem to notice and went on, "Remember, Will?" she turned to Randy, "I borrowed his car. Mine had a flat and he had come home late." She spooned some fruit onto a plate. "He was still sleeping so wasn't around to fix it. I took his car to the grocery and that Ball Buster was in the trunk."

Will was visibly shaking now.

"When I got home, I told him I ought to use it on his lazy ass!" she laughed, and Randy laughed along with her. When he turned to Julie, the laughter petered out.

"Getting a beer," Will said and disappeared into the galley.

"He probably doesn't even remember. It was years ago, maybe six," Diane's math mind whirred. "Definitely six. Heather was still in her car seat. Said he found it in our road."

"Where is it?" asked Julie.

"It was dented and filthy, so I think he threw it away. I only remember because of the funny name, and me teasing him," Diane laughed again. "I thought we should donate it to Toys for Tots, being a month before Christmas. But who wants a dented bat?"

Julie saw Randy studying her, wondering what she was thinking.

She put her hand on her belly, "I think I better get off the boat. You all go ahead with lunch. I'm going to go lie down."

"I'll come with you, babe."

"No, just help me off the boat. This guy wants me all to himself awhile," she hoped her smile was convincing.

Randy hopped off and extended his hand to her. Once she was off the boat, he whispered, "What is it? Let me help you."

"Later, please just . . . We'll talk later." He knew her well enough to let her be.

Once in the house, she let out her breath and let the conversation and Will's reaction turn in her mind.

She had never told Randy her suspicions about the bat being the murder weapon. After that first nightmare of Randy bashing Rick, she didn't want to know where the bat was, didn't let herself think about it. Red Wilder was convicted, so the Ball Buster was inconsequential. Back then, Randy had a new life and didn't need to hear her silly theories, especially since they pointed in his direction.

Once they reunited, it was the furthest thing from her mind . . . except the one nightmare that she had quickly buried away.

But now . . . Will? How should she handle this?

Diane came in the door, "You okay?"

"Yeah, I think we better get home. Closer to our hospital." Again, she hoped her smile was working.

"Oh, yay! Right? Yay?" Julie nodded and Diane flew into action. "Let me get Randy. You should be home, alright!"

There was a flurry of activity: the kids jumping around, Randy practically carrying her to the car, Diane reminding her to breathe when it was time . . . Will standing back, silent and white-faced.

Chapter 39

NOVEMBER 28-29, 1981
WILL

When Will arrived, party sounds were spilling out the windows. He followed the decibel rise into the kitchen.

"Will, buddy, long time, man!" Craig shook his hand.

Eddie pushed his glasses up and handed him a beer, "You're late, you missed the fireworks!"

"What? Fireworks, really?"

"I'll fill you in," Craig took him by the elbow and led him into the empty living room. "Why do party people always crowd into the kitchen?"

"One of life's little mysteries. Now, what's this about fireworks?"

"Rick showed up, unexpectedly. I think he was looking for Cups, you know . . ." Craig pointed to his nose and snorted. "Julie was outside when he pulled up."

"Damn it! Please tell me he didn't hurt her."

"Not like all the times before."

"How many times before? She told me a couple times . . . I knew it." Will slammed his beer on the table. Foam bubbled out and spilled over.

"Not sure how many, but a lot more than a couple. She hid it all well. First, I guess, to protect him, later out of embarrassment that she let it happen."

"Protect him? What the hell?"

"Didn't want people thinking badly of him. She loved him big time, man."

Craig sank his weary body into the sofa, rubbed his hand across his mouth. "I've listened to her stories about it the last couple months but never actually witnessed it before." Will sank down with him, brows twitched together. Fast things zipped behind his eyes.

"When I came out, I guess she tried to holler . . . He had her backed against a car, one hand sealed over her mouth and the other holding her arm, so tight she's got finger-shaped bruises."

"I knew he was still trouble . . . tried to tell her that on Thursday!"

"I tried to talk him down. Other people came outside. Val yelled she was calling the cops. That's when Julie talked him into getting out of Dodge."

"Julie did."

"Yep, she still holds his key, man. Astonishing."

"Where is she?"

"Bathroom, I think. Go easy, Will, she's fragile right now."

"She's tougher than I ever imagined. How does she keep taking all this?" he took a long swig of his beer and pondered what should happen next.

II

After their porch talk, Julie went back inside to see what Colleen wanted her to take home. Will offered to help transfer and would spend the night at Julie's. That was his idea. He wanted to be sure Rick didn't show. Craig was cool, but he was no match for Rick in anger mode.

He pulled his car into the driveway in front of Julie's and got out. His left foot came down on something and slid from under him. He grabbed hold of the car door, pulled himself upright, and looked down. An aluminum baseball bat was lying on the ground. *A good way to break your neck!*

He picked it up and was transported back to his high school days—best home run hitter on the Dulaney High School team. He held the bat as if on home plate.

Here's the pitch, a low fastball. Fairburn swings! Good golly, it's another home run!

Will heard the bat connect, a clean, crisp *clink!* And the ball soared!

Then his daydream morphed—it was Rick's head that he was connecting with. "You've gone too far this time, you son of a bitch!" he murmured to himself. Not that he would ever really do it, but thinking about it felt *good!*

Laughing at himself under his breath, he threw the bat into the back of his Audi and went inside.

The next morning, they slept late, something Will rarely did at home. Little ones curbed that habit. When they rose, Craig made them his famous omelets while Julie tended to the coffee, tea, and toast.

He enjoyed wallowing in the single life for a day, but he wouldn't trade his life for anything: beautiful wife, two adorable kids, fantastic job, house, boat. He was blessed. He wanted that for Julie.

"So, you given any thought to my idea?" he asked after he shoveled the last of his breakfast into his mouth.

Julie sat back and stretched her long legs out in front of her, "I have."

"And?"

"Will, it's a wonderful offer, very tempting, but . . ." she looked at Craig, at the sink elbow deep in dishes, "I've just settled in here. I've bounced around so much the last couple of years, I wake and wonder where I am."

Will's eyes squeezed shut for a moment, "I worry about you."

"I'm ok, Craig is here with me, it's not like I'm living alone."

Craig threw his dishtowel over his shoulder and came back to the table. "I've been calling her Ruby Tuesday. Can't keep up with where her head's at day to day. She's been spinning her wheels," he gave her ponytail an affectionate yank.

"I'm testing out my freedom. And, for now, this is where I want to be. Until I figure out what's next. I may even go back to school."

Will stood, "The offer is open if you change your mind."

Julie reached up to him. He pulled her up and hugged her, squeezed until she squeaked.

"A little too tight, there buddy!" she laughed.

"Hey, maybe I'll stay for the Colts game."

That earned a "Yay!" from Julie.

"Hope they don't get trounced again. It's been painful to watch," Craig said.

After the Colts' humiliating loss to the Jets, Will was ready to head home. He finished his beer, hugged Julie, and left. A frigid gust of wind whipped by as he opened the car door and he struggled to pull it shut. The engine roared to life, and he pulled on his leather gloves and gave it a couple minutes to warm. Shivering, with his forehead against the wheel, he wished there was something he could do for his sister, wished he had done something from the start.

Get over it, man, nothing you can do. Will backed the car out to the street through a swirl of gold and red leaves and turned left. The road took him behind Julie's house. He saw the upstairs light go on and Julie's silhouette against the curtains.

Then he saw the Bronco, backed into a small nook amongst the neighbor's bushes. He couldn't see the man in the driver's seat but didn't have to. He knew who it was.

Two can play this game. Rick hadn't seen him yet, so he swung the Audi onto a parking pad and waited. *What are you gonna do, you psycho?*

When the light in the window blinked off, he heard the Bronco's engine cough to life. Its headlights sent a weak beam through the moonless dark.

No hurry, give him some leash.

Will followed, lagging far behind, to York Road. On Sunday night, there wasn't much traffic to camouflage his pursuit. They drove north through the underpass in Cockeysville and past the new mall.

The next stop didn't surprise him, The Pioneer House. Will watched Rick go inside. His walk had a sway to it—the guy was plastered on something.

Will entered through the back and sat on the far side of the bar, ordered a drink, and kept watch on his ex-brother-in-law. *Can't believe I liked the guy! Julie fell for his country boy charm, then I swallowed the Kool-Aid.*

The bartender nudged the old fellow sitting to Will's right, "George, look who just walked in."

George shook his head, "Trouble with a capital T."

Will looked sideways at Trouble. He would lay odds that was Red Wilder. He was an ugly guy—thin reddish hair, beady eyes, mottled skin. Built like a fireplug, but he walked with a swagger that said, "I'm hot shit, don't cross me."

A girl straggled in behind him. Her bunny fur coat was open to show breasts popping out the top of a ripped tee, and her jeans were so tight, they looked painful.

The couple made a beeline to the bar. She waved down the bartender; he tapped Rick on the shoulder. Will could only hear snippets of conversation over the jukebox music, but it was obvious Trouble wasn't happy. While the girl sucked on a beer, he ranted . . . something about money and keeping his end of the bargain.

Rick stood up. He was four inches taller and broader, but he was wobbling, so the intimidation factor didn't play well. Will saw him point at the door and throw a couple bills on the bar. Trouble followed him outside.

Will slipped a ten under his glass and went out a couple minutes later.

Rick and the guy were standing next to the Bronco, having a heated discussion.

Will kept his head down, got in his car parked in the far corner near the street. They hadn't noticed him. He watched them as they got into the Bronco and drove around to the back of the parking lot. Will couldn't see what they were doing, but he kept his distance. Then the windshield glowed and smoke drifted out the cracked window.

After 20 minutes or so, the Bronco pulled forward and Trouble got out with a shoebox in his grip. Before he shut the door, he said, " . . . off the hook, if you follow through." He walked over to a Buick parked around the side, and got in. As Will passed, he saw a match glow inside the Buick.

The Bronco continued to the exit and turned onto York Road. Will followed him a short way down, onto a narrow lane, and then onto an even narrower dirt drive. *Enough is enough, I'm not getting lost up here.* He blinked his high beams. The bronco slowed, stopped. Will pulled in right behind him. Rick swung the door open, got out, and peered into the lights, hand above his eyes.

Will grabbed the bat from the back seat. He left the car running, headlights on, and stepped into their beam with the bat raised.

"Stay away from my sister, you son of a bitch!"

"Will?"

"I saw you there, watching her."

"No, man, I just . . ." he lowered his hand, "felt bad. Wanted to see that she was okay."

Rick spread his arms out hip height, two broken wings.

Will looked him in the eyes, "You come anywhere near her I'll kill you!"

When Rick brought his left hand back to center, the light glinted and caught Will's attention. *Fucker has a gun!*

His mind whirred, but not as fast as his honed athlete's reflexes; he took two steps forward and swung. Connected.

The gun hand crackled as bones broke. A shot rang out and the trees made sudden sounds of flight. Rick spun, knees buckling, eyes wide with surprise.

The bat came down against Rick's skull. Not a crisp, clean *clink!* But a horrifying *thwack!*

"Oh, God! What have I done?"

Will knelt next to the crumpled man. Rick's confused eyes stared up. His breath came in raspy hitches. A damaged hand raised toward Will, and the gun clattered to earth.

Barely discernable, "Tell her . . ."

Will started to lift him, and was amazed that Rick stood on his own. With his right hand, Rick pulled himself into the Bronco.

BEYOND THE BROKEN WINDOW

Will thought he said something. It sounded like "soulmate." Then he slumped back against the seat, unconscious, still breathing that raspy sound.

What do I do now? He should take him to the ER. *But how this looks!* If Rick died, he could be tried for murder, end up bunkmates with Floyd! He thought of all he had to lose. The image of the looks on his kids' faces threw him into action.

Take care of the gun first. With his gloved hand, he picked it up and gingerly slid it between Rick's feet under the driver's seat. Then he picked up the bat, wiped the blood off with a rag from the back of the Bronco and threw it in his trunk.

Looking ahead, he saw nothing but trees on either side as the lane continued a declining slope. *Make it seem like a car accident.*

Will put Rick's foot against the gas pedal, just enough pressure to move the Bronco forward. He turned the wheel a bit to the left and slipped the shift into drive. The bronco lurched forward and the door clanked against its jam as momentum picked up.

Will watched until it rammed against a tall oak trunk and came to a stop.

He'd never make it to the hospital, anyway. He'll be dead before they find him. Moving quick now, he scuffed all the footprints, jumped in the Audi, and backed away.

As he drove, his thoughts raced. *Need an alibi, get home for the alibi. Get rid of the bat. Take the boat out, dump it in the channel. Tomorrow first thing.*

JUNE 1987

Julie stood in the shadow of the Charlie Brown tree and conjured up memories of her nightmare marriage. Images swam through her, some she had blocked completely from her mind until now: Rick's face looming over her while mashed potatoes dripped from her hair, his hand slamming against her skin as she cowered in the shower, sudden slaps, horrendous accusations spit into her face . . .

. . . and crawling in desperation to reach the door, knowing he would never let her go. He always caught her, dragged her back to crush her with his twisted love. She would never be away from him; he was part of her still. For better or worse, those years had shaped her future, molded who she had become.

She thought about Will. A recollection surfaced of Diane calling, concerned, asking about Will getting home late that night. Julie had figured he wanted a few more hours of single life before heading home. Of course, she never said that to Diane. Now she remembered wondering if Will was having an affair. After the wedding weekend, he had been preoccupied with something for months—emotional one minute, aloof the next—not the levelheaded Will she knew. She was so wrapped up in the trial and her own emotions, it barely registered.

Julie walked back toward her car. At her mother's morning glories, she turned for a final look. Those crows were still chattering, chiding her for not seeing the forest for the trees.

From what Diane said of the timing, the bat was in Will's car the night of the murder. Will's car had been parked in front of Julie's where the bat would have dropped. Christmas of 1981 was now a blur, but another memory surfaced. Will, Russ, and she were having their Bailey's shot after dinner . . .

Russ asked, "Anything new on the trial?"

"Detective Minelli has been keeping me up to date. Wilder's lawyer turned down a plea of manslaughter one; five to fifteen. So, they are going to try him for murder two. Twenty-five to life."

"Huh, same as Floyd got."

"Joe told me the gun was fired so they may have had a case for self-defense, but Wilder still says he didn't do it."

Will had been hitting the bottle all day and his tongue was loose, "Self-defense gets five to fifteen . . . Huh, fifteen years in prison." He sat and rubbed his hand across his mouth, "Sometimes bad guys do things that end up good. Sometimes good guys have good reasons for something bad."

"What are you babbling about?" she asked.

Russ cocked his head at Will, "Mr. Philosophy here."

"Just saying . . . sometimes you find yourself in a situation. Good and bad get . . . blurred. Good intentions can turn bad all by themselves. Like with self-defense."

"Well, whatever you are trying to say, this time the bad guy is going down," Julie raised her cup.

"And you, my love, can breathe again," said Russ.

"I'll drink to that," said Will, and looked at her over his cup, suddenly clear-eyed, a look of release.

She didn't care if Wilder had been sentenced for a crime he didn't commit. He was guilty of the drug and robbery charges and so much more. During the months leading up to the trial, Dawn had confided something to Julie that she told no one before, not even Rick . . .

FEBRUARY 1973

Her eleventh birthday was three days away and her momma was out at that very minute with Aunt Meg to buy her a present. It was a mild day for February and she was playing in the barn in her new dress when she heard the car. Red Wilder, high and fuming, had come looking for Rick. She wandered out as he was going up the back steps.

"Hey, Reddy, you lookin' for Rick, he ain't home," she said.

"Where is he, then?"

"He don't live here no more. Moved out to an apartment."

"Well now, ain't that nice? You know where that apartment is?" He approached her all smiles.

"Yep. You know my birthday is in three days? I'm gonna be 11!"

"You wanna tell me where that fuckin' apartment is?"

"Towson somewhere . . . Don't know."

He was in front of her now and she backed toward the barn, wishing she'd brought Clyde out with her. She could hear him barking in the house.

"I think you better go."

Just as she stepped back into the barn, he grabbed hold of her wrist and leaned in, "Aww, come on, I wanna give you a birthday kiss."

Before she knew it, his mouth was on hers and his tongue pushed in. She felt an odd heat rise in her, and she didn't like it.

"You growing up alright," Red put his hand on her chest, "look at that, you getting titties!"

She looked up at him, secretly proud. Then his hand went around the back of her neck, "Tell me where that cocksucker is."

"Don't know." She was trembling; his hand was a vice.

With a practiced flick, his switchblade appeared and touched her neck,

"You gonna pay his debt for him? Huh?"

Terror rippled through her, tears sprang to her eyes, and her bladder let go.

Red scrunched his nose up at the pungent smell of her urine, "Good thing you ain't a couple years older, I'd be teachin' you a *real* lesson!" He pushed her to the muddied ground and gave her a swift kick. "You keep this to yerself."

Red Wilder was where he belonged.

Julie knew her brother almost as well as her husband. Randy would have told her by now if he had done the deed, but Will would take it to his grave. Why confront him? Make him reveal his darkest moment? Whatever the circumstances of that night were, she was sure Will had started with good intention. Like he said back in December 1981, a bad thing happened, but for a good reason. He was her knight in tarnished armor.

A woman pulled into the drive and got out. She waved at Julie, "Can I help you?"

Julie pulled herself from her thoughts, "Hi. I used to live here, just reminiscing."

"Would you like to come in?"

"No . . . no thanks," she gestured toward the giant fir. "I planted that. You wouldn't believe how little it was, barely made it through its first year. It was my first Christmas tree."

"Oh, my kids will love to hear that story. We love that tree! We have a couple families of finches living in it," as if on cue a tiny bird poked its head out, trilled a little melody and took flight.

"At Christmas you should see how beautiful it is all lit up! The kids can see it from their bedroom window."

Julie remembered its little branches barely holding a few ornaments and smiled, "Yes, I believe it has grown up just fine."

Epilogue

JULY ~~1987~~ 1990

J ulie stood at the edge of their yard and hollered over the sound of splash-
ing and laughter from the pier that jutted into the Magothy River, "Time
for cake!"

In no time, a dozen wet children scampered past her smelling of river
water and sunscreen, a lovely earthy clash of scent, algae and coconut, that
never failed to warm her.

Russ, Ruth, Diane, and Will followed, dragging a few stragglers by the
hand and Harry held tight to Evelyn's hand, helping her navigate the steps to
the backyard.

"Oh, my!" said her mother, "So many children! Now which ones are
mine?"

"They all are in one way or another, dear," her dad answered.

"Well, isn't that marvelous?" Evie said to Julie as they walked the rest
of the way to the house, "I've been told we have cake! Are you the one with
cake?"

"Yes, Mom, birthday cake for your grandson, Kyle. He's my little boy,
remember? And there's the newest." Julie pointed to Randy, who stood on
the back deck, cooing to their newborn daughter in his arms.

"That's baby Evie. My granddaughter. Of course, I know that!" Evie
said matter-of-factly.

Harry smiled and patted her arm.

Colleen came out the back door, with ten-month-old Michael on her hip. "Okay, here comes the cake. Chef Gravy outdid himself. Everybody, sing!"

Linda followed behind, carrying the cake. Teenage Rusty, beside Linda, held his hands up to shield the candle glow from the light summer breeze.

The crowd erupted in a cacophony of song and three-year-old Kyle beamed and bopped up and down on his toes.

Will came up behind Julie, smelling himself of river and sun, slipped his arm around her shoulders, "Great party as always, Jules."

She reached up and gave his hand a squeeze, "Come on. You can be the ice cream man."

A vision flashed in her mind—almost too quickly to comprehend—of a handsome young man with dark curls leaning out of an ice cream truck window. She shook it away, led Will to the ice cream station and handed him the scoop.

Then Julie knelt and hugged her beautiful son, "Happy birthday my love, the first piece is yours."

Once all the cake had been doled out, she navigated her way through the sticky crowd to Randy.

"She's probably ready to eat, too. My boobs are telling me so."

Randy handed the baby over and wrapped his arms around Julie, "Your boobs are very smart . . . and nice to look at, I might add."

He tilted her chin up and kissed her, and a flutter, winglike, stirred within her. Still, after all this time, his touch had that effect, so gentle and profound.

"Now let me go hug that birthday boy," Randy moved into the fray, scooped Kyle up and swung him in the air.

Julie snuggled baby Evie to her, breathed in that undefinable newborn smell, and gazed joyfully at the family and friends gathered at her home, and at her son, the center of attention in his father's sturdy grasp; his arms flung high like branches reaching for the sky.

Acknowledgements

It is with deepest gratitude and love, that I thank my sister, Susan Beauchamp, and my dear friend Chris Plumstead who have been with me on this labor of love from the first chapters. Thank you for your endless reading and rereading, suggestions, and encouragement. Thanks also to my early readers-Susan, Lisa, Connor, Joyce, and Marina. Every leap is easier when you are holding someone's (virtual) hand!

For his literary advice I am indebted to Carl Behm, Professor Emeritus at Towson University and to Twink Behm; you opened your home and hearts to me. Thank you for your time and wisdom.

Thanks to my editor, Cheryl Dishon. Your literary expertise and suggestions helped me fine tune this story and take it to the next level.

Thanks to Marty Ostendorf for his help with printing and editing.

For their medical expertise, I thank Mary Lou Craig, RN and Joyce Josefson, BSN, RN, CM.

For expertise in law enforcement and forensics, I thank Jerry Lyons, Retired First Grade Detective–NYC Police and my husband, Greg Strouse, Pres. Master Security, Inc.

A shout out to all my Facebook friends who helped me nail down spelling, details, and dates of Baltimore Landmarks.

For their understanding, patience, and support, I thank my husband Greg and daughter Lyla and the rest of our large, loving family. You are my sunshine and I love you with all my heart.

And, of course, I am thankful for a lifetime of love and support from my three brothers—Jim and Charles who also assisted with their engineering and geek knowledge and Eddie, my spirit guide (who sends his love from beyond and interferes with my electronics to make his presence known) You are my knights in shining armor.

To those women and men who have been or are in abusive relationships, remember you are not alone. You are worthy of love without pain. As Julie said, "It's different when you're in it." Find a way to untangle the roots and move forward.

If you or someone you know is experiencing relationship abuse in any form, help is available.

The National Domestic Violence Hotline provides free, confidential support 24/7/365. Text START to 88788, call 1-800-799-SAFE (7233), or chat online at TheHotline.org. You are not alone.

An excerpt from the prequel to *Beyond the Broken Window.*

Playing With Fire

I decided to write this on paper so the world will know the truth, well my world at least, the hell with the rest. My world has whittled down to a few, and most of them don't even know I'm alive. I guess you could say that girl I used to be is dead, but once in a while she crawls out of the dark and surprises me.

She was born in darkness on October 29, 1936, a night with no moon and an icy wind whipping up the valley and shaking the trees. I don't remember, but my big brother told me—it was a wicked night.

Rich was four and excited for Halloween, so witches were on his mind. When Momma started her wailing, it scared the bejesus outta him. He thought for sure it was something evil come to get him, and went running to find a bigger brother. Instead, he run straight into Pa coming out of his room with blood on his arms and holding a squalling bundle.

"Meet yer sister, squirt," Pa said to him and leaned down so he could see me, "This here's Bonnie. Finally got me a girl." The evil thing turned out to be me.

Rich told me that I was all bloody and sticky-looking, but when I looked at him with shiny eyes, he loved me, plain and simple. He was the best brother . . . dead now. Killed in Korea, only 20 years old. But he told me that story every time I was hurting, told me I was born in dark and brought him light, that I was strong and could withstand and overcome. He was right. I withstood all I could, and then I overcame with fire.